The Rhyming Gospels

*A poetic paraphase of Holy Scripture
by Bernard Williams*

Limited first edition

D1569374

**HANNIBAL
BOOKS**

Hannibal, Missouri 63401

Copyright Bernard Williams
FIRST EDITION PRINTED DECEMBER, 1990
ISBN 0-929292-14-6
All Rights Reserved Printed in the United States of America by
Lithocolor Press, Inc.
Bible Editor, James C. Hefley, Ph.D.
Poetry Editor, Mary Grace
Design Editor, Cyndi Allison

Introduction

Dr. Larry L. Lewis

I was a seventeen-year-old ministerial student when I first met Bernard Williams. He was then the political science professor at Hannibal-LaGrange College and mayor of Hannibal—known around the world as the hometown of "Tom Sawyer" and "Huck Finn." More importantly, Professor Williams represented the very best in Christian education—a teacher who modeled his life after the Christ of the Gospels.

Every course I took under him was profitable, but the lecture I remember best was delivered in the hallway when he discovered I hadn't gone to church the previous Sunday: "Young man, if you don't have enough gumption to get out of bed to hear someone else preach, you ought to go back to the farm and start hauling hay!" I can still hear his stinging rebuke. From that day to this, I have never missed a Sunday in church unless I was ill.

Way back then Bernard was rhyming college dress codes, parking regulations, and chapel announcements. I'm afraid I took his greatness for granted. It was not until I returned as president of Hannibal-LaGrange, thirty years later, that I truly understood why they called him the poet laureate of Hannibal. He had a rhyme for every occasion. He could make poetic music of the most mundane event.

I led two evangelistic meetings and a Bible study at the church where he was—and still is—an active deacon. At the close of every service, Bernard would hand me back my sermon in rhyme! I have never seen anything like that before or since.

One day I suggested to Bernard that he do the New Testament in rhyme. This had never been done and I felt such an effort would be well received by English speakers throughout the world. The Lord used that idea to prompt *The Rhyming Gospels* and *The Rhyming New Testament,* which is to follow.

3

Now that I've seen Bernard's rendition of Scripture in rhyme, I'm even more amazed at what God has done through this dedicated man. He has accurately rendered the text with great care, assuring that the original meaning was preserved in the paraphrase. As one who believes the Bible to be the inspired, infallible Word of God, he is anxious that there be no distortion or perversion in his presentation of the text.

I commend this marvelous work to all who love and respect the Word of God. I believe it will bring new insights and meaning as well as great inspiration to all who read it.

Acknowledgements & Appreciations

It was just a few short years ago
Larry Lewis asked this question:
"Why don't you rhyme the Scriptures?"
I took this as a suggestion.

At that time he was president
Of the college up the street.
He had taught a Bible class
In which my wife and I had seats.

Each evening as he taught, I'd put
All his teachings into rhyme.
I would write it as he said it,
As I heard it at that time.

I showed him some of the verses.
It was then he said to me,
"Why don't you rhyme the Scriptures?
Your work I'd like to see."

I did not start the project then,
But gradually the idea grew.
I thought if I would try it out
I would read the Bible through.

I would study God's Word closer
Than I'd ever done before,
For to make the verses rhyme
I must read them o'er and o'er.

I am not a language scholar
And I don't know any Greek,
So I have to use translations
When through God's Word I seek.

I used the American Standard Version,
The Nineteen Hundred-one edition.
I also used the King James Version,
As part of this rendition.

In some cases it was necessary
To paraphrase a verse or two,
But I've not changed the meaning;
I've tried to keep that true.

My purpose is not new Gospels,
Or to set forth my own views,
For there is just one Gospel
And this one's Christ's Good News.

As I've written in this manner
By God I've been blessed,
I pray my God will be honored
And His Holy Name confessed.

I wish to express appreciation
To Mary Elizabeth, my dear wife.
In reading and correcting errors
She gave hours of her life.

I am grateful to Jim Hefley
Who these rhymes have compared
With the words of the Bible
Before they would be shared.

Also to Jim's wife, Marti
And to Cyndi Allison,
I say thanks to both of you
For the editing you have done.

I must remember Mary Grace
Who faithfully checked my rhymes,
And talented Amy Worthington
Who made the copy shine.

Thanks to all the many others,
Who in this work had a hand,
I say thanks to everybody
As God's Word spreads 'round the land.

Bernard Williams

The Gospel According to Matthew

Chapter 1

1 The book of generation
Of Jesus, David's son,
Who was a son of Abraham
By whom Israel was begun.

2 By Sarah, Abraham had a son;
Isaac was his name.
To Isaac was born Jacob
And to Jacob, Judah came.

3 Judah's son was Perez.
When Perez became a man
He had a son named Hezron,
And to Hezron was born Ram.

4 Ram begat Amminadab,
Nahshon was his son.
Nahshon then begat a boy
Whom he named Salmon.

5 To Salmon was born Boaz,
By his wife Rahab,
Who had a son named Jesse,
By faithful Ruth, from Moab.

6 To Jesse was born David
And into David's life
Came the smart boy, Solomon
By Uriah's former wife.

7 Solomon begat Rehoboam
Against whom Israel did rebel.
Rehoboam's son Abijah
Did not serve God very well.

8 To Abijah was born Asa,
To him Jehosaphat.
Who had a son named Joram,
Then Uzziah was begat,

9 Uzziah's son was Jotham,
To Jotham Ahaz was born.
To Ahaz Hezekiah came,
A son he did not scorn.

10 Next Manasseh, then came Amon,
Then Josiah, Amon's son;
11 Josiah had Jechoniah
Who went to Babylon.

12 In captivity in Babylon
Life wasn't very stable.
Here Shealtiel was born
And to him Zerubbable.

13 To Zerubbable was born Abiud
And to Abiud, Eliakim;
14 Eliakim's son was Azor
And Zadok was born to him.

To Zadok was born Akim,
Eliud was Akim's son,
15 Then into Eliud's home
Was Eleazar's life begun.

Eleazar was Matthan's father;
Jacob came to him one morn;
16 Then Joseph, husband of Mary,
Of whom Jesus Christ was born.

17 From Abraham to David
The generations are fourteen;
From David to the deportation
Fourteen more are seen.

From captivity in Babylon,
Fourteen generations more;
Then Christ came to earth;
Fourteen again the score.

18 The birth of Jesus came like this:
Joseph thought he'd been deceived.
For although engaged to Mary
He found she had conceived.

19 A righteous man was Joseph,
To serve God he did aspire.
He balked to marry her, but to
Disgrace her had no desire.

20 An angel spoke in a dream.
This message he received:
"Joseph, take Mary as your wife,
For by the Spirit she's conceived.

21 "Jesus will be the Saviour's name,
He'll save His people from their sin.
In Him God will live on earth
And touch the lives of men.

22 "All of this has come to pass,
Recall what God has willed:
23 A virgin with child shall be
This prophecy fulfilled.

"This virgin shall bring forth a son,
Immanuel shall be his name.
Immanuel means, 'God with us,'
He'll ever be the same."

24 Joseph arose from his sleep,
And obeyed the Lord's command.
He took Mary as his wife,
Just as the Lord had planned.

25 He kept Mary as a virgin
Until her first born came.
He called this son, Jesus,
And blessed be His name.

Chapter 2

1 Jesus was born in Bethlehem
When Herod was the king,
Wise men from the east arrived,
This message they did bring:

2 "Where is the one that has been
born
To be the King of the Jews?
We come from afar to worship
Him,
His star brought us the news."

3 When Herod heard them speak,
Their words troubled his mind.
4 He called the priests and scribes
together
In order Christ to find.

"Where should Christ be born?
Tell me, tell me," he said.
5 "In Bethlehem," they answered,
"From the prophet, we read:"

6 "Bethlehem, in the land of Judah,
You're not least—you'll do well.
Out of you shall come a ruler
Who will govern Israel."

7 "When did this star appear?"
Herod asked the wise men three.
8 "Now go and find the child,
and report right back to me."

9 Hearing this from the king
The Magi were released,
And lo, they saw the star again
Which they'd seen in the east.

The star moved on before them, til
It stood over the boy.
10 When the wise men saw the guid-
ing star
They rejoiced with great joy.

11 They walked into the house and
saw
The infant with His mother;
They fell down there and wor-
shipped Him.
This child was like no other.

They opened up their treasure,
Presented gifts of gold,
They gave Him frankincense and
myrrh,
12 Then in a dream were told:

"Do not return to Herod, but
Go back another way."
They went home, thereby heeding
What the vision had to say.

13 Now when the wise men had
departed,
Joseph dreamed that very night.
An angel came to him and said,
"Haste, to Egypt make your flight.

"Stay there until I speak again
For Herod is quite riled.
He'll make a search throughout the
land;
He intends to kill this child."

14 Joseph awakened from his dream;
They left that very night.
They were on their way to Egypt
Before the day was bright.

15 The three remained in Egypt
Until Herod's life was done.
This prophecy was then fulfilled,
"Out of Egypt I called my Son."

16 When Herod saw he had been
  tricked,
With rage the king did shout,
"Kill all the boys in Bethlehem
And in the land about."

17 This fulfilled that prophecy,
Old Jeremiah said,
18 "A voice was heard in Ramah,
There was weeping for the dead.

"Rachel weeping for her children,
Those children which she bore,
She would not be comforted
All her children were no more."

19 After old King Herod died
The angel again appeared,
And in a dream to Joseph said,
20 "They are dead whom you feared.

"Take the child and his mother
To Israel go back."
21 But when they reached Judea
Joseph did not unpack.

22 When he heard that Archelaus ruled
The Judean countryside,
Joseph went to Galilee
And in Nazareth did abide.

23 It was in Nazareth Jesus lived
For twelve years past eighteen.
Thus another prophecy was fulfilled—
He was called a Nazarene.

Chapter 3

1 In the wilderness of Judea
John the Baptist began to stand
2 And cry to everyone,
"God's Kingdom is at hand."

3 Isaiah spoke of this man, John,
When as a prophet he did state:
"Prepare the way, the Lord is coming,
Make His paths clean and straight."

4 John wore a robe of camel's hair,
A belt around his waist;
His food was locusts and wild honey,
For them he had a taste.

5 From all Judea, people came,
And from Jerusalem,
6 As they confessed their sins,
John baptized them.

7 The Pharisees came out to hear,
The Sadducees did too,
John said, "You brood of vipers, who
Brought warnings unto you?

8 "Bring forth fruit unto repentance,
9 Don't suppose that you can say
We have Abraham for a father,
That's enough our debts to pay.

"Listen as I tell you,
that from these very stones
Children God can raise
From Abraham's bones.

10 The axe is at the tree—
At its very root,
Thrown into the fire,
Are those who bear not fruit.

11 "I can baptize you with water
for repentance sake,
But after me will come One
Whose sandals I'm not fit to take.

"With the Holy Spirit
He will baptize you;
Not just with water,
But with fire too.

12 "His threshing fork is in His hand,
And He will clear the floor.
He'll gather wheat into His barn;
He'll burn chaff o'er and o'er."

13 Then Jesus came from Galilee
And said, "John baptize Me."
14 John shied and said, "Tis I, Lord,
Who should be baptized by Thee."

15 Jesus said, "Permit it now
That righteousness be fulfilled."
John then baptized our Lord, and all
The heavens could not be stilled.

16 When Jesus rose up from the
  water
The heavens opened above.
God's Spirit came upon Him
In the form of a dove.

17 Then from heaven came a voice,
John heard it tell,
"This is my Son whom I love,
And He pleases me well."

Chapter 4

1 Jesus went into the wilderness
Where the devil he would meet;
2 He fasted forty days and nights,
Then He desired to eat.

3 The tempter came and said to Him,
"If you are the Son of God,
Command these stones to be made
bread,
This act should not seem odd."

4 Answered Jesus, "It is written
Live not by bread alone,
But by each word that comes from
God,
Directly from His throne."

5 They went then to Jerusalem,
And to the temple's top,
6 The devil said, "Cast down
yourself,
The angels won't let you drop."

7 Jesus said, "Again it is written
Within the Holy Word.
You shall not tempt the Lord your
God,
With actions so absurd."

8 The devil bore Him to a mountain
Where all the kingdoms He could
see.
9 "Jesus, all of this give I You,
If You will worship me."

10 Then Jesus said to him, "Begone,
For although my way is lonely,
It's written, 'You shall worship God,
And you shall serve Him only.'"

11 The devil turned and left Him
There on the mountainside,
Then angels came to Jesus,
Their attentions they applied.

12 Hearing John was in prison
Christ withdrew to Galilee.
13 He moved down to Capernaum,
which
Is located by the sea.

14 Another prophecy was thus fulfilled,
Which by Isaiah said,
15 "The land of Zebulon and Naphtali
Beyond Jordan's river bed,

"Where many Gentiles live;
As you go toward the sea
Where people live in darkness,
Light came to Galilee,

16 "To those who sit in darkness with
Death's shadow all about.
A light has dawned upon them, and
Sin's darkness it will rout."

17 Jesus then began to preach.
He said, "All men repent,
For heaven's kingdom is at hand,
The time is now far spent."

18 Walking by the sea one day
He saw Simon and Andrew
Casting a net in the water,
As fishermen often do.

19 He said, "Come and follow me,
I'll teach you to fish for men."
20 Immediately they left their nets
And followed Him right then.

21 Moving along the shore
He saw two other brothers.
They were the sons of Zebedee,
James was one, John, the other.

Father and sons were in a boat
Making nets as good as new;
When Jesus called unto them
22 They left and followed too.

23 Going about all Galilee,
In the synagogues He taught
The good news of the kingdom,
To Him the sick were brought.

Now as the people came to Him
He healed diseases of all kind,
He healed their bodies and their
souls
And gave them peace of mind.

24 The fame of Him to Syria spread;
They flocked from far and near,
Seeking to be freed from pain
And Christ's good words to hear.

Demonics and paralytics came
And epileptics too;
He healed the ailing, one and all;
Their health was made anew.

25 From Decapolis and Jerusalem,
From Judea and Galilee,
Great multitudes followed every
     move
Wherever He might be.

Chapter 5

1 When Jesus saw the multitudes
Moving like a mighty tide,
He went unto a mountain,
His disciples by His side

2 There he opened up His mouth
And He began to teach,
3 "Blessed are the poor in Spirit,
Heaven's kingdom they will reach.

4 "Blessed are they who mourn,
They will find joy and mirth.
5 Blessed are the meek and lowly,
They will possess the earth.

6 "Blessed are those who hunger
And after righteousness do thirst,
Surely they shall be satisfied
As Satan's bonds they burst.

7 "Blessed are the merciful,
Mercy they will be given.
8 Blessed are the pure in heart,
They will see God in heaven.

9 "Blessed are the peacemakers,
They're my children, God will con-
     fess.
10 Blessed are the persecuted
For the sake of righteousness.

11 "Blessed are you when reviled,
Or if against you men may lie;
If persecuted on account of Me
I'll wipe the tears from every eye.

12 "Rejoice and be very glad;
Your heavenly reward is great;
Prophets were persecuted before
     you
The Holy Scriptures state.

13 "You are the salt upon the earth
But if it's lost its taste
Cast it out to be trodden down,
And throw it away as waste.

14 "You are a light unto the world—
A city set on a hill,
Hidden not from God or man
A light that spreads goodwill.

15 "Men do not light a lamp
Then hide the lamp away,
They put it on a lampstand so
The house will shine as day.

16 "Before men, let your good works
     shine,
So all the world can see,
And glorify your heavenly Father
Who cares for you and me.

17 "I came not to abolish the Law,
Or what the prophets wrought.
I am the fulfillment of that Word,
Contrary to your thought.

18 "The law shall be unchanged
Till heaven and earth pass away.
Not one letter will disappear,
This is the truth I say.

19 "Whoever breaks but one command,
No matter large or small;
And teaches others to do the same
In heaven he'll be least of all.

"But whosoever follows the commands
In heaven will be great;
20 But you must surpass the Pharisees
To enter heaven's gate.

21 "The Law says, you shall not sin,
And those who do, alas,
22 If you are angry without cause,
A like judgment God will pass.

"Or if you say, 'You fool,' then the
Results are very dire,
For then you have enough guilt
To justify hell's fire.

11

23 "If you approach the altar, yet
A brother you have riled,
24 At the altar leave your gifts
And go be reconciled.

"Once you have done this, then return
And your brother bring along.
God will give a blessing
As you right a wrong.

25 "Make friends with every foe
Before the sun is risen,
For if he then takes you to court
You may be sent to prison.

26 "And you will stay in jail until
You pay back all you owe,
You'll pay back every cent before
The judge will let you go.

27 "Do not commit adultery,
In Scripture this you'll find.
28 If you look lustfully at a woman,
You've sinned within your mind.

29 "If your right eye leads you to sin,
Tear it out and throw it away.
'Tis better to be blinded
Than in hell to forever lay.

30 "If then your right hand causes grief,
Dispose of it as well.
'Tis better one part perish
Than the body go to hell.

31 "The Scripture says, 'let he who would
From his wife divorce,
Give to her a certificate—
Not throw her out by force.'

32 "But I say this unto you, when
This question must be faced,
Do not divorce your wife at all
Unless she is unchaste.

"For if she's not unchaste she'll live
In immorality,
And whoever marries such as she
Commits adultery.

33 "Again you've heard the ancients say,
'You shall not make false vows.'
One must keep those he's made as if
Before the Lord he bows.

34 "But I say this unto you: swear
Not by God's Holy Throne.
35 Nor by earth or Jerusalem,
Which is the Great King's own.

36 "You cannot change hair's color, so
Make no oath by your head.
37 Just say yes-yes, or say no-no,
No more needs be said.

38 "You've heard, if someone plucks your eye,
Or if they knock out a tooth,
You should retaliate in kind,
But that is not the truth.

39 "Do not resist the evil one,
But this you ought to do:
If he should strike your right cheek, then
Present the left one, too.

40 "If anyone would sue you, and
He takes your shirt away,
Then let him also have your coat
Is what I have to say.

41 "If someone makes you walk a mile,
What I say to you,
Not only go this mile,
But double it, walk two.

42 "Give to him who asks of you,
Turn not from him who'd borrow.
Stretch out to all a helping hand,
Share one another's sorrow.

43 "You've heard that it's been said to love
Your neighbor; hate your foes.
44 But I say love your enemies,
And pray for even those.

45 "So like your heavenly Father be,
You really know you should.
For He causes it to rain
On both the evil and the good.

46 "If you would love only those
Whose love you can claim,
What reward do you think you'll get?
For cheats do the same.

47 "And if you greet your brother
only,
You'll find this to your shame:
You do no more than others do,
Even Gentiles do the same.

48 "Your heavenly Father's perfect,
and
When all is said and done,
You must be just like Him, if you
Are to be called His son.

Chapter 6

1 "Don't give your gifts just so
You will be seen by men
Or no rewards you will receive
From your Father in Heaven then.

2 "When you give alms, blow not a
horn
As the hypocrites blow hard.
They may be praised by men, but
they
Will have no further reward.

3 "But when you give an alm
To one who is in need,
Let not your left hand know
Of your right hand's deed.

4 "Do only this deed in secret, so
Your Father in heaven will see.
He'll know what you have done,
And he will reward thee.

5 "Don't loudly pray in public places
To make others aware.
6 Go to your room and close the door
And meet your Father there.

7 "Do not pray like the pagan
Who prays in volumes ample.
8 Your Father knows your needs,
9 So follow this example:

" 'Our Father who art in heaven
Hallowed be thy name.
10 Thy kingdom come, Thy will be
done,
On earth and heaven the same.

11 " 'Give us this day our daily bread,
12 Forgive as we forgive,
13 Prevent temptation so that we
May free from evil live.'

14 "If you forgive others, then
God will forgive you too.
15 But if you do not forgive,
God won't forgive you.

16 "And when you fast let not gloom
Accentuate your face.
Fasting to be seen by men
With God gets you no place.

17 "Instead, when fasting wash
your face,
And look as you usually do.
18 Fast to be seen of your Father,
Who will render you your due.

19 "Store not your treasure on this
earth
Where moth and rust destroy,
Where thieves break in and steal
away
Those objects of your joy.

20 "Lay up your treasure in heaven,
where
You have a better deal.
There moth and rust cannot destroy
Or thieves break in to steal.

21 "For where your treasure is,
you'll find
There your heart will dwell.
So if your treasure in heaven lies,
God will protect it well.

22 "The lamp of the body is the eye,
Through it we have our sight.
Therefore if your eye is clear,
You will be filled with light.

23 "But if your eye is bad, then your
Whole body will be dark;
There'll be no light within you, no,
Not even one small spark.

24 "No one can serve two masters,
this
Should come as no surprise.
One will be held in high regard,
The other he'll despise.

"You cannot God and mammon
serve,
No this you cannot do.
25 And for this very reason I
Will say these words to you:

13

"Do not be anxious for your life,
Or what today you'll drink and eat.
Think not how you clothe your body.
Life is more than clothes and meat.

"Life is much more than food,
And the body more than clothes.
26 Look at the birds of the air
Who neither reap nor sow.

"They never store away supplies,
Yet these the Father feeds.
Are you not worth more than they,
Won't God supply your needs?

27 "You may be fretful and
    distraught,
Be burdened down with care.
But you can't add a moment to
Your life, so why despair?

28 "The lilies do not toil or spin,
Yet grow in glorious ease.
29 Yet Solomon in all his wealth
Was not arrayed like these.

30 "If God so clothe the grass, that is
Today and burned tomorrow,
Will He not also care for you
Of little faith, in sorrow?

31 "Therefore don't be concerned
    about
What food you have to eat,
Nor worry about what you drink
Or if your clothes are neat.

32 "For all these things the Gentiles
    seek,
But your heavenly Father knows.
33 Seek ye first His kingdom, and
God will provide all those.

34 "Do not be anxious for tomorrow,
Leave it upon the shelf.
Each day has its own troubles, let
The future care for itself.

Chapter 7

1"Do not judge or you shall be
    judged.
2 The way you judge your brothers
Is the same standard they will use
When you are judged by others.

3 "You see the specks in others' eyes
Yet you pay no mind,
To the log in your own eye
That you refuse to find.

4 "You have no right to point.
5 You hypocrite, retract
Your own log first and then you can
Your brother's speck extract.

6 "Do not feed holy things to dogs
Or cast pearls before the pigs.
Swine will only trample them, then
    turn
And tear you up as twigs.

7 Ask and it shall be given you,
Seek it and you shall find.
Knock and it shall be opened by
Our Lord so good and kind.

8 "For everyone who asks, receives,
He who seeks shall find.
God will open many doors
To those of inquiring mind.

9 "Would a father give a stone
If his son asked for a cake;
10 Or if he asked to have a fish,
Would give to him a snake?

11 "If you then who are evil
Know to give your children good,
How much the heavenly Father will
When asked; you know He would.

12 "If you would have kind treatment
This then you must do,
You must treat other people as
You'd have them treat you.

13 "Enter by the narrow gate,
Hell's gate is broad and wide,
It leads to sure destruction and
There flows the teeming tide.

14"The gate that leads to eternal life
Is quite narrow and small.
And only a very few
Will find the gate at all.

15 "Beware of prophets who are
    false,
Those with an evil heart;
They dress like sheep, these wolves;
They will tear you apart.

14

16 "You will know them by their fruit,
As they do what they please.
You do not gather figs from thistles
Or find a grape on a thorn tree.

17 "Likewise you'll find that a good
tree
Will always bear good fruit.
18 A good tree cannot bear bad fruit,
Or a bad tree follow suit.

19 "Every tree that you find that
Has no good fruit upon it,
Will be cut and thrown upon the
ground.
There the fire will burn it.

20 "Thus, it will be by their fruit
That they will be known.
21 For not everyone who says 'Lord,
Lord'
The Kingdom will be shown.

"You will not be able to enter
Heaven's Kingdom until
You listen to what my Father says
And you follow His will.

22 "Some say, 'Did we not prophesy
And in your name cast out
Great demons and work miracles,
and
Spread your word about?'

23 "I will tell them, 'I know you not,
Depart at once from Me.'
For you who practice lawlessness
My kingdom will not see.

24 "Therefore the one who heeds My
words
And hears when I knock,
Is like the man who's very wise
And built his house on rock.

25 "The rains poured down, the
waters rose,
The strong wind blew along,
And yet the house did not fall—its
Foundation was too strong.

26 "Each one who hears My words
and yet
Who for Me will not stand,
Is like a very foolish man
Who built his house on sand.

27 "The rains came down, the floods
rose up,
The winds blew at the wall
And that man's house fell in a heap,
Great was the house's fall."

28 When Jesus finished teaching, the
Crowds were amazed to see
His teachings were not like the
scribes,
For He taught with authority.

Chapter 8

1 The multitudes then followed
Christ
When He walked down the hill.
2 A leper came to Him and said,
"You can heal me if you will."

3 Jesus said to him, "I will."
One touch and he was clean.
The leprosy left immediately,
And not a trace was seen.

4 Jesus said, "Tell no one, and
Yourself to the priest present
The offering Moses prescribed
As a testimony for this event.

5 Jesus entered Capernaum, where
A centurion met Him there.
6 He said, "My servant is paralyzed
And needs your tender care.

7 "Yes," said Jesus, "I will come,
Your servant I will heal."
8 The centurion said to Him,
"Lord, this is how I feel:

"I am not really worthy
For you to come through my door,
But if you will just say the word,
My servant will be sick no more.

9 "I am a man of authority,
With soldiers at my command,
If I say go or I say come,
They do what I demand."

10 Jesus marvelled at the man.
He said, so all could hear,
"Nowhere in all of Israel
Does faith as this appear.

11 "And this I say to you—they
Shall come from east and west,
Recline at the table with Abraham
And sit with heaven's best.

12 "But the subjects of the kingdom,
Will be thrown outside,
Weeping and gnashing of teeth,
In darkness to abide."

13 Jesus said to the centurion,
"It is done, go on your way,
As you believe, you have received,
Your servant is healed today."

14 Then Jesus went to Peter's home,
Whose mother lay sick in bed,
15 He touched her and she then
    arose—
The fever left her head.

16 When evening came that day to
    Him,
Many demon possessed were
    brought.
He cast the evil spirits out
And did the healing they sought.

17 A prophecy was thus fulfilled
Which Isaiah gave one day,
"He healed all our infirmities
And took all diseases away."

18 When Jesus saw the crowd He
    said,
"Let's seek the other side."
19 A scribe said, "I'll go with you, to
Whatever places you reside."

20 Jesus said, "The fox has
Its hole, and the bird its nest,
The Son of Man has nowhere He
Can lay His head to rest."

21 "When my father has been buried
I'll follow you," one said.
22 Christ answered, "Follow me and
    let
The dead bury the dead."

23 Then Jesus got into a boat,
They rowed across the deep.
24 A great and fearful storm arose
But Christ was fast asleep.

25 The disciples came and woke
    Him, saying,
"Save us, we are sinking."
26 Jesus said, "Ye of little faith
You must change your thinking."

He then arose, rebuked the wind,
The sea became very calm.
27 "What kind of man is this," they
    said,
"Who holds winds in His palm?"

28 Then they arrived at Gadara
Which was on the other side,
Two violent men approached Him
    and
There was nowhere to hide.

These men, possessed of demons,
Let no one down the road,
But they both came to Jesus from
The tombs of their abode.

29 "Behold," they cried out saying,
    "What
Have we to do with you,
You are the Son of God,
Would you torment us too?"

30 The demons pleaded with Him, "If
You are going to cast us out,
31 Permit us to possess the swine
Who are feeding 'round about."

32 Jesus said to them, "Begone!"
Into the swine they went.
The whole herd rushed into the sea;
There their life was spent.

33 The herdsmen fled, fast to town,
And there told all the facts—
Of how the herd was drowned
And about the demoniacs.

34 The whole town then came out,
To meet Jesus that same day.
They pleaded for Him to leave,
And be quick on His way.

Chapter 9

1 Once more He got into the boat,
And crossed the sea again,
He came to His own city, but
Before He settled in,

2 They brought to Him a paralytic
Lying on his bed.
"Have courage, your sins are for-
    given,"
Christ turned to him and said.

3 Some scribes said to themselves,
"This man speaks blasphemy."
4 Jesus knew their thoughts and
    said,
"Why think such things of Me?

5 "Why do you think such evil
    thoughts?
For which is easier to say,
Your sins are all forgiven,
Or get up and walk away?

6 "But so that you may know I have
The power to pardon sin,
I say to this paralytic, 'Rise,
Take your bed, go home again.'"

7 He arose and went to his home,
8 The crowd was filled with awe,
They gave glory to their God
Because of what they saw.

9 As Jesus passed from that place,
A man named Matthew He did see,
Sitting at his tax collection booth.
Jesus said, "Come follow Me."

As ordered, Matthew followed Him,
10 And invited Christ to eat.
Many people gathered who
He wanted Christ to meet.

As Christ reclined at the table
More tax men and sinners came,
They joined with Jesus at the feast.
11 The Pharisees thought this a
    shame.

They said to His disciples,
"He eats with those who sin?
With tax collectors and their kind
Who are not clean within?"

12 When Jesus heard this comment
He said, "Cannot you see
The well need no physician; it's
The sick who needeth Me.

13 "But go and learn just what this
    means,
Compassion is what I do desire.
I have no pleasure in sacrifice
Which you burn on the altar fire.

"I did not come to call the righteous,
But sinners to repent.
It was to such as these that by
My Father I've been sent."

14 John's disciples came to Him,
And said, "Why do we fast?
Your followers eat all the time
And not one meal goes past."

15 "Friends of the bridegroom,"
    Jesus said,
"Can never look downcast
While with them is the bridegroom.
    When
He's married they will fast.

16 "No one puts an unshrunk patch
On an old garment he wears,
For the patch would pull away and
    he
Sould have a bigger tear.

17 "Men would never put new wine
Into wineskins used before.
New wine would burst the skins and
Out the wine would pour.

"Instead, if one possess new wine
Which he'd like to have served,
It should be put in fresh wine-skins,
Then they are both preserved."

18 While Jesus was thus teaching
A ruler came to Him,
He said, "My daughter died, and
Things look sad and dim.

But if you will quickly come
And take her by the hand,
I know that she will live again—
Death yields to your command.

19 Jesus rose to follow him,
His disciples went along,
20 A woman came up behind Him;
She was not very strong.

She'd had a hemorrhage for years,
And in great weakness did dwell.
21 She said, "If I can touch His garment
I know I'll be made well."

She reached out and she touched
His cloak,
22 Then Jesus turned and said,
"Your faith has made you well, and you
Are freed from your sick bed."

23 When Jesus came to the ruler's house
He saw the crowds stand weeping.
24 He said, "Depart, the girl's not dead,
No, she is only sleeping."

All the people laughed at Him
For they knew she was dead,
25 But Jesus placed His hand on her
And she rose from her bed.

26 The news of this went all about,
It spread throughout the land,
Word of this act of mercy from
The Saviour's healing hand.

27 As Jesus passed on from there
Two men who both were blind,
Cried, "Have mercy, Son of David,
To us be very kind."

28 When Jesus came into the house
He met them at His table.
He said, "Do you think I can heal?"
They said, "Yes, Lord, you're able."

29 He reached out and He touched
their eyes.
He said, "Be it done for you.
According to the faith you've shown,
I restore your sight anew."

30 And when their eyes were opened,
To them He sternly said,
"Let no man know of this."
31 But the news quickly spread.

32 They brought a dumb man unto
Him
Who wore a demon yoke.
33 When Jesus cast the demon out
The dumb man plainly spoke.

The multitudes, astounded said,
"He does all things quite well,
Nothing like this was ever seen
In all of Israel."

34 The Pharisees were jealous and
They said, "We have no doubt
That from Satan comes His power
To cast the demons out."

35 Jesus went to all the cities,
And the small towns too,
Proclaiming the kingdom gospel,
What people ought to do.

He healed not only sickness, but
Disease of every kind.
36 He had compassion on fainting
multitudes
And gave them peace of mind.

Like sheep without a shepherd,
they
Were helpless and harassed.
37 Christ said, "The workers are so
few
To reap the harvest vast.

38 "Therefore you should beseech
the Lord
To send workers to the field.
So we can gather all the grain,
And take the fullest yield."

Chapter 10

1 He called to His disciples, gave
Them power to cast out
Great demons and to heal disease,
Then sent them all about.

2 These are the twelve apostles'
names;
Simon Peter, and Andrew his
brother,
James the son of Zebedee,
His sibling, John, another.

3 The next apostles Jesus called
Were Philip and Bartholomew,
He then called Thomas to Him and
The tax collector, Matthew.

James the son of Alphaeus,
4 And Simon were apostles made.
Then Thaddaeus and Judas, too,
By whom He was betrayed.

5 Jesus sent out these apostles
Said, "Away from the Gentiles keep,
Don't go to the Samaritans,
6 Go to Israel, My lost sheep.

7 "And as you go preach, say,
God's kingdom is at hand;
Heal the sick, raise the dead,
Help all throughout the land.

8 "Also cleanse the leapers,
Demons you must cast out.
Freely give what you've received
To remove all fear and doubt.

9 "Do not acquire gold or silver
Or copper to buy your feed,
10 Do not take two pairs of sandals,
One tunic is all you'll need.

"Do not take a staff with you,
The worker is worthy of his hire.
11 Whenever you enter a city
You must always then inquire,

"Where a worthy man's home is,
There you must abide.
12 Let your peace be upon it
If he welcomes you inside.

"If you find such a house
Such blessings will be due.
13 If that house is unworthy
Let your peace return to you.

14"And if they will not heed your
words;
If you they'll not receive;
Shake the dust from your feet, and
That house and city leave.

15 "When judgment comes on that
town,
God will have no pity.
Sodom and Gomorrah will
Fare better than that city.

16 "Among the wolves I send you,
Although you go as sheep,
Be therefore wise as serpents,
While dove-like innocence keep.

17 "You must beware of sinful men,
Who give you a bad report.
They'll scourge you in the
synagogues
And drag you into court.

18 "You will be brought before the
kings
And governors for My sake.
You'll be a testimony to them all,
And My words to Gentiles take.

19 "When you're delivered up to
them,
Don't fear and do not worry,
It shall be given what to say
When you're before the jury.

20 "It is not you who speak
But it is your Father's Spirit,
Who lives and therefore speaks in
you
So all the world can hear it.

21 "Brothers will deliver brothers,
A father will accuse his child.
Children will rise against their
parents,
Capital charges will be filed.

22 "Everyone will hate you then
Because you are my friend.
If you are faithful to My name
You'll be saved in the end.

23 "When persecuted in this city,
Go tell another of their sin.
You'll not visit all of Israel
Till the Son of Man comes again.

24 "A disciple is not above his
teacher,
Nor a master above his slave.
25 From his teacher or his master
Each should learn how to behave.

"If the master is called a devil
How much more his household,
26 But everything will be revealed,
Hidden things will be told.

27 "What I say to you in darkness,
Speak out so all can hear.
Proclaim upon the housetops
What is whispered in your ear.

28 "Do not fear those who kill the
body
But not the soul as well;
Fear Him who kills both soul and body
And destroys both in hell.

29 "Do not two sparrows cost a
penny?
And yet it will be found,
That it is known by your heavenly
Father
When these fall to the ground.

30 "The hairs are numbered on your
head,
31 Therefore, please have no fear.
You are worth much more than
sparrows,
To God you are so dear.

32 "Those who confess me before
men
I'll confess to my Father on high.
33 Those who deny me before men
Before my Father I'll deny.

34 "I did not come here to bring
peace,
I came to bring a sword.
35 A man will rise against his father,
On him wrath will be poured.

"A daughter will speak against her
mother,
Her mother-in-law she'll fear.
36 From within your own household
Many enemies will appear.

37 "If love for parents is greater than
The love you have for Me,
You are not worthy of the blessing
That I would bring to thee.

38 "Nor is a person worthy
Who will not take up his cross
And follow in My footsteps,
Counting all things else but loss.

39 "He who finds life within himself
Will see it slip away.
But if he gives his life for Me
He'll live again someday.

40 "He who will receive you,
Also receiveth me,
And receives the one by whom I'm
sent
As you should clearly see.

41 "He who receives a prophet
In a prophet's name
Receives what a prophet gets.
Yes, he will receive the same.

"He who receives a righteous man
Receives a righteous man's award.
42 A cup of water in My name
Will not lose its reward."

Chapter 11

1 After giving these instructions
Jesus left there to teach.
He went into the cities
God's message He would preach.

2 When John, in Herod's prison
heard
Of works that Christ had done,
By his disciples he sent word,
3 "Are you the coming One?

"Are you the true Messiah
Or do we look for another?
Are you the one God sent
The Savior and no other?"

4 Jesus said to them, "Report
what you hear and see.
5 The lame can walk, lepers are
cleansed,
And the blind are set free.

"The deaf can hear, the dead are
raised,
And there is so much more;
The gospel is preached to everyone,
Even to the very poor."

6 Blessed are those who do not
doubt
7 I say unto you, take heed.
What did you go out to see,
A broken and shaking reed?

8 "What were you looking for:
A man in soft trappings?
Those who wear rich apparel
Are in the palaces of kings.

9 "Why then did you all go out?
To see a prophet you say;
You saw more than a prophet
When you went out that day.

10 "This is the one of whom it's
    written,
'I send ahead of you
My messenger, and behold, he
To prepare your way; it's true.'

11 "I say unto you truly, that
Of all born of women,
None greater than John the Baptist
In this world is risen.

"Yet if you look into God's heaven
This is what you'll see,
The least one in God's kingdom
Is greater still than he.

12 "God's kingdom suffers violently
From John the Baptist until now.
Evil men would take it by force,
They wish to seize it somehow.

13 "All the prophets and the Law
Said one would come some day
To smooth the path for the Lord,
Elijah would prepare the way.

14 "I tell you John is Elijah,
I would make this very clear,
15 He who has ears to hear it
Then I say, 'Let him hear.'

16 "What shall I say of this
    generation?
To what does it compare?
It is like children in the market
Who call to their friends there.

17 "They say, 'We played for you
    and yet
You did not dance or cheer.
And when we played a dirge for you
You did not shed a tear.'

18 "When John arrived upon the
    scene
He neither drank nor ate.
Because of this the people thought
A demon caused his state.

19 "The Son of Man did come.
And He did eat and drink.
They said, 'A glutton and a
    drunkard,
Of Him is what we think.

"'Here's a man with sinners
Who has close ties.'
But the proof is in the action,
And is deemed wise."

20 Then He reproached the cities
    where
His mighty works were done,
For they had not repented
Or listened to God's Son.

21 "To Chorazin and Bethsaida, woe
For all the ill you do,
If Tyre and Sidon saw the works
Which were performed in you,

"Long ago they would have
    repented,
In ashes and sackcloth.
22 In judgment they will better fare,
For you have made God wroth.

23 "Capernaum, which exalts itself
Will be brought down to hell.
If the miracles had been done in
    Sodom
That city would still be well.

24 "When all of you in judgment
    stand
This I will truly state,
Their punishment will be tolerable
While yours will be quite great."

25 Then said Jesus, "I praise you,
    Father,
Lord of earth and heavenly skies,
That you've seen fit to hide these
    things
From the intelligent and wise.

"But unto babes you have revealed
Things which are good and right.
• 26 Yes, Father you have done this,
    for
It's pleasing in your sight.

27 "The Father has given all to Me,
He only knows the Son;
Unless I reveal to you the Father,
He will be known by none.

28 "Come unto Me you burdened
down
And I will give you rest.
29 Assume My yoke and learn from
Me
Of humble heartedness.

"In doing so, your soul will find
Great peace and be all right.
30 You'll find my yoke is easy and
The burden to be light."

Chapter 12

1 Jesus walked across a field
Upon a Sabbath day,
His disciples plucked the grain and
ate
As they walked along the way.

2 The Pharisees, who were looking
on
Were shocked at what they saw,
Said, "Your disciples are doing things
That are against the Law."

3 Jesus turning, said to them,
"Why, have you never read
4 How David and his companions
Ate consecrated bread?

"He began to eat the bread.
God's house he entered in.
By law, only priests could eat
This bread and not sin.

5 "Or have you not read in the Law,
That priests the Sabbath break?
They work the temple on the holy
day
And not the least blame take.

6 "Someone greater than the temple
Stands before you here today,
If you would only stop and listen
You'd hear what He has to say.

7 "If only you knew what this
means,
'It's mercy I desire,
Not sacrifice'; you'd not have brought
The guiltless under fire."

8 Jesus said, "The Lord of the
Sabbath
Is the Son of Man."
9 He left, and in the synagogue saw
10 A man with a shriveled hand.

Those gathered there said, "Jesus
can
You on the Sabbath heal?"
They asked the Lord to trick him and
Perhaps a fault reveal.

11 Jesus then replied to them,
"If your sheep falls in a pit
Even if it is the Sabbath day
You will take care of it.

12 "A man is worth much more than
sheep,
And therefore deeds you may
Do lawfully although they be
Done on the Sabbath day."

13 Then Jesus said unto the man,
"Stretch out your hand, My
brother."
The man stretched out his hand
and it
Was whole just like the other.

14 The Pharisees were very angry,
They really were annoyed,
So they went out and discussed how
This man could be destroyed.

15 But Jesus was aware of this,
So He withdrew from there,
Many people followed, and
He healed with loving care.

16 He asked them not to make Him
known,
17 But now it came about
That which was spoken by Isaiah
Was being carried out.

18 "My servant, whom I have
chosen,
Is pleasing to My soul,
He is beloved, and upon Him
I'll put my Spirit whole.

"He will to Gentiles proclaim justice
19 From Him no fighting word.
And even out upon the street
His voice will not be heard.

20 "He will not break a battered reed,
Or smoldering wick put out,
Until He makes justice victorious
21 And His name Gentiles shout."

22 They brought to Him one with a demon,
He was both blind and dumb;
23 When he was healed by Christ they asked,
"Could this be David's son?"

24 When the Pharisees heard these words,
To the people they did shout,
"By the demon's ruler, Beelzebub,
He casts the demons out."

25 Jesus said to the Pharisees,
"Divided kingdoms fall.
A house or city that is split
I say can't stand at all."

26 "If Satan casts out Satan, then
He cuts himself in twain;
By doing so, you understand,
His kingdom can't remain.

27 "And if I by Beelzebub
These demons put to rout,
By whom do your children claim
To be casting demons out?

28 "But if it is by God's Spirit
I am casting demons out,
God's kingdom has come unto you,
Of this I have no doubt.

29 "Can you enter a strong man's house
And tear his place asunder;
Unless you bind the strong man first?
His house you then may plunder.

30 "He who is not with Me is against Me.
He who does not gather scatters wide.
31 Except for blasphemy against the Spirit
Every sin can be set aside.

32 "If you speak against the Son of Man
You still can be forgiven,
But if you speak against God's Spirit
You'll never get to heaven.

33 "Make tree and fruit both good, or make
It rotten to the root.
For every tree upon the earth
Shall be known by its fruit.

34 "You brood of vipers, being evil,
Couldn't speak truth if you would.
The mouth speaks what is in the heart—
Your heart has nothing good.

35 "The evil man brings forth evil,
From his evil treasure chest.
But the good man from his treasures
Brings forth his very best.

36 "I say that every careless word
That any man shall say;
He shall give an account for it
On that great judgment day.

37 "For by your words you stand condemned,
Or by them justified,
For the words that you speak
Tell how you feel inside."

38 Said some scribes and Pharisees,
"Teacher, your words are fine,
But if we are to believe you,
Then please give us a sign."

39 In answer, Jesus said to them,
"An evil generation
Will always crave to see a sign
For every situation.

"Yet no sign shall be given them
But as Jonah in the whale,
40 A span of three days and three nights,
Confinement it entailed.

"Even so shall the Son of Man
Spend three days in the grave.
Then God will raise Him up again
And men's souls He will save.

41 "The men of Ninevah will rise
To condemn this generation,
For when Jonah preached to them
They listened throughout the na-
tion.

"When Jonah spoke to all of them
They did not laugh or sneer.
Instead they repented, but now
One greater than Jonah is here.

42 "The Queen of the South will also
rise
To condemn this generation.
She travelled far to hear Solomon,
The wise king of our nation.

"You close your eyes and do not see,
Against Me you shut your ear.
You do not realize that a greater
One than Solomon is here.

43 "When an unclean spirit leaves a
man
It travels through dry spaces,
It is seeking somewhere to rest,
Yet never finds such places.

44 "The spirit then says, 'I'll return,
Go back to my old home;
If I can get right back inside
I will not have to roam.'

"He finds it swept, but empty,
45 Brings seven devils more,
Who came to rest inside that man;
He's worse off than before.

"That is the way it will be
With this generation, full of sin.
You may throw an evil spirit out,
But more will enter in."

46 While He was speaking to the
crowd,
His family sought Him out.
47 They wanted to take Him home
with them,
For they were filled with doubt.

48 Jesus said to all,
"Who is my mother and brothers?"
49 Then stretched He forth His hand
Toward the disciples and many
others.

50 Then Jesus spoke these words to
them,
"He who does my Father's will,
He is my mother, sister, brother,
And his life with wisdom fill."

Chapter 13

1 That same day Jesus left the
house
And sat beside the sea.
2 As usual crowds gathered 'round
Wherever He might be.

So Jesus got into a boat,
And in it sat to teach.
The multitudes who gathered there
Stood quietly on the beach.

3 He spoke to them in parables.
"Behold! A sower tilled the land,"
Some thought it just a story
But some would understand.

4 "Some seed fell by the wayside,
The birds had a feast so royal.
5 Other seed fell on rocky ground
Where there was little soil.

"These seeds sprang up too quickly,
They were tender little shoots,
6 But when the sun came up, they
withered,
Because they had no roots.

7 "And others fell among the thorns;
The thorns soon choked them out.
Good seed can't grow among the
weeds,
There is no room to sprout.

8 "But others fell on good rich soil,
They grew quite strong and sturdy.
Some yielded up a hundred fold,
Some sixty and some thirty."

And thus His story ended, but
He added one comment,
9 "He with ears let him hear
What this parable meant."

10 His disciples came to ask Him,
As the crowds they viewed,
"Why do you speak in parables
When you teach the multitude?"

11 In answer Jesus said to them,
"To you it is made known
The secrets of heaven's kingdom,
     but
To them it has not been shown.

12 "Whoever has shall more be
     given—
Abundance comes his way;
But he with naught or little shall
Have all taken away.

13 "I speak therefore in parables
As I go through the land,
For many in the crowds do not
See, hear, or understand.

14 "This is what Isaiah meant,
The thing he had in mind
When he said, 'You will keep on
     hearing,
But meaning, you'll not find.

" 'You will continue seeing,
But you will not perceive,
15 For this people's heart is dull
And their ears they don't believe.

" 'They've tightly shut their eyes
     and they
Have also clogged their ears
Lest that they learn and under-
     stand
A thing they seem to fear.

" 'Then with their heart they'd un-
     derstand,
They'd repent and turn again
And I should heal them, everyone
And cleanse them from their sin.'

16 "But blessed are your ears and
     eyes
Because you hear and see,
17 Righteous men and prophets
     wanted
The truth I bring to thee.

18 "This is the meaning of the
     parable
Which I told you today,
19 The seed along the paths of the
     heart
Satan would snatch away.

20 "The seed sown in a man upon
The dry and rocky ground,
Although it is received with joy,
21 No root in him is found.

"When persecution rises up
He immediately falls away,
He has nothing to hold on to
When trouble comes his way.

22 "The one on whom the seed was
     sown,
Which in the thorns were hurled,
Is the man who hears the word but
     sees
The worry of the world.

"He is deceived by riches,
And My words are choked out,
He becomes an unfruitful plant
Because of his fears and doubt.

23 "And that seed which was sown
     upon
the rich and fertile lands,
Is like the man who hears the word
And deeply understands.

"He indeed will bear much fruit,
Thirty times more than sown,
Others sixty times as much,
Or a hundred fold is grown."

24 He then told another parable,
"Heaven is like a field.
The farmer planned carefully;
He desired abundant yield.

25 "When the planting day was over
And the men went home to eat
His enemy came in the night, and
Sowed tares among the wheat.

26 "The wheat sprang up and
     brought forth grain
But the tares all came up too,
27 The servant said to the owner,
'Sir, what are we to do?'

" 'Did you not sow good seed
And cultivate with care?
Sir, we do not understand
Why it should be full of tares.'

25

28 "To his servants, the landowner said,
'An enemy has come by.
In my fields he sowed the tares so that
The tender plants would die.'

"The servants asked, 'Shall we pull them up,
What would you have us do?'
29 He said, 'If you pull them up,
You'll pull the wheat up, too.

30 "'Allow the two to grow together
Until the harvest day,
Then gather tares and bind them.
To you reapers I will say:

" 'Put the tares in bundles,
And throw them in the fire.
But put the wheat into my barn.
This is what I desire.'

31 "Heaven's kingdom is like a mustard seed.
32 This seed is very small,
But when this tiny seed is planted
It grows up very tall.

"It outgrows all the other plants,
Birds fly to it for rest.
They sit upon its branches, and
In it they build their nest.

33 "Or heaven's kingdom is like leaven,
Which a woman puts in dough,
It only takes a tiny bit
To make bread rise, you know."

34 Jesus spoke to them in parables;
He used parables to teach.
This method Jesus liked to use
When people He would reach.

35 So what was spoken by the prophets,
Of things that God had willed,
Saying, "I will speak in parables,
Hidden things will be fulfilled."

36 Then Jesus went into a house
To rest from many cares.
His disciples came and said to Him,
"Explain to us the tares."

37 He said, "The one who sows good seed,
He is the Son of Man.
38 To sow good seed throughout the world
Is God's own holy plan.

"The good seed are the kingdom's sons,
The tares, the evil ones.
39 The enemy is the sly old devil,
Such evil deeds he's done.

"The harvest comes at the end of time.
God's angels do the reaping.
40 They gather tares and other things
Which are not worth the keeping.

41 "The Son of Man sends angels forth
To gather up the rocks—
All of those evil ones who are
So many stumbling blocks.

42 "He will cast them into the furnace,
Where in the fire they'll burn,
They will weep and gnash their teeth
If the Son of Man they spurn.

43 "The righteous will shine brightly, like
The sun they will appear,
In the kingdom of their Father.
Who has ears, let him hear.

44 "Heaven's kingdom's like a treasure which
Lies hidden in a field,
To get that treasure many would
All their possessions yield.

"A finder sells all he has, and with
The funds that field he buys,
Which contains the precious treasure
That he does highly prize.

45 "Or it is like a merchant, who
Seeks pearls with no flaw,
One day down at the market place
Just such a pearl he saw.

46 He sold everything to buy it,
Gave everything he had,
For to own a pearl so fine
Would make him very glad.

47 "The kingdom's also like a net
That's cast into the sea.
It catches every kind of fish,
Both good and bad, you see.

48 "When the net is full they pull
The net out of the bay,
The good fish go in buckets.
The bad they throw away.

49 "So it will be at the end of time,
Angels from the sky
Will take the righteous from the
wicked.
None evil will get by.

50 "The wicked will be cast into a
furnace,
With a fire down underneath,
There they will weep and mourn.
There they will gnash their teeth.

51 "Have you understood my ex-
planation?
Do you know what I have said?"
They said to Him, "Yes Lord,
Our souls you have surely fed."

52 He said, "Every scribe who is
instructed
Is like the head of a household,
He brings forth from his treasure
Good things, both new and old."

53 After telling all these parables
Jesus left that place.
54 He went into His home town,
where
Old neighbors he would face.

He went into their synagogue
Where He began to teach.
They asked, "Where did He get
such power and wisdom
And receive the right to preach?

55 "Is not this man the carpenter's
son,
Or maybe He's some other?
His brothers live among us.
Is Mary this man's mother?

56 "His sisters are all with us,
Of our town they are apart,
Where did he get these teachings?
He thinks He is so smart?"

57 They took offense at Him, and
they
Then tried to put Him down.
He said, "A prophet has no honor
In His own house and town."

58 He did not many miracles there
Because to believe, they wouldn't;
Not because of lack of love
Nor because He couldn't.

Chapter 14

1 Herod the Tetrarch had heard of
Jesus
And this is what he said,
2 "This man is John the Baptist, he
Has risen from the dead."

3 Herod had put John in prison,
And had threatened to take his life,
For Herod had married Herodias,
Who had been his brother's wife.

4 John had said to Herod,
"This thing is not right,
God's holy law you've broken,
You've done evil in His sight."

5 Herod thought to put John to
death
But he feared the multitude.
They regarded John as a prophet,
The one whom God had imbued.

6 But when Herod had his birthday,
Herodias' daughter danced.
She pleased Herod very much,
By her he was entranced.

7 Then Herod promised, with an
oath,
To give what e'er she'd ask:
"If you just say the word
I will perform the task."

8 Having been prompted by her
mother,
Who wanted John the Baptist dead,
She said, "On a silver platter
Bring me John the Baptist's head."

9 Though it grieved Herod mightily
To grant this wicked request,
He commanded that the deed be
done
To save food with his dinner guests.

10 He sent and had John beheaded,
He did it that very night,
11 The head was brought in on a
plate
For the daughter and mother's
sight.

12 John's followers came for his
body,
For burial took it away.
Then they went to Jesus, and
Told Him what happened that day.

13 Jesus then took to a boat;
He went to a desert part
To be alone with His Father
And talk to Him heart to heart.

The multitudes followed Him on
foot,
They came out of every city,
14 When He looked out and saw the
crowds
On them He had great pity.

He healed their sick throughout the
day.
15 When evening finally came
He still moved amongst the throng
Healing their sick and lame.

The disciples said to Jesus,
"There is nothing to eat out here.
Send the crowd away to buy food
In the villages which are near."

16 But Jesus said to them.
"Though it is the close of day,
You give them food to eat,
They need not go away."

17 But His disciples said to Him,
"Here's five loaves and two fishes.
This is barely food enough
To fill a few dishes."

18 Jesus said, "Bring them to Me,
19 Have all sit on the grass."
Then He prayed to the Father and
The food they began to pass.

20 They all ate and were filled.
There was food for everyone.
And there were twelve full
baskets left
When everyone was done.

21 There were five thousand men
that day,
Along with them their wives,
Not only did they feast on fish,
Their children ate, besides.

22 He then told His disciples,
"Take the boat, go ahead of Me,
While I send the crowd away
From the beaches by the sea."

23 So the disciples left Him, and
The crowds all went away.
Jesus went up into a mountain
To be alone to pray.

24 Meanwhile the boat, out on the
sea,
Was battered by wind and wave.
The mighty gales blew very strong,
The outlook seemed quite grave.

25 In the fourth watch of the night
Jesus came walking on the sea,
26 The disciples cried out in fear,
"It is a ghost we see."

27 Immediately Jesus spoke to them,
"Take courage, it is I;
Do not be afraid of anything,
There is no need to cry."

28 Then Peter bravely answered,
"Lord,
If it is really you,
Command me to come to thee
And walk on water, too."

29 Jesus said to Peter, "Come."
From the boat he started out,
30 He felt the wind, he saw the
waves
And then began to doubt.

As Peter's fears within him rose,
He sank into the sea.
He cried out to the Master,
"I perish, Lord, save me."

31 Jesus stretched forth His hand,
From the waters pulled him out.
He said, "Peter, where is your faith:
What caused you to doubt?"

32 And when they got into the boat,
The wind ceased to blow.
33 They said, "You are the Son of
God,
This thing we surely know."

34 When the boat reached the land,
They pulled upon the shore.
They found they were in
Gennesaret,
Where they'd been once before.

35 As soon as He was recognized
People came from all around,
They brought to Him the sick
Wherever they were found.

36 They asked Him to heal them;
They were so very sure,
That if they simply touched Him,
They'd have an instant cure.

Chapter 15

1 Scribes and Pharisees from
Jerusalem came,
To accuse Him was their mission:
2 "Your disciples don't wash before
they eat,
And this breaks our tradition."

3 Jesus answered them and said,
"Why break ye God's commands,
You've added tradition to His words
To escape what He demands.

4 "God said, 'Your father and your
mother
Are always to be respected.
You shall not evil speak of them,
Or let them be neglected.

"The one who curses his parents
And does not meet their needs,
He certainly shall die unless
The Law of God he heeds.

5 "You say to them, 'I'd like to help,
But everything that's mine
Is dedicated to my Lord, I can't
Take from God divine.'

6 "You invalidated the Word of God
For the sake of your tradition,
You make His Word of no effect
By making your addition.

7 "You really are hypocrites,
You've heard Isaiah's prophecy,
8 'These people honor one with
their lips,'
But their heart is far from Me.

9 "'They worship Me in vain, and
Their works I'll not accept,
For the doctrines that they teach
Are really men's precept."

10 He called the people and to them
said,
"Hear me; be not beguiled:
11 Not what goes into your mouth
But what comes out defiles."

12 His disciples came and said to
Him,
"The Pharisees you've offended
By the things you said to them:
Should your words be amended?"

13 Jesus said, "The plants My
Father did not plant
Shall be pulled up roots and all.
14 They are blind and if they guide
the blind
Into the ditch both will fall."

15 And Peter answered, said to Him,
"Explain to us your word."
16 Jesus said, "Do you not
understand
The things that you have heard?

17 "Things you put into your mouth
Pass through and are eliminated,
18 But things that come from out
your mouth
In your heart have originated.

"The things you eat cannot defile,
For these soon go to waste,
19 But evil thoughts born in the
heart
Can bring a bitter taste.

29

"Out of the heart comes evil
    thoughts,
Of murder, lies, and theft,
And slander and adultery,
All leave a soul bereft.

20 "All things defile a man,
But to eat with unwashed hands
Will not defile a soul and won't
Infringe on God's commands."

21 Jesus then withdrew from there
To a district outside Tyre.
22 A woman from that region came
And cried out her desire.

"Have mercy, Son of David, for
My daughter is possessed.
A demon cruelly treats her, and
She therefore has no rest."

23 Jesus did not answer her,
He gave her no reply.
His disciples said, "Send her away
Or after us she'll cry."

24 When Jesus answered, "I was sent
To Israel's lost sheep,"
25 She knelt and said, "Please help
    me Lord,"
And she began to weep.

26 Jesus answered and said to her,
"You can't take children's bread
And throw the crumbs to dogs until
The children have been fed."

27 She said to Him, "Lord, I know
    this
But even dogs do feed
When crumbs fall from the table,
And thus they meet their need."

28 Jesus answered, "Your faith is
    great,
Be it done as you desire."
Her daughter was healed that
    moment
Then Jesus left from Tyre.

29 When He departed from this
    place
He walked the shore of Galilee,
Then He went into the mountains
And sat where all could see.

30 Great multitudes came unto Him,
'Twas here that they did meet;
Bringing both the lame and blind,
They laid them at His feet.

Jesus had compassion on them,
Their pleas were not ignored,
He healed the lame and crippled,
To the blind, sight was restored.

31 The multitudes greatly marveled
When they heard dumb men
    talking.
They glorified the God of Israel
When they saw lame men walking.

32 Jesus called His disciples and
    said,
"They've been with Me now three
    days.
I must not send them out hungry
Lest they faint along the way."

33 His disciples were dumbfounded,
They looked Him in the face.
Asked, "Where would we find bread
For so many in this place?"

34 To His disciples Jesus said,
"Just what food have you got?"
"Seven loaves and a few fishes,
You know that's not a lot."

"Bring them to Me," Jesus said,
"These loaves that you have found,
35 Tell the people who are here
To sit upon the ground."

36 He took the seven loaves and
    fishes,
And giving thanks, He broke.
He gave them to the disciples who
Passed it among the folk.

37 All the crowd was satisfied,
They ate and had their fill.
They picked up seven baskets full
Left over on that hill.

38 Four thousand men there were
In the crowd on that day,
Plus their wives and children
Who ate and went their way.

39 When Jesus sent the crowd away
According to His plan,
He then got into a boat
And went into Magadan.

Chapter 16

1 The Pharisees and Sadducees,
Thought Jesus they would test.
"Show us a sign from heaven," they
      said,
"We make this one request."

2 Jesus said, "You read the signs,
About you in the air.
In the evening when the sky is red
You say the weather's fair.

3 "Then when the morning does
      appear
There will be storms you say,
Red and threatening is the sky,
Yes, it will rain today.

"You can discern the weather just
From looking at the sky;
Why then can you not see the signs
That are always very nigh?

4 "An evil and adulterous generation,
To see a sign is their wish."
He said, departing, "They're given
      no sign
Except Jonah and the fish."

5 The disciples came to the other
      side,
They had forgotten to take bread,
6 "Beware the leaven of the
      Pharisees,"
To His disciples, He said.

7 The disciples thought, "It is
      because
We've brought no bread along."
8 But Jesus was aware of this,
And said, "Your faith's not strong.

9 "Do you remember not, or is it
You do not understand,
How five loaves fed five thousand
As I filled their demand?

10 "Or when we had just seven
      loaves
Four thousand men did sup;
And when all of the mouths were
      filled,
We picked seven baskets up?

11 "How is it you don't understand
I do not speak of bread?
But beware the leaven of the
      Pharisees,
That is what I said."

12 The disciples understood the
      bread
Was not the eating kind,
But the doctrine of the Pharisees
Was what Jesus had in mind.

13 Jesus came into Caesarea,
To the district of Phillipi,
Asking, "Who do people say I am
When I am passing by?"

14 "Some say you're John the Bap-
      tist,
Elijah, others say,
Jeremiah, or another prophet,
Has come and walks our way."

15 To the disciples He then said,
"Now I would hear from you,
Who do you believe I am?
Now make your answer true."

16 Simon Peter answered boldly,
Gave answer clear and loud,
"You are the Christ, the Son of God,
With His might you're endowed."

17 Jesus answered and said to him,
"Simon, you are truly blessed,
For My Father has revealed to you
This truth which you've confessed.

18 "And I tell you, you are Peter,
On this rock My church I'll build,
Hell may beat against it, but
My church cannot be killed.

19 "I'll give you the keys to the
      kingdom,
According to God's will,
The things that you bind on earth
Will be bound in heaven still.

"The things which you loose on
      earth
Will be loosed in heaven too,
So use the keys I've given
For the work I have for you."

20 Then Jesus strictly charged them,
"You are to tell no one
That I am Jesus Christ, the Lord,
That I am God's Holy Son."

21 Then He began to show His
    disciples
That by whom he'd be killed,
That He would suffer many things;
The prophecy would be fulfilled.

How He must go to Jerusalem
And there die for men's sin.
He would be three days in the
    grave,
Then He would rise again.

22 Peter began to rebuke Him,
    saying
"You can't go to a cross,
You are God's Messiah, and He
Won't let you suffer loss."

23 Jesus said, "Get behind Me,
    Satan,
For you're a stumbling block to Me.
You do not have the mind of God,
But the thoughts of men in thee.

24 "If any man would follow Me
He must himself deny
Take up his cross and follow Me
For Me, be willing to die.

25 "Whoever wants to save his life
Will lose it every time.
But he who loses life for me
Will find new life sublime."

26 "There is no profit to a man
If the whole world he'd gain,
For if his soul is lost in sin
His work is all in vain.

"What will you pay for your soul?
    What will
You do when life is o'er?
27 The Son of Man will come in glory
And even up the score.

28 "Truly I say to you today
There are some standing here
Who shall not taste of death until
Christ's kingdom shall appear."

Chapter 17

1 After six days Jesus called
Peter, James, and John nigh,
And took them along as He
Climbed up a mountain high.

2 There he was transformed before
    them;
His face shone like the sun,
His garments became white as
    light,
While they watched, this was done.

3 Behold there appeared before them
Elijah and Moses from the past,
The prophets discussed with the
    Lord
The things they knew would last.

4 Then Peter spoke to Jesus,
"To be here's very good,
We'll build a shelter for each of you
If you think we should."

5 As he spoke a cloud came by,
A voice came from the cloud,
It said, "This is My beloved Son
Of whom I am very proud.

"Listen to what He has to say."
6 The disciples fell to the ground.
7 Jesus said, "Rise up, fear not,"
8 They rose, only Christ was found.

9 As they came down from the
    mountain top
To His disciples, He said,
"Tell no one of this vision
'Til I am raised from the dead.

10 And His disciples asked of Him,
"Why is it the scribes say
Elijah first must come again
Before Christ comes our way?"

11 He said, "Elijah does come first,
By Him all is restored.
12 I tell you he has already come
But his message was ignored.

"They did to him what e'er they
    pleased,
He suffered at their hand."
13 That He was speaking of John
    the Baptist,
The disciples did now understand.

14 When they came to the crowd, a man
Approached the Lord and kneeled.
15 He said, "My son's an epileptic,
Have mercy and have him healed.

"He suffers very much. Sometimes
He falls into the fire.
Sometimes he falls into the water
With consequences dire.

16 "I brought him to your disciples,
But he's not healed, you see."
They did not know what to do
And how to cure his disease.

17 "Unbelieving and rebellious people,
How long with you shall it be
How long shall I be patient?
Bring hither the boy to me."

18 Jesus spoke sharply to the demon
He came forth from the boy.
When the father saw the cure
He was filled with great joy.

19 His disciples came and said to Him,
"Why could we not cast it out?"
20 Jesus answered, "You lack faith,
You still harbor doubt.

"If you have just a grain of faith,
Faith like a mustard seed,
You can say to this mountain, 'move,'
And it will move indeed."

21 "I tell you truly, be assured,
No demon of this class;
Except by prayer and fasting,
From a possessed man will pass."

22 When they were all in Galilee
To His disciples He said,
"The Son of Man will be betrayed, and
Into men's hands be led.

23 "But though I be killed, I
Will rise on the third day."
Still the disciples were distressed
At what they heard Him say.

24 When they came into Capernaum
The tax collectors to Peter said,
"Does your Master pay the tax
That is levied on His head?"

25 Peter answered, "Yes," to this,
Then went into his abode.
Jesus spoke to Peter saying,
"What think you of the tax code?

"Do kings on earth collect customs
From their daughter or their son?
Or do they take it from strangers
Or perhaps some other one?"

26 Peter answered, "From strangers."
Jesus said, "Children are exempt.
27 But lest we offend the rulers, and
They say we're in contempt,

"Take a fishing line and hook,
And throw it into the sea,
You'll find a coin in the fish's mouth
To pay the tax for me."

Chapter 18

1 At that time the disciples came,
On Jesus they did call,
"In the kingdom of God's heaven who's
The greatest one of all?"

2 Jesus called a child to Him,
3 "I say this unto thee,
Unless you become as this child
Heaven you will not see.

4 "If you are humble like this child
Great in heaven will you be,
5 He who receives a child in My name
Is also receiving Me.

6 "If you should cause little ones to stumble,
Make one child to fall down,
Better a stone hang from your neck
And in the sea you drown.

7 "Woe to the world's offenses which
Are strewn along the way.
Woe to those who scatter them
They'll surely have to pay.

33

8 "If hand or foot leads you to sin
Cut it off from you.
Better to live life with one limb
Than go to hell with two.

9 "And if your eye leads you to sin,
You would do very well
To pluck it out instead of keep
The two and go to hell.

10 "Do not despise these little ones,
For this I say to thee,
Their angels up in heaven
The Father's face they see.

11 For I also say this to you,
I've come to seek the lost,
The Son of Man's for everyone,
He'll pay what e'er the cost.

12 "If a man has a hundred sheep
And one sheep goes astray,
He then will leave the ninety-nine
To seek it night and day.

13 "And when the man finds that
lost sheep
He'll feel so very fine.
He will rejoice more over it
Than the other ninety-nine

14 "It's not your heavenly Father's
will
That any one should perish.
He is the master of the world,
The children He doth cherish. ·

15 "If your brother sins against you,
Then you must draw him aside,
Perhaps you'll win him over.
At least you'll know you've tried.

16 "But if he will not listen, then
Take with you one or more,
With them as your witness
Talk the problem o'er.

17 "If he still will not listen, bring
The matter to the church.
Let God's people hear the matter,
For a true solution search.

"If he still remains obstinate,
If counsel he does flout,
Withdraw the hand of fellowship
And put the brother out.

18 "I say what e'er you bind on earth
In heaven shall be bound;
If on the earth you turn it loose,
In heaven it is found.

19 "Again I say unto you,
If two of you agree,
On anything you ask
It shall be done for thee.

20 "If two or three of you are
gathered
Together in My name
I'll be there in the midst of you
For that is why I came."

21 Then Peter came and said to Him,
"If against me my brother sins,
Shall I forgive him seven times
Then not forgive again?"

22 Jesus said, "When you forgive,
At seven times don't stop,
Forgive him seventy times seven
And forgiveness then don't drop.

23 "The kingdom of heaven may be
compared
To a king who was settling accounts,
There were some who owed little and
Some who owed large amounts.

24 "One owed ten-thousand talents,
which
25 The man could not repay.
'Sell his wife and children,'
He heard his master say.

26 "The slave fell down before him,
and
Prostrate before him lay.
'Give me time, have patience, and
The debt I will repay.'

27 "The master felt compassion and
Forgave the debt immense.
28 The slave then found a fellow man
Who owed him a hundred pence.

"The slave seized him by the throat,
Said, 'Pay me all you owe.
I'll have you pay my money now
Or off to jail you go.'

29 "His fellow servant before him fell,
He begged on bended knees.
'I will repay you all I owe,
Give me some time, oh, please.'

30 "His pleading words fell on deaf
ears,
His words had no avail.
He refused to grant him any time,
And had him thrown in jail.

31 "Other servants saw what had
happened
And they were deeply grieved.
So they reported to their master
Who felt he'd been deceived.

32 "He called that slave unto him,
and
He said, 'You evil one!
Should you not show compassion
After all that I have done.

33 "Because you've given no mercy,
No mercy you'll be shown.
34 You will be held a captive there
Until you pay your loan.'

35 "So shall the Father do to you
If you forgive not each other,
Or show no mercy to your fellow
man,
And love not one another."

Chapter 19

1 He turned away from the crowds
After these words He did deliver,
He left Galilee for Judea,
Just beyond the Jordan river.

2 The multitudes still followed Him
And so He healed them there:
Compassion He had for them
And tender loving care.

3 Some Pharisees came, testing Him,
On Jesus they did call.
"Is it lawful to divorce your wife
For any cause at all?"

4 He turned and answered the
Pharisees,
And this is what he stated:
"Have you not read the Scripture,
God male and female created?

5 "For this a man shall his parents
leave
And cleave unto his wife.
These two shall then become one
flesh,
And live as if one life.

6 "They are no longer two, but one,
Is what I have to state,
What God has joined together
Let no man separate."

7 The Pharisees not satisfied,
Then asked of Moses' command,
"Why could any man divorce his wife
By a certificate in her hand?"

8 He said, "Because your heart is
hard
Moses allowed divorce,
But from the beginning of creation
This wasn't God's planned course.

9 "If you divorce your wife, but not
For immorality,
And then you take another wife
You commit adultery."

10 Then His disciples said to Him,
"If the relations of man and wife
Are as you say then, is it best
To lead a single life?"

11 But Jesus answering said to
them,
"By some My words are rejected.
Only to those who have been given
Will these words be accepted.

12 "There are eunuchs born that
way
And some are made by men.
Other eunuchs were self made
To keep themselves from sin.

"He who is able to accept these
words
Then let them be accepted
But if these words he cannot accept,
Then let them be rejected."

13 Children were brought to Jesus,
so
That o'er them He'd pray.
They were rebuked by His disciples,
Who would send them away.

14 But Jesus said, "Let them alone,
And let them make their pleas.
The kingdom of God's heaven
Belongs to such as these."

15 He laid His hands upon them,
His love with them did share,
And when he had blessed them all
He took His leave of there.

16 Then one came and before Him
knelt,
Saying, "Teacher what must I do,
A life eternal I would gain;
Can you give me a clue?"

17 The Master looked on him and
said,
"Why ask Me what is good?
In heaven is the perfect One,
Obey His laws you should."

18 "Which of the laws?" the young
man asked.
Jesus gave this reply,
"You shall not kill or steal, nor shall
You ever tell a lie.

"Adultery you'll not commit,
19 Honor your father and mother
And you shall treat your neighbor
just
As you would treat your brother."

20 The young man sadly said to
Him,
"I have done all of this,
Yet there is something lacking,
What else is it I miss?"

21 Then to the young man Jesus
said,
"If complete you would be
Give your possessions to the poor
And come and follow Me."

22 The young man heard this; on
his face
There came a sad expression,
For he did not desire to give
Away his great possessions.

23 "It is easier for a camel
24 To go through a needle's eye
Than for the rich to enter heaven,
It is something you cannot buy."

25 When His disciples heard this
They were very much amazed.
They turned to Him and asked,
"Just who then can be saved?"

26 Jesus, looking at them, said,
"With men this can't be done,
With God all things are possible,
Through Christ, His Holy Son."

27 Then Peter said to Him, "We've
left
Our homes to follow You;
What will the future hold for us
When life on earth is through?"

28 Jesus said unto Him, "When
I sit upon My throne,
Those who have faithfully followed
Me
Will have one of their own.

29 "Everyone who has left a home
And lands and family,
And who for My sake serves the
Lord,
Makes Me their priority;

"That one shall receive eternal life,
Have on him blessings cast.
30 But many last will be the first,
And many first be last.

Chapter 20

1 "Heaven's kingdom is like a land
owner
Who went one morn to hire
Some workers for his vineyard,
This was his desire.

2. "And when he had agreed
With some laborers about their pay,
He sent them into the vineyard
To work throughout the day.

3 "About nine in the morning
He went outside again,
Saw men idle in the market,
And he thought this was a sin.

4 " 'You go into my vineyard
And what is right I'll pay
If you will labor faithfully
The hours that remain today.'

5 "Then at noon and three o'clock
He did the same thing o'er.
6 Then at five in the afternoon
7 He hired workers more.

8 "Then when the evening came, and
The working day was past,
He said, "Pay to the men their
    wages,
Pay first those who came last.

9 "Those hired at the hour of five
A coin each received.
10 The others thought they'd get
    more,
This all of them believed.

11 "When they received the same
    amount
They were quite upset.
They grumbled to the owner,
12 'Sir, did you not forget,

" 'These hired last worked just one
    hour
Yet they got equal pay?
Remember we have borne the
    burden
And scorching heat all day.'

13 "But he answered one of them,
'Friend, I do no evil deed.
I paid you the exact amount
Upon which we agreed.

14 "Take the earnings that are yours
And be along your way,
15 My way is not against the law
To give all equal pay.

" 'A little envious you may be
At what has come to pass
16 But you will find that it is true
The first shall come in last.' "

17 Jesus went up to Jerusalem,
He took His disciples aside,
He said, "I want to tell you
    something,
These things I will not hide.

18 "We will go to Jerusalem,
There the Son of Man will be given
Into the hands of priests and scribes
Who for his death have striven.

19 "He'll be delivered to the Gentiles
Who'll mock, then crucify,
On a cross of execution
The Son of Man will die.

"Three days He will lie in the grave,
Then rise upon the third.
All of this will happen
Just believe my word."

20 Then the mother of James and
    John
Came forward at their bequest,
She knelt down before Jesus
To make known her request.

21 Jesus looked down upon her,
Asked, "What is your desire?"
She said, "To serve in your kingdom
My two sons do aspire.

"Command one to stand at your
    right,
For both I want the best,
The other put at your left hand,
This, then is my request."

22 Jesus, turning to James and John
Said, "You know not what you ask.
Can you drink from the cup I drink?
Are you able for the task?"

They said to Him, "Lord we are
    able."
23 He said, "My cup you'll share,
But who will sit beside My throne
My Father chooses there."

24 The ten others heard of this and
    were
Indignant as could be.
25 Jesus said, "You know Gentile
    rulers
Have authority over thee.

26 "But if great you would be, then
    like
A servant you must behave.
27 Who among you would be first
Must serve just like a slave.

28 "The Son of Man did not come
    down
To be served by men like thee,
But to give His life as ransom
So that men could be set free."

29 As they went out from Jericho
A great crowd followed behind,
30 And sitting by the roadside
Were two men who were blind.

Now when they heard that Jesus
Was going to pass that way
They cried, "Son of David have
mercy
On both of us today."

31 The crowd rebuked the two blind
men
And ordered them, "Be quiet!"
"Have mercy on us, Son of David,"
Once more the men did cry it.

32 Jesus stopped and called to them,
"What do you want from Me?"
33 They said, "Lord, let our eyes be
opened,
For we desire to see."

34 In pity Jesus touched their eyes
And they received their sight.
They followed Him along the way,
The first they'd walked in light.

Chapter 21

1 On toward Jerusalem they went
On that bright and sunny day,
And as they neared Bethphage, to
two
Disciples He did say,

2 "Go to the village opposite,
And there you'll surely see
A donkey tied next to a colt,
Loose them, bring them to Me.

3 "If anyone asks questions, say,
'Of these our Lord has need.'
He will allow them to be sent;
You will not have to plead."

4 Thus what was spoken by the
prophet
At that moment came true,
5 "To the daughter who is in Zion
Your king now comes to you.

"Gentle, mounted on an ass,
Even on a donkey's foal."
He rode upon a beast of burden
To show His servant's role.'

6 The disciples went into the village.
7 The donkey they untied.
They took the animals to Jesus
And He got on to ride.

8 Their coats the crowd spread on
the path,
Cut branches from the trees.
9 They went before and after Him
As they shouted out with glee,

"Hosanna to the Son of David
Who comes in our Lord's name;
Hosanna in the highest heaven!"
To Jerusalem they came.

10 His entrance stirred up the city,
The crowd asked, "Who is this?"
11 "He is the prophet from Galilee,
He's Jesus of Nazareth."

12 Jesus then went to the temple,
Cast out who bought and sold.
Overturned the money changers'
tables
With actions very bold.

13 He said, "It's written, that My
house
Shall be called a house of prayer,
But you have made it a robbers' den;
God's holy wrath you'll bear."

14 The blind and lame then came to
Him,
He healed each one He met,
15 But when the priests saw what
He'd done
They all were quite upset.

The children cried out in the
temple,
"Hosanna to David's son!"
The scribes were much indignant
Because of what He'd done.

16 They said, "Do you hear what
they say
When their voices they raise?"
He said, "Yes, have you never read
'From babes you have true praise?' "

17 He left and went to Bethany
And there He spent the night.
18 In the morning when He returned
The sun was shining bright.

19 Along the way He hungered.
He spied a green fig tree;
He went to get some figs,
Leaves only could He see.

Said Jesus unto that fig tree,
"No more will you bear fruit."
At once the fig tree withered, from
The top down to its root.

20 The disciples marveled, saying,
"The fig tree looks so sick.
What has caused it to wither, and
Why did it die so quick?"

21 He said, "Not only can you do
What was done to this tree,
But you can cause a mountain to
Be cast into the sea.

"Truly, I say to you, if you
Have faith and never doubt,
22 Then everything you ask in
     prayer
Is sure to come about."

23 When He came to the temple, the
Priests took Him to task,
"By what authority do you
Perform is what we ask."

24 But Jesus answered, said to
     them,
"I'll ask you one thing, too,
And if you will answer Me, then I
Will likewise answer you.

25 "The baptism of John, was it
From men or heaven received?"
"If heaven," they reasoned, "He'll
     ask why
Then did we not believe?

26 "But if we say it was from men,
We fear the multitude,
They believed John to be a prophet,
This is how John is viewed."

27 The chief priests answered Jesus
     with,
"We really cannot say."
He said, "I'll not say who approved
The works I've done today.

28 "A man who had two sons told
     them,
'Work in the vineyard find.'
29 The first answered, 'I will not go,'
But then he changed his mind.

30 "The second son he also would
Have to the vineyard sent.
He said, 'Yes, Father, I will go,'
But this son never went.

31 "Which of these did the father's
     will
Is what I ask of you?"
"The first son did, for he repented,
Did what he was asked to do."

"Your answer is correct," He said,
"That is why it's true
That harlots and tax men will
Reach heaven before you.

32 "John came to you in
     righteousness,
Him you did not receive
But sinners flocked to him, and they
Repented and believed.

33 "A man possessed a vineyard, and
Around it built a wall.
He dug a wine press into it,
Then built a tower tall.

"He rented it to tenants, then
A journey he did start,
34 When all the grapes were
     ripened, he
Sent slaves to get his part.

35 "The tenants took the slaves, and
     then
One of the slaves they beat,
And then they killed another one,
The third they did mistreat.

36 "The owner sent more men to
     them,
Even more than the original group;
They treated them in the same way
That they treated the first troupe.

37 "The owner said, 'I'll send my son,
Their deference he'll command.'
38 The growers said, 'This is the
     heir,
Kill him and seize the land.'

39 "So they cast him from the
vineyard,
And then they killed him, too.
40 When the owner of the vineyard
comes
What will the owner do?"

41 "He'll destroy them," they said,
"Their evil deeds they'll rue,
To others he will rent the land
They'll pay when it is due."

42 Jesus said, "Have you not read,
'The stone the builders rejected
Became the cornerstone when it
Was by the Lord selected?'

43 "The kingdom God will take from
you
And give to a nation He can trust.
44 On whom this stone may fall,
they will
Be scattered like the dust."

45 The chief priests and Pharisees
Both heard and understood
That it was of them Jesus spoke.
46 They'd seize Him if they could,

But they did not seize Him,
For they feared the multitude
Who thought Jesus was a prophet
And with God's power endued.

Chapter 22

1 Again He spoke in parables,
2 Said, "Heaven may be compared
To a king by whom a wedding feast
For his son was prepared.

3 "The king sent his servants to
Bring in the wedding guests.
But they refused to come at all
And honor his requests.

4 "He sent more slaves and said,
'Tell them
I've killed the fatted bulls.
Now everything is ready for you,
Come and eat your full.

5 "But they paid no attention, to
Their own affairs retreated.
6 The rest killed some slaves
Which first they mistreated.

7 "Then He was very angry, and
In fact was much annoyed.
His armies went against those and
Their cities were destroyed.

8 "The king then said, 'The feast is
ready,
But those who were invited
Weren't worthy to partake of it
For my son they have slighted.

9 " 'So therefore go to the
highways,
And everyone you meet,
Invite them to the wedding feast,
To freely come and eat.'

10 "His slaves went out as they
were told,
And brought both bad and good.
The wedding hall was filled with
guests
Who at the table stood.

11 "The king came to the wedding
hall.
And looked at all the guests.
One had not on wedding clothes,
He was not in proper dress.

12 "He said, 'Friend how did you
get in
Without the proper clothes?'
And that man could not say a word
Or a defense propose.

13 "The king said to his servants,
'Bind his hands and feet,
Cast him into the darkness,
Where weeping men he'll meet.'

14 "Although quite many are invited
From both the rich and poor,
Amongst them very few are chosen
To enter through the door."

15 The Pharisees then got together,
And they devised a plan
By which to ask a tricky question
And trap the Son of Man.

16 They sent their followers to Him,
The Herodians came along,
They said, "You teach the way of
God,
You never do a wrong.

40

"And you defer to no one, and
In service you aren't lax,
17 Therefore would you please tell
   us if
We should pay Caesar's tax?"

18 He said, "Why do you test Me?
   For
I know your tricks are many.
19 Show Me the coin used for the
   tax."
They showed to Him a penny.

20 Then Jesus said, "Whose face is it
Which on the coin does appear?"
21 They said, "Why it is Caesar's,"
A fact they found quite clear.

"Then render unto Caesar those
Things that to him belong.
Give God things that belong to God,
And you will not go wrong."

22 On hearing this they marveled at
The things He had to say.
And since they could not trick the
   Lord,
They turned and went away.

23 On that day some Sadducees,
Who scoff at the resurrection,
Also tried to trap Him, and
Asked Him a further question:

24 "Moses taught that if a man
Should some day lose his life,
And if he has no children, then
His brother should take his wife,

"In order to raise up offspring
In his brother's name,
For to have his family die out would
Be very much a shame.

25 "Now there were seven brothers,
   and
The first died with no offspring.
The second brother took the wife
To live beneath his wing.

26 "He also died without increase.
She became the third one's wife
And still no child was conceived,
They brought not forth new life.

"The brothers all had her to wife.
She was the wife of seven.
27 And last of all the woman died.
28 Whose wife is she in heaven?"

29 "The Scriptures," Jesus
   answered them,
"You do not understand,
Nor do you know the power of God
Which is at His command.

30 "In resurrection not a man
Will be in marriage given,
Instead they will be like angels
Who live in God's great heaven.

31 "As for the resurrection, how
Is it that you've not read
What God has spoken unto you,
The things that He has said?

32 " 'I am the God of Abraham,
The God of Isaac, too.
I am the God of Jacob and
Another thing is true:

"God is God of the living, He
Is not God of the dead.
And all of you would know this if
The Scriptures you had read."

33 The multitudes heard this, and at
His teachings were astonished,
34 But when the Pharisees heard He
Had the Sadducees admonished,

They got their heads together and
Devised another test.
35 They sent a lawyer to ask of Him,
36 "Which commandment is the
   best?"

37 "That you shall love the Lord
   your God
With all heart, soul, and mind;
38 This is the first and greatest
   commandment
Which in God's word we find.

39 "The second is like unto it,
And this I give to you:
To love your neighbor as yourself,
Yes, this you ought to do.

40 "Upon these two commandments hang
The Prophets and the Law."
The Pharisees made no reply
For they were filled with awe.

41 Now while the Pharisees were gathered there,
Jesus said, "I ask of thee,
42 What do you think of the Christ?
Tell me whose Son is He?

They said, "The son of David, in
Our Scripture we have read."
43 "Then how does David call Him Lord?"
"In Spirit," Jesus said.

44 " 'The Lord said to my Lord, you shall
Sit close at My right hand
Until thy foes are at thy feet
And on them you will stand.'

45 "If David calls Him Lord, then how
Is He the son you stated?"
46 They could not answer him and so
The questioning abated.

Chapter 23

1 Then Jesus spoke to the multitude,
And to His disciples there.
2 He said, "The Pharisees and scribes
All sit in Moses' chair.

3 "Observe the things that they tell you,
But copy not their deeds,
4 They put such heavy loads on you,
But care not for your needs.

5 "They do their deeds to gain attention, they
Make their phylacteries wide.
And lengthen the tassels which
Are on their garments tied.

6 "At feasts they seek places of honor,
In synagogues, the important seat.
7 They expect respectful greetings when
In the marketplace they meet.

" 'Rabbi,' is a favorite, but
8 Use not this name for others.
For there is only one teacher,
The rest are your brothers.

9 "And since your Father is in heaven,
On earth, therefore call none.
10 Do not be called a master, for
Your master's Christ, God's Son.

11 "The man who would be great among you
Shall be the one who serves,
12 He then who would exalt himself
Will get what he deserves.

13 "Woe to you scribes and Pharisees,
You all are full of sin.
You shut the doors of heaven
Against all other men.

14 "Woe to you scribes and Pharisees
You pretend to be so holy.
You make long prayers in the streets
And evict from homes widows lowly.

15 "Woe to you scribes and Pharisees,
This is quite plain to tell,
When you would make one proselyte,
You make a child of hell.

16 "And woe to you blind guides who say,
To swear by the temple is nought,
But if you swear by the temple's gold
Then keep your oath, you ought.'

17 "You are both fools and blind men
And your ignorance you cannot hide.
Is the gold any greater than the temple
By which it's sanctified?

18 "You say, 'To swear by the altar's
 nothing,'
Instead it has been stated,
If on the altar's gifts you swear
Then you are obligated.

19 "These things are very clear and
 yet
You're like the blind, I've found.
The altar blesses the offering, not
The other way around.

20 "If you swear by the altar, it's by
What's on it, and again
21 If you swear by the temple
You swear by what's within.

22 "And he who swears by heaven,
 then
Swears by God and His throne.
23 Woe to you scribes and Pharisees
Who'd make heaven on your own.

"Woe to you scribes and Pharisees,
You tithe of mint and dill.
This is quite commendable,
Still you fail to do God's will.

"The truth is you're neglectful of
The weight in matters of the Law
Justice, mercy, and faithfulness;
You haven't practiced at all."

24 "You blind guides strain at a
 gnat, and yet
A camel swallow up.
25 You all are hypocrites, who
 cleanse
The outside of the cup.

"The inside's full of robbery,
You cleanse what can be seen.
26 If you first cleanse the inside,
 then
The outside will come clean.

27 "You are like the whitewashed
 tombs,
Which outside look quite well,
But inside lies uncleanness
And in them dead bones dwell.

28 "You truly are hypocrites.
Righteous you seem to men.
But your hearts are full of evil,
And you are full of sin.

29 "You build the prophets' tombs,
 and to
The righteous honor give.
30 You say, 'If we'd lived in our
 fathers' day
We'd have let the prophets live.'

31 "Thus you bear witness against
 yourself:
You are your father's son.
32 Now all your guilt fills to the full,
For you'll do as he has done.

33 "You serpents, brood of vipers,
 you
Know not how to do well.
How are you to escape the judgment
When you're condemned to hell?

34 "I send you prophets and wise
 men
But you show them no pity.
Some you scourge and crucify,
Some you drive from your city.

35 "All of the guilt will fall on you,
For all the wrong you've done.
You've shed the blood of the in-
 nocent
Since Adam's second son.

"You killed the son of Barachiah,
Zechariah was his name.
Killed him in front of the altar, and
For this you have no shame.

36 "Upon this era evil comes.
37 The prophets you have killed.
Jerusalem! Jerusalem!
They were the ones God filled.

"I long to gather you like chicks,
Beneath a mother's wing.
But you will not come, and to Me
Yourselves you will not bring.

38 "Behold your house is desolate.
39 You'll not see Me until
You say, 'The One who comes is
 blessed
To do God's holy will.' "

43

Chapter 24

1 Jesus came out from the temple
And was going on His way.
His disciples said, "Look at the buildings
That stand along the way."

2 Jesus answered and said to them,
"All of you look around.
No stone will be left standing,
They will all be torn down."

3 As He sat on the Mount of Olives
The disciples came privately.
Saying, "When will this thing come to pass,
And what will the signs be?"

What will be the sign of your coming?
When will the world come to an end?
Tell us today, dear Master,
Your answer to us send.

4 Jesus answered and said,
"Let none lead you astray,
5 Many will say they are Christ,
But heed not what they say.

6 "You'll hear of trials and wars,
Don't let them frighten you
For all these things must come to pass
Before life on earth is through.

7 "Nation will rise against nation;
Kingdom against kingdom powers;
Famine will rage o'er the land,
Earthquakes and pestilence will devour.

8 "But these are just the beginnings,
They are the pangs of birth.
9 They will persecute you because of Me
And try to wipe you from the earth.

10 "Many will fall from faith,
They will even betray their brother.
Instead of loving you will find,
Hatred for one another.

11 "Then prophets false will soon arise
And lead many astray.
12 And due to lawlessness increased,
Men's love will die away.

13 "He who endures to the end,
He shall be saved, no doubt.
14 This gospel will reach all the world,
Then the end will come about.

15 "When you see the abomination of desolation
Which Daniel spoke to thee,
16 Let those who are in Judea
To nearby mountains flee.

17 "Let no one on the housetop
Go inside to take something away.
18 Let no one in the field
Go back for his coat, I say.

19 "Woe to all who are with child
Or nurse babies in that day.
20 Hope that your flight is not in winter,
Nor on a sabbath day.

21 "Great tribulation there will be
Like never seen before,
Nor will its like be seen again
Until life on earth is o'er.

22 "Unless those days had been cut short
No life would have been spared,
But those days will be shortened
God for His own has cared.

23 "If anyone should say to you,
'Behold, the Christ is here,'
Or if they say, 'No, there He is,'
Believe not what you hear.

24 "False christs and prophets will arise and they
By miracles gain respect.
By wonders and signs they would
Deceive even the elect.

25 "Behold! I've told you in advance,
26 So whatever they should try,
Do not go forth and follow them,
Do not believe their lie.

27 "As lightening comes from the east
And flashes to the west,
So shall on earth the Son of Man
His coming be impressed.

28 "Wherever there is dying flesh,
The vultures gather 'round,
It shall be so in tribulation,
Wherever death is found.

29 "When tribulation's over, and
Those dreadful days pass by,
The sun won't shine, the moon won't glow,
Stars will fall from the sky.

"The powers of heaven will be shaken,
The signs will be very clear.
30 Then the signs of the Son of Man
In clouds there will appear.

"All the tribes on earth shall mourn,
They'll shout as they see
The Son of Man coming on clouds
With power and great glory.

31 "He will send forth heaven's angels,
With trumpet blast they'll call
All of the elect together
From heaven's corners all.

32 "Now you can from the fig tree learn,
It gives a sign so clear,
When branches put forth fig leaves, then
You know that summer's near.

33 "So when you see these things, you'll know
That Christ is at your door.
34 These things will take place before
This generation is o'er.

35 "Though earth and heaven pass away
My words retain their power.
36 But when these things will come about
None knows the day and hour.

"The angels know not the time,
Nor God's holy Son.
The Father only knows these things
And when they will be done.

37 "The coming of the Son of Man
Will be like Noah's day.
38 They paid no heed to God's Word til
39 The flood bore them away.

40 "Two men shall toil in the field,
41 Or two women grain may grind.
When the Son of Man shall come,
One will be left behind.

42 "Therefore you must always be alert,
For you know not the hour or day.
If you're not ready when He comes
You'll be left behind, I say.

43 "If the head of the house had known the hour
The thief came in the night,
Then he would have tried to stay awake
To guard with all his might.

44 "For this reason you be ready,
So that regardless of the hour,
The Son of Man will find you faithful
And before Him you'll not cower.

45 "The faithful servant who's ready
46 When the Master comes,
Will hear the Master say to him
47 'You will share in My kingdom.'

48 "But if the servant says in his heart,
'It is long before He returns,'
49 Begins to beat his fellow slaves
And no food or drink he spurns.

50 "The Master of that servant will come
One unexpected day.
At an hour he's unaware of,
While he is still at play.

51 "He will cut the servant to pieces and
With hypocrites he'll be placed,
He shall gnash his teeth and weep,
For the judgment he has faced.

Chapter 25

1 "The kingdom of heaven may be
  compared
To ten virgins who one day,
Took lamps to meet the bridegroom
  and
They planned to light his way.

2 "Five of these maids were foolish,
The other five were bright.
3 The foolish maids took their
  lamps with
No extra oil for their light.

4 "The wise maids not only took
  their lamps,
But also took oil in a flask,
So if perhaps they had to wait
They still could do their task.

5 "The bridegroom was delayed in
  coming
And many lamps grew dim,
6 At midnight there arose a shout,
'He's coming, come meet him.'

7 "Up the virgins quickly jumped
When they all heard the shout.
8 The foolish said, 'Give us some oil
Our lamps are going out.'

9 "The wise virgins answered, 'No,
We've not enough for you.
Go to the dealers, buy some oil.
This is what you'll have to do.'

10 "While they were gone the
  bridegroom came,
All those ready went in
And when the guests were all inside
The door was shut again.

11 "Later the other virgins came,
Saying, 'Lord, open the door.'
12 He answered, 'I know you not'
I'll open it no more.'

13 "Therefore, I say to be alert,
You know not the day or hour.
To set the time of the Lord's return
Is not within your power.

14 "The kingdom is like a man who
  for
A while would be away,
He called his servants together and
Said, 'I must leave today.'

15 "To one he gave five talents,
To another he gave two.
Then said he to still another,
'I'm trusting one to you.'

16 "The one who had five talents
  made
Investments and they soared;
17 And he who had two talents soon
Had gained two talents more.

18 "The slave who had one talent,
When no one was around,
Took the talent he'd received
And hid it in the ground.

19 "When the master's journey
  ended, and
Back home he did arrive.
20 The one who had five talents said,
'Look, Master, I've gained five.'

21 "His master said to him, 'Well
  done,
You've been steadfast with few.
I'll give you charge of many things,
I'll share my joy with you.'

22 "The one who had two talents
  said,
'You trusted two to me,
And Master I now have two more
Which I can show to thee.'

23 "His master said, 'Well done,
Just as I knew you would.
Your authority will be increased,
You'll share in what is good.

24 "Last said the slave who was
  given one,
'One talent I received,
I knew you would want it back,
This is what I believed.

25 " 'I was afraid if I used it
The talent might be lost,
And if I could not return it, then
I could not pay the cost.

" 'Therefore I took your talent,
Hid it where none could see,
But now that you have returned, I
Will give it back to thee.'

26 "His master said then to him,
'You wicked lazy worker.
You knew how to behave.
You proved to be a shirker.

27 " 'You should have put it in the
bank,
Or otherwise invest,
Then when I came home again
I would have gained interest.

28 " 'Take the coin away from him,
Give it to him with ten.
29 He who has shall gain much more
And be great in the eyes of men.

" 'He who does not have much at all
And what he has won't use,
Even the little that he has
That lazy man will lose.

30 " 'Now into outer darkness,
Where there's gnashing of teeth
and weeping
Cast that worthless slave,
Because he did no reapng.'

31 "When the Son of Man in glory
comes,
With angels all around,
He will sit on His glorious throne,
32 All nations will bow down.

"He'll separate them as a shepherd
Divides the goats and sheep.
33 The sheep will be on His right
hand,
On the left the goats He'll keep.

34 "To those on the right the King
will say,
'Come blessed from every nation,
Inherit the kingdom prepared for you
From the foundation of creation.

35 " 'When I was hungry you gave
Me food,
With a stranger you always shared.
When thirsty you did give Me a
drink,
36 You clothed Me because you
cared.

" 'When I sat in a prison cell
You came to visit Me.'
37 Then the righteous will answer
Him,
'Lord, we never saw Thee.

" 'When were You hungry
And we You did feed?
When were You thirsty
And drink was our good deed?

38 " 'When did we see You a
stranger,
And invite You inside?
When were You naked
And we clothed You?' they cried.

39 " 'When did we go and visit You,
When in prison You sat?
Or come when You were sick,
When have we done that?'

40 "The king will answer them, 'It
was
When caring for your brothers,
You proved your love for Me those
times
That you were serving others.'

41 "Then to the ones on his left hand
He'll turn and say, 'Depart,
With the devil and his angels go,
Those with an evil heart.

42 " 'I hungered, you gave me no
food,
I thirsted, you did not care.
43 I was a stranger, you shut me
out,
I was naked, you left me bare.

" 'And when I sat in a prison cell
You turned your face away.'
44 'Lord, when did we commit these
things?'
Those on the left will say.

45 "The Lord will then reply, 'When
The poor you did not feed,
And when you turned away from
them
You did not meet My need.'

46 "Eternal punishment they'll find,
They will be turned away
From the kingdom of the Son of Man
On the final judgment day."

Chapter 26

1 With this Jesus' words were ended,
To His disciples He did say,
2 "You know within two days the passover
Will be under way.

"The Son of Man will be betrayed
And will be crucified."
3 Chief priests and elders met to plot
How Jesus should be tried.

The high priest then was Caiaphas and
4 He was in on the plot,
They said, "We must seize Him by stealth,
We must wipe out this blot.

5 "Do not seize Jesus at the feast,
Or a riot will occur."
The priests and elders agreed to this,
On this they did concur.

6 Going to Simon the Leper's home
Jesus ate in his dining room.
7 A woman came up and on Him poured
A vial of expensive perfume.

8 The disciples were indignant:
They thought she showed poor taste,
9 "The money could have gone to the poor,
But now it's gone to waste."

10 Jesus said, "Why trouble her
For a good deed done to Me.
11 The poor will always be with you,
Soon I'll be gone from thee.

12 "When she poured perfume on My body
For My burial she did prepare.
13 Where'er the gospel then is preached
This story will be told there."

14 Then one of the twelve named Judas went
Unto the priests and asked,
15 "Just what will you give me if I
Assist you in your task?"

They said, "We'll give you thirty silver pieces."
And then they weighed them out.
16 Judas sought to betray the Lord
When there were few about.

17 Now on the first day of the feast
The disciples came and said,
"Where shall we make the meal, where will
We eat unleavened bread?"

18 "Go into the city,"
You'll find a certain man,
Say, 'I'll keep the passover at your house,
My time is now at hand.' "

19 The disciples did as they were told,
The passover they prepared.
20 That evening He sat at the table with
His twelve disciples there.

21 As they sat eating, Jesus said,
"In what I say believe:
I'll be betrayed by one of you."
22 Then they began to grieve.

They began to say to Him,
"Lord it's not I, I pray."
23 He said, "He who dips his hand with me
Is the one who will betray.

24 "The Son of Man is to go just like
In Scripture it is sworn.
It would have been best for the betrayer
To never have been born."

25 Said Judas, who was betraying Him,
"You don't think it is I?"
"Yes, you have spoken,"
Was Jesus' reply.

26 And while they were eating there,
Jesus took some bread,
He blessed it, then He broke it, and
To His disciples said,

"Take this bread and eat it,
This is my body broken."
He passed the bread to His
   disciples
Once these words were spoken.

27 He took the cup, gave thanks,
   and said,
"This I want you to do,
Drink from this cup, it is My blood
Which is shed for each of you.

28 "This is My blood of covenant
Which will be shed for all,
Through it sins will be forgiven
If on Me in faith they call.

29 "But I will not drink from this
   cup,
I will not drink with you,
Until in heaven's kingdom we,
Will drink sweet wine anew."

30 After they had done these things
They arose and sang a hymn.
Jesus went to the Mount of Olives
And the disciples followed Him.

31 Before He prayed, Jesus said,
"You'll stumble away from Me.
It's written, 'I will strike the
   shepherd,
And all the sheep will flee.'

32 "But I tell you I will rise again
And go to Galilee,
I'll go before you, then you shall
Go there and meet with me."

33 Peter answered and said to Him,
"Though others desert you today
I will remain forever true;
I will never go away."

34 Said Jesus sadly to Peter,
"Before the cock shall crow,
Three times you will deny me,
   saying,
"'The Christ I do not know.'"

35 Peter said, "My Master, no,
I shall not you deny,
I never shall forsake you, e'er
If with You I must die."

The others disciples said the same,
36 Then they came to Gethsemane.
He said, "Sit here while I go pray
And with the Father be."

37 He summoned Peter with Him
   and
Two sons of Zebedee.
He was grieved and distressed,
38 He said, "Keep watch with Me."

39 Then from them Jesus drew
   apart,
He fell down on His face.
Praying, "Father let this cup pass,
   not
Of my will, but your grace."

40 He found the disciples sleeping
   and said,
"Peter had you not the power
To keep your eyes wide open,
And watch with Me one hour?

41 "Keep watching and keep
   praying, lest
Temptation enter you.
I know your spirit's willing, but
The flesh is weak, 'tis true."

42 A second time He went away,
Prayed, "Take this cup from Me.
I'll drink it if it is your will,"
I will not turn from Thee."

43 He came again and found them
   sleeping.
They could not stay awake.
44 He left again and prayed once
   more,
The same prayer He did make.

45 He came to the disciples and
Said, "Sleep on and be allayed.
Behold, the hour is at hand,
The Son of Man is betrayed.

46 "Arise and let us go, the one
Betraying Me is near."
47 And while He was speaking did
A crowd of men appear.

Led by Judas, an apostle,
Followed by a motley horde,
Sent by chief priests and elders,
Carrying clubs and a sword.

48 "A sign I'll give you," Judas said,
"Thus your task I will ease.
The one to whom I give a kiss
He is the one to seize."

49 And Judas went and said, "Hail,
    Master,"
And kissed Him on the cheek.
50 Jesus then to Judas said,
"My friend, what do you seek?"

Then the multitude came and took
    Him,
51 But one man standing near,
Swung a sword at the high priest's
    slave
And he cut off his ear.

52 Jesus said unto this man,
"Please put your sword away."
Those who depend on might are
    sure
To perish that same way.

53 "Don't you think I could call the
    Father,
And if to Him I cried,
He would send legions of angels
To stand here by My side?

54 "Then how would Scripture be
    fulfilled?
You know the prophets say,
'By evil men Christ will be seized,'
This came to pass today."

55 Jesus said, "You come with
    swords
And clubs like fearful men,
I taught in the temple every day,
You could have seized Me then.

56 "But all of this is taking place
As the prophets said,"
Then all the disciples turned away,
And from that crowd they fled.

57 The ones who had seized Jesus
    brought
Him to the priests and scribes,
And all the elders gathered there
To watch as he was tried.

58 Peter walked behind and came
As far as the courtyard,
He entered in and sat down with
The servants and the guards.

59 The council sought for evidence,
Cared not if it were true.
Though they brought false
    witnesses,
None of it would do.

60 A cause to sentence Him to death
Could not be justified.
Though many spoke against Him, it
Was evident they lied.

Two witnesses came forward, then
61 Said Jesus claimed He'd raze
The temple to the ground and then
Rebuild it in three days.

62 The high priest stood and said to
    Him,
"That's what they say of You,
So would You now defend yourself,
Is what they say untrue?"

63 But Jesus said no word at all,
The chief priest found this odd.
He said, "I adjure you by our Lord,
Are you Christ, Son of God?"

64 Jesus replied to the chief priest,
"Yes, I will answer you,
Although you yourself have said it,
What you say of Me is true.

"Some day you will see Him sitting
At God's right hand of power,
Coming on the clouds of heaven
And you will fear that hour.

65 The high priest rose; he tore his
    clothes;
"He blasphemed!" he did roar,
"We need no further witnesses,
We need to hear no more.

66 "What do you think?" the high
    priest asked
"What will your judgment be?"
The council all replied, "He should
Die for his blasphemy."

67 Then they did spit in His face,
With fists His body they beat.
68 "Prophesy to us, O Christ.
Who hit you?" did they entreat.

69 As Peter in the courtyard sat,
A maiden to him said,
"You too were with the Galilean."
And Peter's face turned red.

70 Peter denied before them all,
"This man I do not know,
I have never met Him."
And he rose up to go.

71 When Peter reached the
gateway, yet
Another girl was there.
She said, "This man was with
Jesus."
72 Peter said, "I know Him not, I
swear."

73 Later, some bystanders said,
"You're one of them we say,
We know this by the way you talk,
It surely gives you away."

74 Then Peter cursed and swore. He
said,
"I do not know this man."
Immediately he heard a cock crow
And Peter turned and ran.

75 Jesus' words Peter then recalled,
"Three times you will deny Me
Before the rooster crows," I say.
Peter left and wept bitterly.

Chapter 27

1 When morning came, the chief
priests and
The elders met as planned,
2 They bound and turned Him over
to Pilate,
The governor of the land.

3 When Judas, who had betrayed
the Lord,
Saw He had been condemned,
He felt remorse deep in his heart
And tried to make amends.

4 He said, "I've betrayed innocent
blood;
Your money I return."
The priests said, "What is that to
us?"
And Judas they did spurn.

5 Judas threw the money at their
feet
Then went and got a rope,
He hanged himself upon a tree
For he had lost all hope.

6 The chief priests picked the silver
up:
"A problem we now face,
To put blood money in our bank,
Would be a great disgrace."

7 They put their heads together, and
To them this plan appealed:
They'd buy a burial place for Him,
One in the potter's field.

8 That's why it's called the Field of
Blood,
9 So prophesy was fulfilled,
They took thirty silver coins, the
price
Set by the prophet of Israel:

10 "And they gave them for the
potter's field
As the Lord directed me."
11 Then Jesus before Pilate stood,
Who said, "I ask of Thee,

"Why were you brought before me
It's your leaders who accuse,
Now your answer I would hear,
Are you the King of the Jews?"

He answered, "It is as you say."
12 Then He would say no more,
Although the priests and elders
made
Accusations by the score.

13 Then to Him Pilate said, "Do you
Not hear how they testify?"
14 But Jesus did not defend Himself,
He did not even try.

15 Now at that feast which came
each year,
The custom was to release
One prisoner that the people chose,
A gesture made in peace.

16 They had a notorious felon,
Barabbas was his name,
Because of his many crimes
He had received much fame.

17 Pilate asked the gathered priests,
"Now what thing shall I do,
Shall I release Barabbas, or
Release this Christ to you?"

18 He knew it was because of envy
That Christ they had arrested.
He never thought they'd choose
    Barabbas,
He thought he had them bested.

19 While Pilate sat on the judgment
    seat
His wife sent him a note,
"Have naught to do with that just
    man—
He upset my dreams," she wrote.

20 The priests said to the multitudes,
"This we would have you do:
21 When Pilate says, 'Whom shall I
    release,'
Ask Barabbas be given you."

When Pilate asked, "Whom do you
    want?"
"Barabbas," they all cried.
22 "What then shall I with Jesus do?"
"Let Him be crucified."

23 "What has He done?" asked Pi-
    late, but
The crowd just shouted more,
"Let Him be crucified!" they said;
They cried this o'er and o'er.

24 Pilate saw he could not prevail,
The crowd was in an evil mood.
He feared a riot would soon begin,
He feared the multitude.

He called for a bowl of water, and
In it he washed his hands.
"Of His blood I am innocent;
Fulfill your own demands."

25 "His blood be on us and our
    children,"
All the people cried.
26 Barabbas was released; Jesus
    scourged, and delivered
To be crucified.

27 The soldiers seized Him and into
The palace He was led.
28 They put a scarlet robe on Him,
29 And with thorns crowned His
    head.

They put a stick in His right hand,
And jeered Him in disgrace,
"Hail to the King of Jews," and they
30 Then spit upon His face.

31 They beat and mocked Him there,
They took the robe He wore,
They led Him away to be crucified,
His own clothes He now bore.

32 As they went out, they met a man
Walking along the way.
The soldiers forced Simon of Cyrene
To bear the cross that day.

33 They came to a place called
    Golgotha,
Which means hill of the skull.
34 They gave Him wine and gall to
    drink,
But the pain He would not dull.

35 Then the soldiers rolled some dice
Once He was crucified.
They cast their lots for Jesus' clothes
He'd hang there 'til He died.

36 Then they sat down to watch
    Him there
Where none could block their views.
37 O'er His head the charge was
    read,
"This is Jesus, King of the Jews."

38 Two robbers were also crucified,
One on His left, one on His right.
To all the people passing by,
It was a gruesome sight.

39 Abusing words were hurled at Him,
40 "You there upon the cross
Who would destroy the temple,
Your life is at a loss.

"You who claim to be God's Son,
The so-called Son of Man,
You who claimed to save others
Now save yourself if you can."

41 The elders and chief priests mocked,
They shouted out with glee,
42 "Come down, youKing of Israel,
And we'll believe in Thee.

43 "He trusts in God, says He's
God's Son, then
Why is it not God's pleasure
To take this king from the cross,
If He is such a treasure?"

44 The robbers crucified with Him
Threw insults at Him, too;
They said, "If you're the Son of God
Save Yourself, then save us, too."

45 The sixth hour came and darkness
fell,
And it was hard to see.
46 Cried Jesus at the ninth hour,
"My God, why have You forsaken Me."

47 Some of the crowd who stood nearby,
Said, "This is what we heard,
He called upon Elijah; will
Elijah hear His word?"

48 One ran and soaked a sponge with
wine,
And put it on a reed,
Then raised it up to Jesus' lips,
Trying to fill a need.

49 But all the rest of them said,
"Leave Him on the cross.
We'll see if old Elijah comes
To save Him from this loss."

50 Jesus cried out loud again,
Then yielded up His spirit.
51 The temple veil was torn in two,
From top to bottom split.

The earth shook and the rocks were
cracked;
52 And tombs were opened wide,
Many bodies of the saints arose
And came out from inside.

53 Out they came from their tombs
And after Jesus rose again
They went into the holy city
And were seen by many men.

54 When the centurion and his soldiers
Guarding Jesus felt the quake,
And saw the things that happened,
They all with fear did shake.

The centurion, as he trembled,
Seeing things he'd not seen before
Said, "Surely this was the Son of
God
Who we should worship and adore."

55 Many women were looking on,
They watched from a distant hill,
They had followed Him from Galilee,
His needs they desired to fill.

56 There was Mary, James and
Joseph's mother,
And Mary Magdalene,
And the mother of the sons of Zebedee
All looked upon that scene.

57 Then in the evening of that day
Joseph of Arimathea came,
58 Asked Pilate for Jesus' body,
And Pilate gave to him the same.

59 He wrapped it in clean linen cloth,
60 He laid it in his own tomb.
Nothing had laid there before,
Out of a rock it was hewn.

He rolled a stone against the door
And then he went away.
He did all that he could do
On that momentous day.

61 Mary Magdalene watched the
burial,
The other Mary, too,
They wanted to know where the
body lay
Of the One they loved so true.

62 The next day the priests and
Pharisees
To Pilate came and said,
63 "You know that when the deceiver
lived,
He said He'd rise from the dead.

64 "Therefore, won't you seal the grave,
Let no one in or out,
Lest His disciples steal His body,
And trouble comes about."

65 Unto the chief priests Pilate said,
"I will approve your plan,
You seal the tomb and set a guard,
Secure it if you can."

66 They went their way and sealed
　the tomb,
In their minds they were sure
That with a guard around the grave
The grave was quite secure.

Chapter 28

1 On that morn after the Sabbath day,
At the breaking of the dawn,
Mary Magdalene and the other Mary
To Christ's grave were drawn.

2 Behold! an earthquake came,
And an angel moved the stone.
The angel sat upon it, and
How bright his garments shone.

3 His appearance was like lightning,
His raiment white as snow.
4 The guards shook for fear of him,
Then fainted in his glow.

5 The angel said to the women,
"Come close, and do not fear,
I know you look for Jesus,
6 He's risen, He's not here.

"Come see where He was lying.
He has risen from the dead.
7 Tell His disciples He goes before you
To Galilee, as He said."

8 So overcome with joy,
From the tomb the women fled,
They ran to find His disciples
To tell what the angel said.

9 Jesus met them on the way.
They worshipped at His feet,
To see the Lord alive again
Was something very sweet.

10 He said, "Be not afraid,
Tell My brethren they will see
Me in My risen form
When they arrive in Galilee."

11 Now while they were on their way
The guards at the tomb did revive.
They went and told the priests,
　"The tomb
Is empty! He's alive!"

12 The elders and the chief priests
　came,
The soldiers they did bribe,
13 They said, "This is what you're to
　say,
Your stories all must jibe.

13 " 'His disciples came and stole
　Him.
His body they took away.
All of you were fast asleep.'
This is what you should say.

14 "If this should come to Pilate's ears
We will take care of you.
We'll keep you out of trouble,
And satisfy him, too."

15 So the soldiers took the money,
Went out and spread the news.
This is the story still believed
By many of the Jews.

16 The disciples went to Galilee,
Which He had designated,
17 When they saw Him they
　worshiped Him.
They were greatly elated.

They all fell down and worshipped Him,
But some were doubtful still.
18 Jesus came up and spoke to those
Who were gathered on the hill.

"All power has been given Me
In heaven and every nation.
19 Go therefore; make disciples
Tell them of My salvation.

"Baptize them in the Father's name,
Of the Son and Spirit, too,
20 Teach them to observe all things
That I have commanded you.

"I will be with you always,
In all the things you do.
I'll provide the power to overcome
Until life on earth is through."

The Gospel According to Mark

Chapter 1

1 The beginning of the gospel
Of Jesus Christ, God's Son.
2 As foretold by the prophets
This good news is begun.

"I send My messenger before You
Who will prepare Your way;
3 A voice cries in the wilderness
And this is what he'll say:

"Make ready for the Lord to come,
Yes, make His pathways straight."
Those who hear and believe His words
Will pass through heaven's gate.

4 John the Baptist baptized in the
    wilderness.
Preaching that men should repent
To have their sins forgiven;
This is why John was sent.

5 The people of Judea came,
To hear John was their quest.
They were baptized in the Jordan river
After their sins they confessed.

6 John wore a cloak of camel's hair,
A leather belt around his waist.
His food was locusts and honey,
For them he had a taste.

7 He preached, "He who comes after me
Is mightier than I.
I am not fit to bow before Him,
Or His sandals to untie.

8 "I baptize you with water, but
He who's coming will
Baptize you and with
The Holy Spirit fill."

It came to pass that Jesus came
9 From Nazareth of Galilee.
He was baptized by John in Jordan
Where all the crowds could see.

10 As He rose up out of the water
The gates of heaven opened wide,
A dove, God's spirit, upon Him sat
11 And a voice from heaven cried,

"You are My beloved Son,
I am well pleased with You."
12 The Spirit sent Him to the
    wilderness,
13 Where wild animals were, too.

For forty days and nights, Satan
Tempted Christ very sore,
Then angels ministered unto Him
When these trials were o'er.

14 After John was put in prison
Jesus went into Galilee,
Preaching the kingdom gospel
15 Saying, "It has come nigh to thee.

"This is the time as prophesied
God's kingdom is at hand,
Repent, you and believe the gospel,
For this is God's command."

16 As Jesus walked along the shore
Of the sea of Galilee,
He saw Simon and his brother
Casting nets into the sea.

17 "Follow Me," He called to them.
"Fishers of men I'll make of you."
18 At once they left their nets
To make Him their Master new.

19 He went on a little further,
Where James and John He met.
These sons of Zebedee were
In a boat mending their nets.

20 They quit the boat to follow Jesus
When the Master called to them,
They left their father, Zebedee,
With all his hired men.

21 They all went into Capernaum,
There on the Sabbath day,
They went into the synagogue
Where He began to teach and pray.

22 They were astonished at His
    teaching,
For unlike scribes, who kept tradition,
He taught with authority
As one who had a mission.

23 That day there was in the synagogue
A man with a demonic spirit.
24 He cried aloud in the meeting
    place,
So loud that all could hear it;

"What have we to do with You,
Jesus, the Nazarene?
We know You are God's Holy One,
Will you destroy us unclean?"

25 Jesus rebuked the spirit saying,
"Be still, come out of him."
26 The evil spirit shook the man,
Then left for regions dim.

27 "What is this thing?" the people
    asked,
For they were all amazed.
"What new doctrine can this be?
That even the evil spirit obeyed?"

28 The news of Jesus traveled fast,
Spread throughout Galilee.
They heard what he had done, that He
Had made a demon flee.

29 Jesus and His followers left
For Simon's house, nearby.
30 For Simon's mother-in-law was sick
With a fever very high.

When Jesus came to her bedside
31 He took her by the hand.
The fever vanished at His touch,
She arose and served the band.

32 Evening came and He remained
After the sun had gone down,
They brought the ill and demon-
    filled
From all throughout the town.

33 It seemed the entire city
Was gathered at the door.
34 He healed many sick
And cast out demons by the score.

He would not let the demons speak,
They could not say one word.
They knew He was the Son of God;
He did not want this heard.

35 Early next morning He arose,
While others were still asleep.
He went out to a lonely place
Where a vigil He would keep.

36 The disciples went to look for Him,
37 They found Him there in prayer,
They said, "Other towns are
    seeking you."
38 Said He, "We'll go there.

"Let us go to towns nearby,
I'll preach and teach the same,
We'll take the gospel to them, too,
For that is why I came."

39 He went into the synagogues
Through all of Galilee.
He preached the gospel, cast
    demons out,
Wherever He might be.

40 A leper came beseeching Him,
Who fell down on his knees.
"You can make me clean," he said,
"Won't you do it, please?"

41 Moved with great compassion
Jesus touched him with His hand.
He said, "I will, so be you clean,"
And the leper felt so grand.

42 At once the sickness left him,
43 Then Jesus sent him on his way,
44 He said, "Tell no one how this
    happened,
How you were cleansed today.

"But show yourself to the priest
As Moses has commanded,
Make an offering for your cleansing
As God's law demanded."

45 But as he went along his way
He spread the news far and near;
Telling all he had been healed,
So everyone could hear.

The news kept spreading through
    the land,
And soon no room was found
To hold the pressing multitudes
That came from all around.

Jesus moved to desert places,
Where people came from everywhere.
To hear Him preach and see Him heal
Before all who gathered there.

Chapter 2

1 Jesus returned to Capernaum
Where He had been before,
2 Again the crowd had grown so large
They even blocked the door.

3 Four men carrying a paralytic
Came hurrying down the street,
Believing that he would be healed
If Jesus he could meet.

4 The crowd prevented their approach,
So a hole in the roof was made.
They let down through the opening
The pallet on which he laid.

5 Jesus, seeing their faith was great,
Said to Him on the cot,
"My son, your sins are taken away
I forgive the entire lot."

6 Certain scribes were sitting there,
Each reasoning in his mind,
7 "To claim to forgive is blasphemy,
To God's authority He is blind."

8 Jesus perceiving in His Spirit
That they were thinking this way,
Said to them, "Why are you
        reasoning so?
9 Which would be easier to say,

"All your sins are forgiven you,
Or take up your bed and walk?
10 So you will know the power of God
And end your idle talk;

11 "I say, 'My son take up your bed,
Take it to your dwelling place.'"
12 The man got up in front of them
Thanking God for His loving grace.

The amazed crowd glorified God:
"We've not seen the like before."
13 But Jesus walked away from them
 To teach again by the shore.

He taught the crowds who came to
        Him,
14 And then as He passed by
He saw the son of Alpheus,
Whose given name was Levi.

Though Levi was a tax collector.
"Follow Me," Jesus said.
And Levi arose and followed Him,
By the Spirit he was led.

15 Then to Jesus, Levi said,
"Come to my house and eat,
There are some other tax collectors
Whom I want you to meet."

And at the table Jesus reclined,
With others at the dinner,
16 The Pharisees questioned Him
For eating with the sinners.

17 Hearing this Jesus said to them,
"The well need no physician,
I came not to call the righteous,
The sinners are My mission."

18 As John's disciples and Pharisees
        fasted,
They said, "We ask of you
Why do we abstain from food
When none of your disciples do?"

19 Jesus said, "Do the wedding
        guests fast
While the bridgegroom is here?
This is not the time for fasting,
This is a time for cheer.

20 "But the day will surely come
When the bridgroom is taken away.
There will be time for fasting
When His absence saddens the day.

21 "You do not use unshrunken cloth
To patch a garment torn,
For it will make a bigger tear
And that garment can't be worn.

22 "New wine isn't put into old
        wineskins
For they will crack and split.
Only a new wineskin should have
New wine put into it."

23 One day while walking in a field
The disciples plucked some wheat.
They rubbed the kernels in their hands
And then began to eat.

24 The Pharisees, quick to see,
Stood aghast at what they saw.
They asked, "Why are they doing this?
It's against the Sabbath law."

25 "Have you never read?" Jesus said,
"What David did when in need?
26 How he went into the house of God
And on the sacred bread did feed?

27 "The Sabbath day was made for man,
Not man for the Sabbath day.
28 Therefore, the Son of Man is Lord
Even of the Sabbath, I say."

Chapter 3

1 Back to the synagogue Jesus went.
A man with a withered hand was
    there,
2 They watched to see if He would heal;
If on the Sabbath He would dare.

They wanted a reason for which to
    accuse
And drive Him from the land.
3 "Rise and come forward," Jesus said,
To the one with the withered hand.

4 "The Sabbath is a holy day,"
    Christ said.
"It's in our law we've heard,
On it shall we do good or harm?"
But they answered Him not a word.

5 He looked on them with anger and
    grief;
Their hearts were hard, He knew.
He said to the man, "Stretch forth
    your hand."
And healing He did do.

6 The Pharisees did quickly leave
King Herod's men to employ,
They formed a plot against Jesus,
Whom they wanted to destroy.

7 Jesus withdrew again to the sea.
Where those who'd hear His word
8 They came from regions far and near
To check the things they'd heard.

9 There He instructed His disciples
To have a boat near shore,
In case the people should press on Him,
As they had done before.

10 There He healed many sick,
They all desired His touch,
Because He healed so many,
His garments they would clutch.

11 Whenever evil spirits saw Him,
They cried, "You are God's Son."
12 "Be silent," Jesus said to them,
"You are to tell no one."

13 He went up into a mountain
And called a special few,
They came as He called
To see what He'd have them do.

14 He ordained them apostles
That with Him they could be,
To send them out to preach and heal;
15 Over demons have authority.

16 Simon, whom He called Peter,
17 And James the son of Zebedee.
John, who was James' brother,
These were a special three.

18 There was Andrew, Peter's brother,
Philip and Bartholomew,
There was Levi, the tax collector,
Also known as Matthew.

There was Thomas, called the doubter,
James the son of Alphaeus.
There was Simon, the Cananaean,
And also Thaddaeus.

19 There was Judas of Iscariot,
This the twelfth apostle made.
He would be the disciple
By whom Jesus was betrayed.

20 When they came into a house,
The crowd pressed from behind.
So many sought to see Him
The disciples could not dine.

21 When His friends heard about this
They came and sought Him out.
They said, "He has lost His mind,
Of this we have no doubt."

22 The scribes there from Jerusalem
Said, "Just as we have guessed,
He casts out demons by Beelzebub
For by Satan He's possessed."

23 He called to them and said, "How can
I be in Satan's band?
24 If a kingdom is divided against itself
That kingdom cannot stand.

25 "If a house divides against itself
You know that house will fall.
26 If Satan rises against himself
He will have no power at all.

27 "No one can enter a strong man's
house
And take his property
Unless he first binds up the man;
That is plain to see.

28 "All sins can surely be forgiven
Even the blasphemies of men,
29 But if you blaspheme against the
Spirit
Youll not be forgiven then."

30 His mother and brothers came,
Hearing someone had said,
"He has an unclean spirit,
By this spirit He is led."

31 Because of the great multitude
They had to stand outside,
In order to get word to Him
They sent someone who cried,

32 "Behold, your mother and brothers
Wait outside to see You."
But as the crowd was sitting 'round
The family could not get through.

33 "Who are my mother and my
brothers?"
His answer then seemed odd.
34 "Behold, My mother, sister,
brother
35 Are those who do the will of God."

Chapter 4

1 Again went Jesus to the seaside,
Crowds gathered as before.
Jesus stepped into a boat,
And pushed it from the shore.

2 Jesus sat down in the boat
Then He began to teach.
He taught them truth in parables
Rather than to preach.

3 He said, "A sower went out to sow,
4 But as the grain was sown
Birds swooped down and plucked it up
Before the grain was grown.

5 "Other seed fell in the rocks
Where there was little soil,
And quickly sprang up tender leaves
With very little toil.

6 "But when the sun rose high
Those precious little shoots
Scorched and withered very soon,
Because they had no roots.

7 "Some seeds fell among the thorns;
The thorns grew up so thick
They kept the seed from bearing;
There was no grain to pick.

8 "Other seeds in rich soil fell
And grew and multiplied;
Thirty, sixty, and a hundred times
Around the country side."

9 When finished teaching, Jesus said,
"He who has ears to hear,
Listen to what I'm saying,
And I'll make the meaning clear."

10 When the disciples and others
were left
They said, "We'd like to know
The meaning of this parable,
Won't you, to us, it show?"

11 To them, He then did say,
"It has been given to you to know
The mysteries of God's kingdom
And the way that you should go.

"But to those who are outside
To them in parables I speak,
12 For though they have eyes to see,
My way they do not seek.

"And though they have ears to hear,
My words they don't believe,
My message they will not accept.
Forgiveness they will not receive."

13 Said He to them quite plainly,
"This you do not understand;
How can you grasp other parables
And be at my command?

14 "The sower spreads the Word of God.
15 The seeds which by the roadside fall
Are like the Word on hardened hearts,
For they cannot grow at all.

"For when the hearer hears,
Satan takes the Word away,
No fruit remains with them
When they face the judgment day.

16 "The seed that's sown in rocky places,
Also does not remain.
17 They receive the words with
    gladness,
But those words they don't retain.

18 "The seed that's planted amidst
    the thorns
Is like those who hear My word,
19 But the cares and riches of this
    world
Choke out all they have heard.

20 "The rest, like those on good
    ground,
Believe what they've been told,
They mature and bear good fruit
From thirty to a hundred fold."

21 Jesus said, "You don't fetch a lamp
Then try to hide the light,
You put it on a lampstand
Where it will shine out bright.

22 "Nothing can be done in secret,
Or be hidden from God's sight.
All you do will be revealed,
Each act will come to light.

23 "If anyone has ears to hear,
24 Mind what you listen to,
The rule by which you judge another
The same will apply to you.

25 "To him who has, more shall be
    given;
But he who hasn't a lot
Will lose the little that he has,
He will lose all he's got.

26 "God's kingdom's like a man who
    casts
Out seed upon the land,
27 And how the seeds sprout and grow,
He does not understand.

28 "First, a little shoot comes through,
The head forms on the blade.
Then finally the grain matures
And another crop is made.

29 "When the time of harvest comes,
And it is time for him to reap,
He puts the sickle to the grain, and
Takes it to his barn to keep.

30 "God's kingdom is like a mustard
    seed,
31 The smallest seed that's found.
32 But it becomes the largest plant
When sown into the ground.

"The branches on the plant are large,
Where a bird can build its nest.
It provides a shade for them
Where fowls can come and rest."

33 With many parables He spoke
As He taught to them His word,
And all those who believed in Him
Understood the things they heard.

34 He spoke in parables to the crowds,
Then explained them privately,
So the disciples would understand
How things were going to be.

35 When evening came, He said to
    them,
"To the other shore, we'll go."
They all got in the boat, and
The disciples began to row.

36 Other boats were on the sea
37 When there arose a gale.
They were afraid the boat would
    sink
Before they could trim the sail.

38 Jesus lay in the stern asleep.
They woke Him with a shout,
"Teacher, we are about to sink,
Why won't you help us out?"

39 Jesus then arose and said
Unto the wind, "Be still."
Immediately the wind died down
And a calm the air did fill.

40 He said to them, "Don't you have
    faith?
Why were you so afraid?"
41 All of them asked, "Who is this
Who the wind and the sea obeyed?

Chapter 5

1 When they reached the other side,
In the country of Gerasene,
2 One came out from among the tombs
Filled with a spirit unclean.

3 This man lived among the tombs,
And no way had been found
To keep him fastened up, although
With chains he had been bound.

4 Shackles he broke into pieces,
Chains he tore apart.
No one could subdue him,
Or ease his troubled heart.

5 He walked among tombs and
     mountains,
He cried out day and night,
He cut and bruised himself with
     stones,
And caused considerable fright.

6 Seeing Jesus from a distance, he
Ran up, with a chilling cry,
7 Said, "What have You to do with me,
Son of God most high?"

"Please do not torment me, for
I know what You're about."
8 For Jesus had been saying,
"Evil spirits, you must get out."

9 Jesus then asked of the spirit,
"Won't you tell me your name?"
He said, "My name is Legion,
For many demons came."

10 The demon pled with Jesus,
"When you would send us out,
Don't send us to the countryside
Where we'll wander all about."

11 A herd of swine stood nearby
Upon the mountainside.
12 "Let us enter them," they pled,
"In the swine we will abide."

13 He gave them His permission and
He said, "So let it be."
The demons moved into the swine
Who rushed into the sea.

14 Those caring for the swine turned
And quickly ran away.
They told in city and country
What had occurred that day.

15 The townsmen came out to see
     the sight.
They saw the man in his right mind
16 They heard how he had been
     healed,
And what had happened to the swine.

They became quite fearful and
17 Begged Jesus to leave their shore.
They feared Jesus' power
And that He would do more.

18 As Jesus walked back to the boat
The healed man sought him saying,
19 "I'll go with you." But Jesus said,
"Go home, these things relaying."

20 When Jesus left, the man proclaimed
In Decapolis and all about
The things that had been done for him
When the demons were cast out.

21 When the Master returned to the
     other side
Crowds met Him on the shore.
Jesus stayed with them, and there
He taught them all some more.

22 A synagogue ruler named Jairus
Came up and fell at His feet.
23 He exclaimed, "My little
     daughter's dying,
Please come," he did entreat.

"Come lay your hands upon her,
Her sickness you can quell.
If only you will come and touch her,
I know she will get well."

24 Jesus started to go with him,
Crowds pressed from every side,
It was very difficult to move
Against the human tide.

25 A woman with a hemorrhage,
For twelve years had endured,
26 She spent all she had on physicians
But still had not been cured.

27 She pushed through the crowd,
     declaring,
"As He is passing by,
28 I'll be healed if I touch His garment,
I must give it a try."

29 She touched Him, and the flow
     dried up,
And she felt immediately,
That she was healed of her affliction
As she knew she would be.

30 Sensing power had gone out from Him,
Jesus stopped, then turned to see.
He said unto the multitude,
"Which of you touched Me?"

31 His disciples answered Him,
"How can you ask this question,
'Which one of you has touched me?'
In all of this congestion."

32 Jesus sought the person who
Had touched His garment's hem.
33 So she came forward and told
     her story,
And confessed it all to Him.

34 "Daughter, go in peace," said Jesus,
"By faith you are made well,
You are healed of your affliction,
To your friends this message tell."

35 While Jesus spoke to the woman
Some men to Jairus said,
"Why bring the teacher to your home?
Your daughter's already dead."

36 Jesus heard what had been spoken.
He said, "Don't fear, believe;
Take Me to your little daughter
And your child you'll receive."

37 He allowed no one to follow Him
Except Peter, James, and John,
38 And when they came to Jarius'
     house
A great wailing was going on.

All the people in the house,
They were loudly weeping.
39 "Why cry you so?" Jesus asked.
"This child's not dead; she's sleeping."

40 All the mourners laughed at Him.
Jesus sent them all away.
Then with His disciples and Jairus
Went in where the child lay.

41 He took the child by the hand,
Said, "Little girl, arise."
At once she sat up in her bed
And looked Him in the eyes.

42 She got up and began to walk,
For she was twelve years old.
All the people were amazed
At the sight they did behold.

43 Jesus gave strict orders to them
That no one should know His deed.
Then Jesus instructed them that
The young girl they should feed.

Chapter 6

1 Jesus went away from there,
Came to His hometown;
2 When the sabbath day was come,
     He went
To the synagogue and sat down.

He began to teach the people
About what God demands.
They were astonished at His
     wisdom and
The miracles from His hands.

3 "Is not this man the carpenter,
The oldest son of Mary?
Are not His brothers with us?
And with us His sisters tarry?"

His neighbors took offense at Him.
4 Jesus said, "It is often told
A prophet is not without honor
Except in His own household."

5 He could perform no miracles
     there,
But laid hands on a few,
And He healed some of the sick,
That was all that He could do.

6 He wondered at their unbelief,
Yet taught with loving care.
7 He called the twelve unto Him,
Then He sent them out in pairs.

He gave them authority over
     unclean spirits,
8 But said, "A bag do not pack.
Take no food or money with you;
Nothing but the clothes on your
     back.

9 "Wear sandals on your feet, but do
Not two tunics don.
10 When you enter into a house
Stay there 'til you move on.

11 "If any place does not receive you,
Or listen to what you say,
Shake the dust from off your feet,
As testimony on judgment day.

"Truly, I say unto you
Sodom and Gomorrah will
Fare better in the judgment
Than those who reject you still.

12 They all went out and preached
  to men
"Repent," they did appeal.
13 Casting out demons, they
  anointed with oil
The sick who then were healed.

14 King Herod heard of Jesus, who was
Becoming well known. He said,
"He has miraculous powers, He's
John the Baptist risen from the dead."

15 But some spoke up, "He is Elijah."
Still other people said,
"He is like a prophet of old,
Or so we have been led."

16 Hearing them talking, Herod
  spoke,
"Although John I did behead,
I repeat, I believe it's John
Who has risen from the dead."

17 Herod had put John in prison
To please Herodias, his wife.
She hated John the Baptist and
She desired to take his life.

She had been wife to Herod's brother
Before she and Herod were married,
18 John had said, "This union is not
  lawful."
19 Herodias wanted John dead and
  buried.

20 But Herod was afraid of John, he
Knew John was a holy man.
He liked John's words although
  sometimes
He did not understand.

21 When King Herod's birthday came
The day was celebrated
By the leading men of Galilee,
All who were highly rated.

22 Herodias' daughter came and
  performed.
She danced before the guests.
She pleased the king so very much
He vowed, "I'll grant your request."

23 Before his guests he swore to her,
"Ask of me what you will,
Up to half of my kingdom;
That wish I will fulfill."

24 She went and asked her mother,
"What shall the king give me?"
25 "Ask that the head of John the
  Baptist,
On a platter be given thee."

She came back to the king and said,
"Oh King, now keep your vow,
I want the head of John the Baptist,
And I want the deed done now."

26 The king regretted what he'd said
But because of his dinner guests,
He feared he'd lose respect, if
He denied the girl's request.

27 The king sent for an executioner
Commanding for John's head.
28 He brought the head in on a platter
Just as the king had said.

He gave the platter to the girl,
She took it to her mother's room.
29 When John's disciples heard of this
They took his body to a tomb.

30 When the apostles came back to
  Jesus,
To report what they'd done and taught.
31 He said, "Let us go aside and rest,
From all the efforts you have wrought."

For many people pressed on them
So close upon their heels,
They felt that they must get away
For rest as well as meals.

32 So they all got into a boat,
And sought a lonely shore,
33 The people saw which way they
  went,
And they ran on before.

34 When the boat came to shore
A crowd was gathered there,
Compassion He had for them, and
God's message He began to share.

They were like sheep without a
shepherd,
35 He taught until the sun was down.
36 His disciples said, "Send them away,
For no food out here is found."

37 He said, "You give them food to
eat."
They asked, "Shall we buy bread?
It would take a lot of loaves
For this crowd to be fed."

38 He said, "How much food do you
have?
Go through the crowd and see."
They reported, "Five loaves, and
two fish."
He said, "Bring them to Me."

39 He broke the people into groups
40 To sit down on the grass.
41 Once He had blessed the bread
and fish
The food He began to pass.

42 They all ate and were satisfied.
43 The leftovers were picked up.
44 There were five thousand men
who on
The loaves and fish did sup.

45 The disciples got into the boat,
While He sent the crowd away.
His followers went to Bethsaida,
46 While Jesus went to the mount
to pray.

47 When evening came they were at sea
And He was alone on land,
48 The wind came up against the boat,
They strained at the oars, each man.

Jesus walked out on the water
In the fourth watch of the night.
49 The disciples thought He was a
ghost
And they cried out in fright.

50 All saw and feared Him, but He said,
"It is I, do not fear."
51 Then Jesus got into the boat
Stayed the winds and gave them cheer.

All the disciples were amazed,
52 But gained no new insight
From the feeding of the loaves and
Their hearts were hard that night.

53 When the boat came to the shore
They were at Gennesaret.
54 As soon as He got out of the boat
By a large crowd He was met.

They brought the sick unto Him,
55 For they were very sure
56 If they but touched His garment
That they would have a cure.

Chapter 7

1 Scribes and Pharisees from
Jerusalem
Gathered in groups to meet.
2 They saw the disciples did not wash
Before they'd start to eat.

3 For Pharisees and Jews did not
Until they washed their hands,
A tradition of their elders, they
Were keeping old commands.

4 When from the marketplace they
came
They stopped and washed again,
And to eat from an unwashed pot
They thought an awful sin.

5 They asked Jesus, "Why don't
your disciples,
Before eating, wash their hands?
According to our traditions
This is one of God's commands."

6 Jesus gave them this reply,
"Isaiah prophesied of you,
'You give me honor with your lips
But your hearts are not true.'

7 "Therefore in vain you worship Me,
For doctrine you are teaching,
Precepts of man and not of God,
My word you are not preaching.

8 "You set aside God's
commandment, so
Traditions you can keep.
9 You spurn God's word for the
sake of
The rules in which you're steeped.

10 " 'Give honor to your parents,' are
The words that Moses said,
The man who would curse them
Will surely join the dead.

11 "You say, 'If one tells his father
     or mother
I've given God all I own,
12 Then no more care to both his
     parents,
By that one must be shown.'

13 "Thus God's Word you invalidate,
Your traditions take its place.
You do many things such as that,
Such actions are a disgrace."

14 He called the multitude to Him
And to the crowd He cried:
15 "You'll not be defiled by anything
That comes from the outside.

"Nothing that enters from without
Can defile a man inside.
What's inside makes him 'unclean,' "
Jesus clarified.

16 "If any man have ears to hear,
Let him hear this true,
And not forget a single word
That I have said to you."

17 When He went in the house, the
     disciples
Asked, "What does this mean?"
18 He said to them, "Are you so
     blind that
Its meaning can't be seen?

"That which goes into a man
Does not corrupt his heart,
19 It goes into his stomach, and
Digested it departs.

20 "It is what comes out of a man
That makes the man unclean;
21 Evil thoughts, thefts, and murder,
Even adultery is seen.

22 "Also from the heart comes deceit,
Envy, foolishness, and pride.
23 Such are the things which can defile,
And come from deep inside."

24 Jesus then left that region,
In Tyre to reside.
He entered quietly into a house,
But He found He could not hide.

25 The news of His arrival spread
Amongst those on the street.
A woman whose daughter was
     demon filled
Came and fell down at His feet.

26 This woman was a Gentile, of
The Syrophoenician race.
She asked Him to cast out the demon;
"Oh, Sir, grant me your grace."

27 He said, "Let the children first be
     filled,
One shouldn't take their bread
And throw it on the ground
So that the dogs are fed."

28 She said, "The children at the table
Are given every need,
But on the crumbs that fall below
The dogs do come and feed."

29 Then Jesus said to her, "Because
Of your answer, go your way.
30 The demon has fled from her, your
Daughter is made well today."

31 From Tyre He soon departed,
To Decapolis came near.
32 They brought one hardly speaking,
For this one could not hear.

They asked Jesus to lay hands on him.
33 He took him from the crowd.
He put His fingers in his ears,
Touched his tongue, then cried aloud:

34 "Ephphatha!" which means 'be
     opened' and
Toward heaven He deeply sighed.
35 The dumb man's tongue was
     loosened—
His ears were opened wide.

36 He ordered them to tell no one.
But loudly they did proclaim.
37 They said, "He does all things
     quite well,
Heals deaf and dumb the same."

Chapter 8

1 Again great masses came to Him,
2 Sat three days at His feet.
He called His disciples aside,
And said, "They need to eat.

3 "If I should send them all away
Before they have been fed,
They have been with me for three days
    now,
And might faint for want of bread."

4 "We're in a wilderness," they said,
"Where could we find enough
To feed a crowd as large as this
With bread or such foodstuff?"

5 He asked, "How many loaves
    have you?"
They answered, "Only seven."
6 He told the crowd to sit down, then
He raised His eyes to heaven.

He gave thanks and broke the bread,
They passed the food around.
They served all of that great crowd
Which sat upon the ground.

7 They also had a few small fish
Which He took up and blest.
8 Everyone ate and was satisfied,
Seven baskets held the rest.

9 There were about four thousand
Who ate the food that day.
10 And after they had had their fill
He sent them all away.

He took a boat with His disciples,
To Dalmanutha went to rest,
11 But Pharisees arived to argue
And seek for signs as a test.

12 He deeply sighed and then He said,
"This generation seeks a sign,
No sign shall be given but
These very words of mine."

13 And leaving them He went away.
He crossed to the other side.
14 They failed to take food, so there was
But one loaf for the ride.

15 Jesus said, "Beware the leaven
Of Herod and the Pharisee."
16 They thought, "Because we have
    no bread
He speaks thus to you and me."

17 Their thoughts known to Him,
    Jesus said,
"Why do you talk of bread?
Do you still not understand,
Or remember what I've said?

"Do each of you have hardened hearts?
You'll never understand, I fear,
18 Having eyes you do not see,
Having ears you do not hear.

19 "When how I broke five loaves
Shared by five thousand souls.
How many baskets were left over?"
"Twelve," they said, "Full of fish
    and rolls."

20 "And when I broke the seven loaves
How much was then picked up?"
They said, "We picked up seven and
Four thousand souls did sup."

21 He said, "You witnessed all of this
Yet do not understand?
You are so very slow to learn
This thing that God has planned."

22 Then coming to Bethsaida,
They brought to Him one blind.
They entreated Him to touch the man
So his sight he would find.

23 Jesus took him by the hand,
He led him out of town.
He put some spittle on his eyes
Then asked him to look aroun'.

He put his hands upon him and
He said, "What do you see?"
24 He said, "I see men walking, but
Each one looks like a tree."

25 Again He laid His hands on him
And other things did appear.
For Jesus had restored his sight;
He saw all things quite clear.

26 Jesus sent him to his home,
Said, "Don't return to town
And also don't tell anyone
Just how your sight was found."

27 Jesus went to Caesarea Phillipi
And as He made His way
He asked, "Who do they say I am?
What do the people say?"

28 They said, "Some say you're John
    the Baptist
Or Elijah come again.
Still others say you're a prophet
To turn us all from sin."

29 "But who do you say I am, now
That many miles we've trod?"
So Peter answered for them all,
"You, Lord, are the Christ of God."

30 He warned the disciples,
"Tell no one about Me."
31 Then He began to teach,
How He must suffer shortly.

He said by elders, chief priests, and
    scribes
That He would be rejected.
He would be killed but after three days
He would be resurrected.

32 All this He stated plainly,
Then Peter took Him aside.
He said, "You cannot let this happen,
These things You did describe.

33 Jesus said, "Get behind Me, Satan;
For you know not God's plan,
Your mind's not on the things of God,
Your interests are those of man."

34 He called the crowd to Him and said,
"One who'd My follower be
He must first deny himself, take up
His cross and follow Me.

35 "If you would save your life,
Your efforts will be in vain.
But if you lose it for My sake,
You'll save it for great gain.

36 "It is no profit to gain the world
For then you are not whole.
To gain the world is poor exchange
37 If in doing so, you lose your soul.

38 "For whoever is ashamed of Me
Before the sinners of this time,
I will be ashamed of him as well
When I return in glory sublime.

Chapter 9

1 "Truly some are standing here
With Me this very hour
Who shall not taste death's sting until
God's kingdom comes in power."

2 And after six days Jesus went
Up into a mountain range,
There before Peter, James, and John
His countenance did change.

3 His garments became radiant,
Beyond the white of bleach;
4 Elijah and Moses appeared and
With Jesus had some speech.

5 Peter spoke and said to Jesus,
"Teacher, to be here's well,
Let us now make three shelters
In which you each may dwell."

6 He knew not what he should say,
For they were terrified.
7 Then a cloud formed over them
A mighty cloud quite wide.

A voice came from the cloud
Saying, "This is My beloved Son,
I would have you listen to Him
And hear what He has done.

"All of you can learn from Him,
From what He has to say."
8 At once they looked around and saw
The visitors had gone away.

9 As they were coming down the mount
To the disciples Jesus said,
"Do not tell of these things until
I've risen from the dead."

10 They seized upon Christ's statement
    and
Upon what they had seen,
"He says, 'I'll raise up from the dead,'
By this what does He mean?"

11 They questioned Him about
    God's Kingdom.
"Why do the scribes all say
That Elijah must come first
Before that glorious day?"

12 "Elijah did come first again,
Just as you have heard.
He put all things in order
According to God's Holy Word.

"It is written of the Son of Man
That He will be mistreated.
He will suffer at men's hands
Until evil is defeated.

67

13 "I say Elijah has already come
And just as it is written,
They did to him what e'er they wished,
By evil men he was smitten."

14 He came back to the disciples,
A large crowd stood around,
There were some scribes who argued
    with them
And made an angry sound.

15 When the multitude saw Jesus, they
Ran up, the Lord to greet.
16 He asked the scribes, "What
    were you discussing
As we came down the street?"

17 One man said unto Him,
"My son has a speechless spirit,
He can hardly speak at all,
And I greatly fear it.

18 "Sometimes he's thrown down to
    the ground,
At times he's dashed about.
He also foams and grinds his teeth.
Please drive this spirit out.

"I asked your disciples to try
But nothing they could do."
19 Jesus said, "Oh faithless generation
What shall I do with you?"

"Bring the boy to Me," He said,
20 But the child fell to the ground.
He started foaming at the mouth
And rolling all around.

21 He asked the father, "How long has
This thing been going on?"
The father said, "Since childhood,
These things he's undergone.

22 "It has thrown him into the fire
And into water, too,
Have pity on us, Lord, if there
Is something you can do."

23 Then to the father Jesus said,
"If in Me you believe,
Then in faith all is possible
And your wish you'll receive."

24 The father of the boy cried out,
"Oh Lord, I do believe.
Help me in my unbelief,
My son's disease relieve."

25 When Jesus saw a crowd had
    gathered
To see what was at hand,
He stood before the unclean spirit
And He gave this command,

"I say, you spirit, deaf and dumb,
Come out of him right now,
You cannot enter him again
For this I'll not allow."

26 The spirit cried and threw him
    down,
Some thought the boy was dead,
27 But Jesus took him by the hand
And to his father led.

28 When they came into the house
His disciples asked privately,
"Why could we not cast it out?
Tell us, what is the key?"

29 Jesus gave to them this answer,
"This kind cannot come out
Unless you spend much time in prayer
And have in you no doubt."

30 They then went out through Galilee,
But He didn't want it known,
31 For He was teaching His disciples
And would have them alone.

"The Son of Man will be delivered
Into the hands of men,
Although they'll abuse and kill Him,
He will still rise again."

32 His words they did not understand
But were afraid to ask,
For He might think them unworthy
For their appointed task.

33 And when they came to Capernaum
He turned to them to say,
"What thing were you discussing as
We walked along the way?"

34 The disciples all kept silent, for
They all felt much shame.
They had discussed who would be
    greatest
When heaven's kingdom came.

35 As He sat down where He was
The twelve to Himself did call.
He said, "If one wants to be first
He shall be last of all."

36 He placed a child in their midst,
Where everyone could see,
And with His arms around the child
37 He said, "I say to thee,

"If you receive a child like this
And accept him in My name,
You also are receiving Me
And He who sent Me the same."

38 "Demons were cast out," said John,
"By one who used your name.
We told him he must stop until
A follower he became."

39 Jesus said, "Don't bother him, if he
Does a miracle in My name.
He cannot speak evil of me,
And a blessing he can claim.

40 For anyone who is not against us,
Is with us, don't you see?
41 Anyone giving water in my name
Will have reward from Me.

42 "Who causes these little ones to
    stumble,
These children who believe in Me;
He would be much better off if he
Were cast into the sea.

43 "If your hand causes you to sin,
Cut it off; cast it from you.
44 Better to live life a cripple
Than go to hell with two.

45 "If your foot causes you to sin,
Cut if off; throw it away.
46 It's better to be lame on earth
Then to walk in hell, I say.

47 "If your eye causes you to sin
To lose it you'd do well.
Better to enter heaven with one eye
Than with two be cast into hell.

48 "There the worm will never die,
In these pits where they dwell.
Neither will the fires be quenched
In all the realms of hell.

49 "Each one by fire will be salted.
50 Some salt is good to taste,
But if the salt has lost its flavor
It's thrown out in the waste.

"Have the salt of God within you,
Have peace with one another.
Don't let the salt lose its taste
When you mistreat your brother."

Chapter 10

1 Jesus went to the region of Judea,
To the Jordan and beyond,
The crowds all gathered 'round,
    and as
He taught they did respond.

2 Some Pharisees came up and asked,
"Tell us, is there a cause
For a man to divorce his wife?
Are there any sacred laws?"

3 He answered, "What did Moses write?
Just what did Moses say?"
4 They said, "Write a bill of
    divorcement,
Then send the wife away."

5 "Because your hearts are hard,"
    He said,
"Moses wrote you this command,
6 But from the beginning of creation
This is not what God had planned.

"Male and female—God made both.
7 When a man leaves his father and
    mother
8 He and his wife become one flesh,
And shall remain with one another.

9 "What God has joined together, then
Let no man separate.
If you are joined in marriage so
Remain in the married state."

10 When they went into the house
The disciples asked Him again.
By asking one more time they hoped
To understand it then.

11 "If a man should divorce his wife,
This I do say to thee,
If he then takes another woman
He commits adultery.

12 "It is the same with a woman,
If divorce she did demand
She would commit adultery then
If she married another man."

13 Some brought their children to Him
So o'er them He would pray,
They were rebuked by the disciples
Who tried to send them away.

14 Jesus looked on with displeasure,
Said, "Bring them to Me, please,
For all of God's great kingdom does
Belong to such as these.

15 "I say unless you, like a child
Upon our God call,
You will not see His kingdom, no
You'll not get in at all."

16 He took the children in His arms.
And blessed all those He held.
He laid His hands upon their heads,
With them His blessing dwelled.

17 As He was starting on a journey
A man ran up to ask,
"How can I gain eternal life,
Just what should be my task?"

18 Jesus said unto the man,
"Why do you call Me good?
No one is good but God alone,
I'd have this understood.

19 "Know all God's commandments
well,
Let no lie come from thee,
Don't murder, cheat, or steal,
Or commit adultery.

"You must give honor to your father,
And to your mother, too."
20 The man said, "I've done this
since youth,
What else is there to do?"

21 Jesus looked and loved him much,
Said, "You need one thing more,
Sell your belongings, then give all
The money to the poor.

"Treasure in heaven you shall have
If you then follow Me."
22 At this the young man turned away
For he was rich in property.

23 Jesus looking at His disciples,
Said something they thought odd;
"It is hard for those who are rich
To find their way to God."

24 At this the disciples were amazed
So He said the words again,
"Children, how very hard it is
God's kingdom to enter in.

25 "It's easier for a camel to
Go through a needle's eye
Than for the rich to enter heaven,
No matter how they try."

26 The disciples were astonished, for
This principle seemed so odd,
But marvelous to comprehend
As are all the things of God.

They asked Him, "Who can then be
saved?"
27 Jesus said, "It's not of man,
But with God all is possible
According to God's plan."

28 Peter began to say to Him,
"We left all to follow You."
29 Jesus then replied to him,
"This may be very true,

"But none has left his house or left
His family for My sake,
30 Will fail to receive a hundred-fold,
For the sacrifice they make.

31 "But many who try to be first
Will end up being last,
And those who are the last today
Are first when judgment's passed."

32 As He went toward Jerusalem
They were a little fearful,
Though Jesus walked ahead of them,
They were not very cheerful.

So again He took them all aside,
Told what would come their way.
33 "We're going to Jerusalem where
Chief priests will have their day.

"The priests and also the scribes
will hold
A mockery of a trial.
They shall condemn the Son of Man
And deliver Him to the Gentile.

34 "They will mock and spit on Him
And they will scourge Him, too.
They'll take His life away, but in
Three days He'll rise anew.

35 The sons of Zebedee, James and
     John,
Said, "We make a request of you."
36 Jesus turned and said to them,
"What would you have Me do?"

37 They said, "When your kingdom
     comes,
And you stand in all your might,
Let one of us sit on your left,
The other on your right."

38 Jesus said, "You don't know
     what you ask,
Nor see things through My eyes.
Can you drink from the cup I drink,
Be baptized as I'm baptized?"

39 "We are able, Lord," they said.
Jesus said, "The cup I drink
You shall also share with Me,
From it you cannot shrink.

"You'll be baptized with My baptism
As in this world you live,
40 But who's to sit at My right hand
Is not for Me to give.

"Who will sit on My right or left
Has not yet been declared.
Only My Father in heaven knows
For whom it's been prepared."

41 When the other ten disciples heard
Of James and John's request,
Very indignant they became,
For they desired the best.

42 Calling the disciples to Himself
He said, "These over you
Are recognized as having power
In things they say and do.

43 "Be this not so among you, if
You would be truly great,
Then you shall be a servant, this
Is what I have to state.

44 "Among you, he who would be first
Must be a slave to all,
45 I did not come to be ministered to
A servant was My call.

"I was sent to serve mankind,
For man's ransom give My life.
So too, if you would be great, you
Must serve and cease all strife."

46 As they arrived at Jericho,
Followed by a tremendous crowd,
Blind Bartimaeus sat by the road
And cried out very loud:

47 "Jesus, oh you son of David,
My request, please fill."
48 The crowd around the Master said,
"Old blind man, please be still."

But louder did the blind man cry,
So that the Lord would hear,
49 Jesus stopped along the road,
Saying, "Call the blind man here."

Those about him said, "Take courage,
Arise, He calls for you."
50 When he came, Jesus said,
"What can I do for you?"

51 The blind man said, "Lord,
I would receive my sight,
I want to see my way again
I ask with all my might."

52 "Go your way," He said to him,
"Your faith removed your load."
Immediately he received his sight
And followed Jesus down the road.

Chapter 11

1 As they came near Jerusalem,
They reached Bethpage and Bethany,
On the slopes of the Mount of Olives
Which all of the crowd could see.

2 He said to two of His disciples,
"Enter the village ahead of you,
When you get there you'll see a colt,
And this is what you're to do:

"Untie the colt, and bring it here,
3 If challenged in your deed,
You are to say to the one who asks,
'For it the Lord has need.' "

4 The disciples went their way and
     found
The colt out on the street.
They immediately started to untie
     it, so
The Lord's request they'd meet.

71

5 Some said, "Why do you do this
thing?
And just what is your mission?"
6 The disciples spoke Jesus' words.
And were given their permission.

7 They spread their garments on
the colt,
Others spread theirs on the ground.
Then Jesus got upon the colt
And they started into town.

8 The road was spread with robes
and branches
Which they'd cut from the field.
As they saw the Lord ride by,
The people reverently kneeled.

9 They cried, "Hosanna, in the
highest!
Blessings to our God and Lord,
10 By Him who in His name comes
David's kingdom is restored."

11 Into Jerusalem He went,
Up to the temple gate,
From there He left for Bethany
As the hour was getting late.

12 Leaving Bethany the next day
He desired a bite to eat.
13 He saw a fig tree down the road
And thought He'd have a treat.

When Jesus came up to the tree
No figs did He find there,
There were only leaves upon the tree,
For it was not time to bear.

14 And to the fig tree, Jesus said,
"You will not bear again,
Never again will you produce fruit
To satisfy the taste of men."

15 Inside the temple in Jerusalem
Were those who bought and sold.
He cast them out, overthrew their
tables
Scattered of silver and gold.

He went to those who were selling
doves,
And upset the seats He found;
16 He suffered none to carry wares
Throughout the temple ground.

17 Then He began to teach and said,
"It's written for all men,
My household shall be a house of
prayer,
And not a robber's den."

18 The scribes and priests heard of
what He said
And wanted Him destroyed,
For by His actions and His teachings
They all were much annoyed.

They feared Him for the crowds all
were
Astonished at His teaching,
It was the poor and humble folk
The Son of Man was reaching.

19 They left the city every day
When evening time did fall,
But they returned the morning next
To go inside its wall.

20 One morn they saw the fig tree
withered
Away and wondered why.
21 "It's the tree you cursed," Peter
recalled,
"The roots are withered, Rabbi."

22 He answered, saying unto them,
"With faith in God you see,
23 You can command this mountain
To be cast into the sea.

"If you believe it will be done,
And in your heart's no doubt.
Ask in prayer what e'er you wish
And it will come about.

24 "I say, therefore what'er you pray
If you in faith believe,
The things for which you ask will be
The things you will receive.

25 "Whenever you stand praying,
forgive
All those who have wronged you
So that your Father up in heaven
Will hear and forgive you, too."

26 I tell you truly, pay attention
At this I have to share,
Forgive your erring brother, or
My Father won't forgive you there.

27 Again they came to Jerusalem,
In the temple they did walk,
Chief priests and scribes came unto
  Him,
And they began to talk.

28 They started by asking Jesus, "Who
Gave you authority
To do the things you have been doing?
We expect a reply from Thee."

29 Unto them Jesus said, "I will
Ask you one question, too,
And if you therefore answer Me
Then I will answer you.

30 "Did John's baptism come from
  heaven,
Or did it come from man?
Tell me from where his authority
  came,
Answer Me if you can."

31 The accusers then reasoned
  among themselves,
"If from heaven we confess,
'Why did you not believe?' He'll say,
'John's preaching in the wilderness.'

32 "But if we say it came from men
We fear the multitude,
For they believe John was a prophet
And with God's power endued."

33 So unto Jesus they did say,
"The answer we don't know."
"Then neither will I answer you,"
He said, and turned to go.

Chapter 12

1 He began to speak in parables;
"Within a vineyard wall,
An owner had a vat and press
Also a tower tall.

"He rented out his vineyard and
Then on a journey went,
2 At harvest time he sent a slave
To collect for him the rent.

3 "The growers beat him viciously,
Then they sent him away,
4 The master sent another servant,
Again they would not pay.

"They treated shamefully this slave
And hit him on the head.
5 The owner sent another servant
They beat him 'til he was dead.

"The owner then sent others, who
They beat and some they killed,
These vine growers still refused
To pay as they were billed.

6 "The owner said, 'I'll try once more,
My plan won't be rejected,
I'll send them my beloved son
He'll surely be respected.'

7 "The growers said to one another;
'Come, let us kill the heir,
We then can seize the inheritance
And we won't have to share.'

8 "They seized him and they killed
  him, and
They cast his body out.
9 What will the vineyard owner do?
I'm sure you have no doubt.

"He will destroy those tenants and
The vineyard give to others.
Be careful how you treat God's word,
I say this to you, My brothers.

10 "Have you not read this scripture,
'The stone which was rejected
By builders is the corner stone
The Lord Himself selected.' "

11 "And it is a marvelous thing, this act
We see before our eyes.
To humble folk God reveals Himself,
Not to those who think they're wise."

12 And they sought to seize Him for
They clearly understood,
He spoke this parable against those
Who thought of themselves as good.

But they feared the multitude,
So they let Him go away,
13 They sent Pharisees and
  Herodians to trap Him
In words that He might say.

14 They said, "Teacher, you are
  truthful,
In your duty are not lax,
You teach the way of God in truth
So should we pay Caesar's tax?"

15 He knew of their hypocrisy,
And said, "Why give Me a test?
To Me bring a penny."
He made this one request.

16 They brought the coin to Him,
    He asked,
"Whose image is seen here?"
They said, "It is Caesar's image
Which on it doth appear."

17 Jesus said, "Unto Caesar render
Things which are Caesar's due,
But don't forget what's owed to God,
You must obey God, too."

18 Some Sadduccees came up to Him,
Who say there is no resurrection,
Questions they began to ask,
Pretending to seek direction.

19 "Teacher, Moses wrote for us
If a childless man leaves this life,
His brother should raise up offspring
By marrying his wife.

20 "There were seven brothers, and
The first one took a wife,
No children came into this home
To bring them joy or strife.

21 "The second brother took her, then
He died with no descendant.
The third brother likewise did, yet
Still there was no infant.

22 "All seven brothers wed her,
The results were all the same.
Last of all the woman died.
No children bore their name.

23 "Now when the resurrection comes,
When they will rise again,
Whose wife will she then be for she
Married all seven men?"

24 Jesus said, "You're all mistaken,
Your reasoning is not sound,
You don't understand the Holy
    Scriptures,
God's power you have not found.

25 "For when they rise up from the
    dead
In marriage they're not given,
But like the angels they will be,
As angels are in heaven.

26 "In fact, the dead do rise again,
As read in Moses' book,
In the passage of the burning bush
When Moses paused to look.

" 'I am the God of Abraham,
Of Isaac and Jacob, too,'
27 He is not the God of the dead
But of the living I say to you."

28 A scribe who heard them arguing
    said,
"Although you've answered well,
What is the first commandment?
This I would have you tell."

29 Jesus answered, "The first is this,
'Oh, Israel, now hear Me.
The Lord our God is one Lord,
There is none but He.

30 " 'You shall love God with all
    your heart,
With body, soul, and mind
31 Then love your neighbor as yourself.
No greater law you'll find.' "

32 "You are correct," the scribe
    replied,
"God is the only one.
And we know that is true,
Beside Him there is none.

33 To love Him with all of our hearts,
With all of our understanding,
With all the strength we have in us
Is what He is demanding.

"To love one's neighbor as himself
Is always very nice,
It's much better than burnt offerings
And more than sacrifice."

34 When Jesus heard his words, He
    said,
"You're near the kingdom door."
And after that the questions ceased,
They pestered Him no more.

35 As Jesus taught in the temple
He asked of everyone,
"How say the scribes that Jesus is
Said to be David's son?

36 "Led by the Spirit David said,
When he was king of the land,
The Lord said to my Lord please come
And sit at My right hand.

" 'Take your place by My side,
Near My throne take your stand,
Until I put your enemies down
And under foot they land.'

37 "If David calls Him Lord,
How can He be his son?
Has the Christ always been
Since creation was begun?"

38 He also said, "Beware of scribes,
They wear robes and long faces,
They have respectful greetings when
They meet in the market places.

39 "They want chief seats in the synagogues,
40 Yet widows' houses devour.
They want honor at their banquets
And pray publicly by the hour.

"They expect to be admired
For their demonstration.
God who knows their hearts will give
Greater condemnation."

41 He sat down by the treasury,
He watched the money which
Was given in large amounts
Donated by the rich.

42 A poor widow then came by,
The givers she would join,
She dropped her gift into the pot,
Just two half penny coins.

43 Jesus called His disciples aside,
"That widow that you see
Has given more than all the rest
Who gave to the treasury.

44 "For out of surplus they did give
And while that isn't bad,
They still had something left to give
While she gave all she had."

C hapter 13

1 As He was going out of the temple
This remark a disciple made,
"Behold what beautiful buildings
Look how their stones are laid."

2 "Yes, look at these buildings,"
Jesus said,
"I just have this to say,
Soon these will be torn down and
Not two stacked stones will stay."

3 As from the Mount of Olives they looked
Four disciples asked Him privately,
4 "Tell us when this thing will happen
And just what the signs will be."

5 Jesus cautioned, "Let none mislead you,
6 Many will come in My name,
'I am He, each will say, and
To be Christ each will claim.

7 "And when you hear of wars and such
You are to have no fear,
For all of these things must take place
Before the end draws near.

8 "Nation will rise against nation
And kingdoms will go to war.
There also will be famines
And earthquakes will be in store.

"All of this will happen, then
It'll happen o'er again,
But the end is not coming yet
It's just the earth's birth pain.

9 "Take heed, you will be delivered up;
Before rulers and kings you see,
Be beaten in the synagogues,
All on account of me."

10 "First to all the nations
The gospel must be taught.
11 Whenever you are arrested,
And to trial brought,

Do not worry beforehand
What you are to say.
Speak as led by the Holy Spirit
Who will guide you all the way.

12 "Brother will betray brother to death,
A father his child will slay.
Children rebel against their parents,
And to death betray.

13 "Because of Me you will be hated,
But if you do endure,
Then you will have salvation, and
Of this you can be sure.

75

14 "But when you see the abomination
Stand where it ought not be,
Then let those who are in Judea
To the high mountains flee.

15 "Let him who's on the housetop go
Not down and enter in.
16 Let him who is in the field not for
His cloak return again.

17 "Woe to those who are with child,
Or nurse babes in that day.
18 Hope it comes not in winter,
For this you need to pray.

19 "Such tribulation will come upon you
Like none that's come before,
Since God created heaven and earth,
In those long days of yore.

20 "Unless the Lord in His great mercy
Had not shortened up the days,
All life on earth would be abolished,
For no one would be saved.

"But for the sake of the elect,
Those people who God chose,
He will shorten those troubled days
And bring them to a close.

21 "If any one should say to you,
The Christ is here or there,
Do not believe a thing they say
Or in their actions share.

22 "For false prophets and false Christs
Will rise up in that day,
With signs and wonders they would lead
The very elect astray.

23 "Take heed of what's been told to you
When these hard times are o'er,
24 The bright sun will be darkened and
The moon will shine no more.

25 "From heaven stars will fall, and the
Heavenly bodies will shake,
26 The Son of Man will come in glory,
His return to earth He'll make.

27 "His angels will be sent forth
To gather His elect.
They'll go to the end of earth and
    heaven
To find all the select.

28 "Learn from the parable of the
    fig tree,
When those new leaves appear
You will know winter's over,
And summer is very near.

29 "When you see these things then
Know He is at the door.
30 I say these things will come to pass
Before this generation's o'er.

31 "Heaven and earth will pass away,
But my words will stand true,
32 But the day and hour only God
    knows,
Not angels, I, nor you.

33 "Therefore, take heed, watch and
    pray,
For the time you do not know.
You should at all times be alert
And be prepared to go.

34 "It is like a man who goes on a
    journey
And when his bags are packed,
He puts his slaves in charge of things
Until he will be back.

35 "He commands the doorkeeper to
    be alert,
To be there to let him in,
Whether it be morning, noon, or night
When he comes home again.

36 "Don't let the Lord find you asleep,
37 I say to one and all,
Always be alert and ready
To hear the Master's call."

Chapter 14

1 The feast of the Passover was two
    days away.
The chief priests made their plan
To seize Him quietly in the night
And to kill the Son of Man.

2 They said, "Wait 'til the feast is over
Lest the people get upset,
For they may cause a riot, which
All of us would regret.

3 While He was still in Bethany,
In Simon the Leper's dining room,
A woman came up behind Him and
Poured o'er Him sweet perfume.

4 The perfume was very costly,
Which she poured on His head.
Some of them were quite indignant
And this is what they said:

5 "Why was this perfume wasted?
Why was it not sold?
The money could be used for the poor."
The woman they did scold.

6 He said, "Let her alone; she's done
A kindly thing for Me.
Do not bother her at all
I am commanding thee.

7 "The poor are always with you, when
You wish, you can do them good,
But you will not have Me always.
8 She has done what she could.

"She anointed My body for burial,
9 And this I say to you,
Where'er the gospel's preached, you
    will
Hear of this woman, too."

10 Judas Iscariot, one of the twelve,
Then sought the chief priests out
In order to betray the Lord,
For the love of money no doubt.

11 The priests received Him, and
They promised they would pay,
Then Judas sought the best time when
The Lord he would betray.

12 The Feast of Unleavened Bread
    approached,
His disciples asked Him, "Where
Shall we prepare for Passover
And for the meal you'll share?"

13 He called in two disciples,
Said, "In the city go.
You'll meet a man with a water
    pitcher,
Follow him, he will know.

14 "And when he goes into the house
Unto the owner say,
'Where is the room where I
Will eat with My disciples today?'

15 "He'll show you to an upper room,
Ready for us to share,
Then get whatever things you need
And the feast for us prepare."

16 The disciples went into the city,
Found things just like He'd told.
They prepared the Passover feast
Which that night they would hold.

17 When evening came He and the
    twelve
18 Around the table took seats.
"One will betray Me," Jesus said,
"One who with Me now eats."

19 Each of them looked sad and asked,
"Surely it is not I."
20 "It is one who dips with Me in
    the dish,"
Was Jesus' reply.

21 "The Son of Man is going to go
Just as the prophets portrayed,
But woe unto that man, I say,
By whom He is betrayed.

"It would've been better for that man
If he had not been born.
Still I know he will betray Me
Even though he's been warned."

22 And while they were eating there,
He took some of the bread,
He blessed the bread and then He
    broke it,
And this is what He said:

"This is My body which I say
I shall lay down for thee.
Each time you eat this bread, I want
You to remember Me."

23 Then He took up the cup, gave
    thanks,
And passed the cup around.
He said, "This is My blood, I say
Which is poured out on the ground.

24 "This is My blood of covenant,
Which I pour out for you,
25 I'll not drink of the vine's fruit 'till
In the kingdom I drink it anew."

26 And after they had sung a hymn,
They went out into the night,
They went unto the Mount of Olives.
It was dark; there was no light.

27 Jesus stopped and said to them,
"You will all fall away,
For the prophets all have written
That there will come a day

" 'When I will strike the shepherd, and
The sheep will not be found.'
When the shepherd leaves the flock
The sheep are scattered 'round.

28 "After I have been raised from
the dead,
I will go into Galilee.
I'll go before you to that place
And there you shall meet me."

29 Then Peter said unto Him, "Lord
I have one thing to say,
I never will desert you, though
The others run away."

30 Jesus turned and said to Peter,
"Your words are very nice,
But you will deny Me thrice
Before the cock crows twice."

31 But Peter kept insisting that
The Lord He'd not deny,
He said, "I'll always stand with you
Even if I must die."

All the rest of the disciples,
Those who were gathered there,
Also said the same words
Saying, "Lord we really care."

32 Coming to the garden of
Gethsemane,
Taking Peter, James, and John,
He said, "Wait here, while I go pray."
Then he went further on.

33 He was troubled and distressed,
34 He said, "My soul is grieved.
I feel I am at the point of death,
From My burden I'd be relieved.

35 "I want you to stay and watch
While to My Father I cry."
Then He prayed, "Lord, if possible
Please let this cup pass by."

36 He was praying, "Abba Father,
Hearken to My plea,
Remove this cup, but I will drink
If it's Your will for Me."

37 He found the disciples sleeping, said,
"Simon are you asleep?
Could you not watch one hour,
Your eyes wide open keep?

38 "Keep watching and keep
praying lest
Temptation find you out.
The spirit is very willing, but
Your flesh is weak, no doubt."

39 He went away and prayed again,
The same words He did pray.
40 When He returned they were asleep
And knew not what to say.

41 He came to them a third time and
Said, "Are you still at rest?
Behold! the hour is now at hand
For Me to meet the test.

Into the hands of sinners is
Betrayed the Son of Man,
42 Arise, let us be going, the
Betrayer is at hand."

43 Judas had a signal planned
So His enemies could work with ease,
44 He said, "Whomever I shall kiss
It's Him you are to seize."

45 He went right up and kissed the
Lord,
And said to Him, "Rabbi!"
46 Then the guards seized Jesus and
His hands began to tie.

47 One of those who stood nearby
With a sword then did appear,
He swung it at the high priest's
slave
And he cut off his ear.

48 "Am I leading a rebellion?"
Jesus said to the men.
"Is that why you come with clubs
and swords
To capture Me then?

49 "I was with you in the temple courts
Teaching every day.
You did not arrest Me then, so
Fulfill what the Scriptures say."

50 When the disciples saw Him bound
They turned and ran away,
Fear gripped their hearts so suddenly,
They were afraid to stay.

51 They seized a man who followed,
Wrapped only in a linen sheet,
52 He left the sheet behind him and
Ran naked down the street.

53 They took Jesus to the high priest,
To convict Him was their aim,
Together all the chief priests,
Elders, and teachers came.

54 Peter followed at a distance,
Went inside the palace gate
He warmed himself at the servants'
    fire,
There he planned to wait.

55 The council would put Him to death,
But no cause could they see.
56 For many testified against Him,
But their words did not agree.

57 Standing to speak against Him, they
58 Said, "We've heard Him exclaim
He'll destroy this temple, but
In three days rebuild the same."

59 In all the things they had to say
They were quite inconsistent.
But they continued testifying,
The priests were so insistent.

60 The high priest then arose and said,
"Please answer what you've heard."
61 But Jesus stood in silence and,
He would not say a word.

Again the high priest questioned Him,
"You claim to be God's lamb,
Are you the son of the Blessed One?"
62 And Jesus said, "I am.

"And you will see the Son of Man
At the right hand of power,
Coming in the clouds of heaven
And you will fear that hour."

63 The high priest tore his clothes
    and said,
"No witnesses we need.
64 You have all heard His blasphemy.
This is an awful deed."

They all condemned the Lord to death
65 And in His face they spit.
They slapped Him and said,
    "Prophesy!"
By the servants He was hit."

66 Meanwhile in the courtyard, Peter
By the high priest's maid was seen.
67 She looked at Peter and said, "You
Were with the Nazarene."

68 Peter said, "I do not understand
The words that you are speaking."
Withdrawing from the fire, a
Safe corner he was seeking.

As Peter slipped out to the porch
A sound pierced the air.
A cock crowed from the darkness,
Just as Jesus did declare.

69 And when the maid saw him again
She said to those nearby,
"See this man is one of them."
But again he did deny.

A little later a bystander said,
"Those words I feel are true,
70 Surely you are one of them,
You're a Galilean, too."

71 Then Peter began to curse and
    swear,
"This fellow I don't know."
The words had hardly left his
    mouth
When Peter heard the rooster crow.

72 Peter recalled what Jesus said,
"Before the cock twice crows,
Three times you will deny Me," and
Weeping, Peter arose.

Chapter 15

1 Very early in the morn
The priests and elders, too,
Held a meeting with the council
To decide what they would do.

"We must take him to Pilate,"
The whole Sanhedrin said.
So after they had bound His hands,
To Pilate was Jesus led.

2 Pilate began to question Him,
"You who they bring today,
Are you the King of the Jews?"
Jesus said, "It's as you say."

3 Of many things He was accused,
Although they were untrue,
4 Pilate said, "Will you not answer
The things they say of you?"

5 Jesus gave no further answer,
To him gave no reply.
This so astonished Pilate that
He gaped and wondered why.

6 In those days it was a custom
That at Passover time,
A prisoner would be released
Who'd hadn't paid for his crime.

7 There was a man named Barabbas, who
Was charged with insurrection.
And also murder, so he was
Imprisoned in that section.

8 The crowd asked Pilate to follow what
The custom said to do.
9 "The one you call King of the Jews,
Should I release to you?"

10 He knew it was because of envy
That Christ was to him led,
11 But the priests stirred up the crowd
To release Barabbas instead.

12 "Then what shall I do with Jesus?"
Pilate to them replied,
13 The masses quickly shouted back,
"Let Him be crucified!"

14 Pilate asked, "What has He done?"
The crowd yelled all the more,
"We'd have you crucify the Man."
They said this o'er and o'er.

15 Then he released Barabbas,
Did as the people urged;
He delivered Jesus to be crucified,
But first had Jesus scourged.

16 The soldiers then took Jesus
Into the inner court.
They called the guards together
And of Him they made sport.

17 They dressed Him in a purple
  robe,
Thorns crowned His head,
18 Acclaimed Him as, "King of the
  Jews,"
Yes, this is what they said.

19 They also beat Him with a reed,
Before Him they bowed down.
20 And after they had spit on Him, they
Took off His robe and crown.

They gave His own clothes back to Him,
They led Him out to crucify.
21 They seized Simon of Cyrene who
Was just a passerby.

They put the cross on Simon's back,
When Christ fell beneath the load.
22 They led Him up Golgotha's hill
Along a steep, dusty road.

23 They offered to Him wine with
  myrrh,
But this He refused to take.
The pain and anguish He would bear,
Man's salvation was at stake.

24 They crucified the Lord and for
His garments they cast lots,
To determine what each man
  would take,
To see what each one got.

25 So Christ was crucified
At nine a.m. that day.
26 "King of the Jews," was what
The written charge did say.

27 They crucified two robbers,
On His left and on His right.
The execution by crucifixion
Was a very gruesome sight.

28 Those passing by tormented Him
With angry words they hazed,
29 "You said You would rebuild the
  temple
Three days after it was razed.

30 "Save yourself, and leave the cross."
31 The chief priests mocked Him, too,
"He may have saved others,
But for Himself He cannot do.

32 "Let this Christ, the King of Israel,
Then from the cross come down
So we may believe He's Messiah, and
That He deserves a crown."

Those crucified on either side
Cast insults at Him, too.
Saying, "Take yourself from the cross
And take us down with you."

33 At twelve o'clock darkness came,
So no one there could see.
34 At three o'clock He cried, "My God,
Why have you forsaken Me?"

35 Some said, "He's calling for Elijah,
At least that's what we think."
36 Someone filled a sponge with vinegar
And offered Him a drink.

He said, "Let's see if Elijah comes
And takes this 'King' away.
That would truly be a miracle
If it came about today."

37 Jesus cried aloud again,
And then He breathed His last.
38 The veil of the temple split apart,
Those watching stood aghast.

39 The centurion who stood by Him,
Saw how Christ had died.
"Truly He was the Son of God!"
Was what the centurion cried.

40 Some women stood far off, and they
Looked out upon the scene.
Mary, mother of James and Joseph,
Salome, and Mary Magdalene.

41 When Jesus had been in Galilee
They'd gone and for Him cared,
Along with many other women
Who with the Lord had shared.

42 When evening came, because it was
The preparation day,
43 Joseph of Arimathea came to Pilate
To take His body away.

44 Pilate wondered, "Is Jesus dead?"
He called a centurion to his side,
And questioned him about His death
To make sure He had died.

45 Pilate gave Joseph the body,
And Joseph took it down.
46 He wrapped the body in a linen
sheet,
Then placed it in the ground.

He put it in a brand new tomb,
Which had been hewn from rock.
He rolled a stone against the opening,
The door this stone would block.

47 Mary Magdalene and the other
Mary,
Observed where He was laid,
So later they could return and then
Their last respects be paid.

Chapter 16

1 When the Sabbath day was over,
The women went to Him,
With spice for anointing as
2 The sun peeked o'er the rim.

3 They were saying to each other,
"Who will remove the stone?"
For they knew it was heavy, they
Could not do it alone.

4 As the women neared the tomb
They saw the stone was rolled.
The entrance was wide open and
The door they did behold.

5 When entering the tomb, they saw
A young man in white there.
They all were much amazed and then
With them the man did share.

6 The young man said these words
to them,
"Don't be amazed, don't fear,
You seek the crucified Nazarene,
He is risen, He is not here.

7 "But go tell His disciples
He goes before to Galilee,
And there you are to meet Him just
As He said unto thee."

8 The women shook in astonishment,
And from the tomb they fled.
For they were awed that Christ indeed
Had risen from the dead.

9 Early, on the first day after
His resurrection came about,
He appeared to Mary Magdalene,
From whom He'd cast demons out.

10 She reported to His disciples
The things that she had seen,
11 But they would not believe the words
Of Mary Magdalene.

12 He then appeared in a different form
To two along the way.
13 But these disciples did not believe
The things he had to say.

14 He then appeared to the eleven,
When at a meal they took part.
He reproached each one of them
For the hardness of his heart.

He said, "I told you before the cross
I would rise from the dead.
Why did you not believe those who
Had seen Me without dread?"

15 "Go into all the world," He said.
"Preach the gospel to all creation.
16 He who believes and is baptized
Will have his soul's salvation.

"But he who won't believe in Me
Will suffer damnation.
This is the message you must take;
Tell it to every nation.

17 "All signs will accompany those
Who believe and follow Me,
They'll cast out demons, speak new
    tongues,
This power I'll give to thee.

18 "Deadly poison, they may drink,
Take serpents in their hands,
And it will not hurt them if they
Are true to My commands.

"They will lay hands upon the sick,
Their touch will make them well,
If in My name they go
And to all My message tell."

19 When the Lord had thus spoken
Into heaven He was received.
At God's right hand He sat down and
His disciples now believed.

20 They went out and preached the
    Word,
Spread the gospel everywhere.
The Lord confirmed their work
    with signs
As the good news they did share.

The Gospel According to Luke

Chapter 1

1 Many have tried to compile a record,
Of what we believe. most surely
2 Ministers and eyewitnesses of the
Word,
They have handed it down to me.

3 I have investigated everything
That has been told to us.
It seems I should put them in order,
Most excellent Theophilus,

4 That you may know the truth about
The things that have been taught;
If you are asked to give an answer,
In ignorance you'll not be caught.

5 Those days King Herod ruled Judea;
A priest named Zacharias came.
His wife was descended from Aaron,
Elizabeth was her name.

6 They were both righteous folk, doing
Whatever they were told.
7 But they had no children, and
Both were getting old.

8 As Zacharias served in the temple,
By lot it became his turn,
9 To approach God's holy altar and
On it the incense to burn.

10 As Zacharias burned the incense,
The people were in prayer,
11 An angel appeared to Zacharias
And with him began to share.

12 He was troubled when the angel said,
13 "Fear not, thy prayer is heard,
Your wife will bear a son, for your
Petition has been heard.

You will name the baby John,
14 And you will have great joy.
Many will rejoice with you
At the birth of this baby boy.

15 "For in God's sight he will be great
And he will drink no wine.
Before birth he'll be Spirit filled,
This lovely son of thine.

16 "He will turn many to the Lord,
Who is like a mighty tower.
17 He'll go before as a forerunner
In Elijah's spirit and power.

He'll turn fathers back to children,
The bad to a right attitude.
He'll prepare men to receive the Lord,
As a prophet he will be viewed."

18 Zacharias said, "I've prayed for this,
Wept many bitter tears,
How can we know these words are true
For we're advanced in years?"

19 The angel said, "I am Gabriel,
In God's presence I do stand,
I have been sent to bring His word,
I've come at His command.

20 "Behold! you shall be silent, you
Shall be able to speak no more
Until these things have come to pass,
And the pregnancy is o'er.

"Because you didn't believe my words,
And your heart is filled with doubt,
You must communicate with signs
Until this comes about."

21 The people waited outside the temple,
For Zachariah's return,
They thought it was taking too long
To just some incense burn.

22 When he came out to where they were
He could not speak, they found;
They knew that he had seen a vision,
He motioned but made no sound.

23 His time of service completed.
He went back to his wife,
24 Soon she became pregnant,
With the beginning of a new life.

25 After five months of silence, she said,
"The Lord has shown His grace.
He's looked on me with favor and
Has removed all my disgrace."

26 In the sixth month, sent from God,
Gabriel to Nazareth came
27 To a virgin engaged to Joseph,
Mary was the virgin's name.

28 And coming in he said to her,
"Hail thou, the favored one.
The grace of God is on you
For you shall bear His Son."

29 Mary was troubled by this
   announcement,
For she was just a lowly maid.
30 Therefore, the angel said to her,
"Mary do not be afraid.

"You have found favor with the Lord,
31 In your womb you will conceive.
You will bear a son named Jesus,
This I want you to believe.

32 "He will be great in God's sight,
God will not leave Him alone.
Son of the most High He'll be called,
He'll receive King David's throne.

33 "He will reign o'er the house of Jacob,
His kingdom will never cease.
It will go on forever and forever;
He'll be the Prince of Peace."

34 Mary said unto the angel,
"How can this be done?
You know I'm still a virgin, how
Then can I bear a son?"

35 The angel answering said to her,
"To you this may seem odd,
The Holy Spirit will come upon you,
Your child's the Son of God.

36 "Behold! the aged Elizabeth:
A son she has conceived.
37 Nothing is impossible with God,
Listen and believe."

38 Mary said, "I am the Lord's
   handmaid,
Be it done as I have heard."
The angel left her there, he did
Not say another word.

39 Mary then rose with haste, and to
A city of Judah came.
40 She entered Zachariah's home
And called Elizabeth's name.

41 The babe leaped in Elizabeth's womb
When he heard Mary's voice.
She was filled with God's Spirit and
With Mary did rejoice.

42 Elizabeth cried out to Mary,
"Blessed of all women are you,
Blessed is the fruit of your womb;
   to what
Is this honored visit due?

43 Why am I so honored
That the mother of my Lord
Should choose among all women
To announce to me this word?

44 "Behold! when you called out
   your greeting
It reached my baby's ears;
The babe in my womb jumped for joy
And my eyes filled with tears.

45 "Blessed is she who believed that
The Word would be fulfilled.
What the Lord has said to you
Is coming as God willed."

46 "My soul magnifies the Lord,"
   Mary sang,
47 "In God my Saviour I rejoice,
48 For He looked on my low estate
And called me with His voice.

"From this time forth all generations
Will hear and count me blessed.
49 For God has done great things for me,
His name I have confessed.

50 "To generations He'll give mercy—
Those who of Him do fear;
51 With His arm He has shown
   strength,
Scattering proud men far and near.

52 "From thrones He has brought
   princes down,
Exalted those of low degree;
53 The rich He sent away empty,
But the hungry He did please.

54 "His servant Israel He has helped.
His mercy He'll remember always.
55 He spoke to Abraham and our
      fathers,
And to His seed as in bygone days."

56 Mary spent three months with
      Elizabeth,
'Til Elizabeth's labor was done.
Then she returned to her home after
57 Elizabeth had her son.

58 When Zachariah's neighbors
      heard
That Elizabeth had a boy,
They came to rejoice with her
And to share in all the joy.

59 On the eighth day after his birth,
It was time for his circumcision.
They wanted to call him Zachariah,
But it was not their decision.

60 His mother answered, "Not so,
John is to be his name."
61 They said, "None in your family
Was ever called the same."

62 They made a sign his father,
And when the father came,
63 Zachariah wrote upon a tablet,
That John would be his name.

64 At once his mouth was opened, and
He shouted, "God be praised!"
65 And all the people gathered there
Were very much amazed.

The news of all these happenings
      spread
Through the country 'round about;
66 They said, "We will wait and see,
For the Lord touched him, no doubt."

67 Zachariah, filled with the Spirit,
Prophesied and thus professed,
68 "The God of Israel has visited us,
May His Holy name be blessed.

69 "He has accomplished our
      redemption,
He's raised salvation's horn.
In the house of His servant David
The Messiah will be born.

70 "As He spoke by His Holy prophets
In times from long ago,
71 Salvation from our enemies,
Those who hate us so.

72 "And now to our fathers
His mercy will be shown;
His holy covenant remembered,
His words will be made known.

73 "The oath He swore to Abraham,
74 From enemies to deliver us,
Has enabled us to serve Him,
And free from fear to be thus.

75 "In holiness and righteousness
You'll serve Him all your days.
76 Your child, a prophet of the
      Highest,
He shall prepare His ways.

77 "To give His people knowledge of
How salvation can be obtained,
78 Because of His tender mercy, His
Forgiveness can be gained.

79 "The sun that sits on high will visit
Those who in darkness sit,
In the way of peace He will guide
      our feet
From the shadows of death's pit."

80 The child grew in strength, and in
The deserts he did dwell,
Until the day of his appearing
To the people of Israel.

Chapter 2

1 Now a decree went out from Caesar
That it was his desire
That a census should be taken
Throughout all of his empire.

2 Quirinus was governor of Syria
When this was handed down.
3 All those who were to be counted
Went back to their hometown.

4 In order to be registered, Joseph
Left Nazareth of Galilee
For Bethlehem, David's city, for
He came from David's family.

5 Mary went with him when
He left to have the census filed.
Engaged to be his wife,
Mary was great with child.

6 Her time came while they were there;
She gave birth to her firstborn Son.
7 She laid Him in a manger,
For the inn had room for none.

8 Out in the fields nearby,
Lived shepherds keeping sight
Of their flocks of sheep
While others slept that night.

9 An angel of the Lord appeared to
them—
And they were terrified,
As God's glory shone 'round about,
But then the angel cried:

10 "Fear not, I bring good news for all,
Great tidings I bring down.
11 A Saviour has been born to you
In Bethlehem, David's town.

"He is Christ the Lord,
12 And here's a sign for you;
"You'll find a baby, wrapped in cloth,
And lying in a manger, too."

13 Suddenly a great choir arrived,
A heavenly host were they.
Praising God with the angel,
The shepherds heard them say:

14 "Glory to God in the highest
Peace on earth to men
On whom God rests His favor."
The angels all left then.

15 The shepherds said to one another,
"To Bethlehem, let us go
And see this thing that has happened
Of which the Lord did show."

16 To Bethlehem they hastened, and
Saw where the baby lay,
Just as the angel said, upon
A manger filled with hay.

17 The shepherds, seeing the child,
made
The angel's message known,
18 And all who heard it were amazed
At what the shepherds were shown.

19 But Mary thought upon these things,
In her heart she kept each word.
20 The shepherds returned to their
flocks
Giving praise for what they'd heard.

21 Then when eight days were fulfilled
For circumcision to be received,
The baby was named Jesus,
The name given when conceived.

22 It came time for their purification,
According to Moses' law;
They presented Him unto the Lord,
Before Him knelt in awe.

23 For it is written in the Law
That every firstborn male
Is holy to the Lord, and he
Must serve Him without fail.

24 A sacrifice they were to make,
As given by God's words,
Two pigeons or two turtle doves:
A sacrifice of birds.

25 Simeon of Jerusalem
Was righteous and devout,
As he waited for the birth
Of the Messiah to come about.

26 The Holy Spirit revealed to him
That he would not die
Until the Saviour came
And he saw him with his eye.

27 When they brought Jesus to the
temple,
To carry out the law,
28 Simeon took Him in his arms,
Praised God for what he saw:

29 "Now Lord, I can go in peace,
According to Thy care,
30 Mine eyes have seen Thy salvation
31 Which for us thou dids't prepare.

32 "Unto the Gentiles He shall be,
A light of revelation,
And to the people of Israel,
A glory to the nation."

33 Joseph and Mary marveled at
What they had seen and heard.
34 As Simeon blessed them, unto Mary,
He gave this further word:

"Behold! because of this child many
In Israel will fall and rise.
Men will oppose Him even though,
His might they realize.

35 "A sword will pierce your very soul,
And thoughts will be revealed,
The evil that is in man's heart
No longer can be concealed."

36 A prophetess in the temple,
Anna was her name,
After seven years of marriage
37 A widow she became.

Now at eighty-four she stayed
In the temple day and night.
She spent her time in prayer and
fasting,
Worshiping God with all her might.

38 She came that very hour and,
She spoke so all could hear,
"The redemption of Jerusalem
Is to be found right here."

39 Completing their sacrifice, they went
To Galilee again.
40 There the child grew strong and wise
In the grace of God and then:

41 His parents went to the Passover
feast
In Jerusalem each year;
42 When He was twelve, He went along
So the ritual He could hear.

43 When the feast was over they
started back,
But Jesus stayed behind;
Mary and Joseph did not know
He had this thought in mind.

44 They travelled all that day
Thinking He was with friends;
They did not look for Him until
That day came to an end.

45 And when they did not find Him, to
Jerusalem they returned;
46 They found Him after three days in
The temple with the learned.

47 Those who had heard Him were
astonished
At the things He understood,
They found Him very wise,
And His answers were quite good.

48 His parents were surprised, and said,
"Son, what made You stay behind?
We have looked for You anxiously
Why did You trouble our minds?"

49 Jesus then replied to them,
"Why did you search for Me?
Did you not know in My Father's
house
Is where I'd surely be?"

50 They did not understand His
statement,
51 But with Him did depart.
Mary treasured all these words
And stored them in her heart.

52 In wisdom Jesus did increase,
And He in stature grew,
Gaining favor with God and man
In all that He did do.

Chapter 3

1 In the fifteenth year of Tiberius' reign,
When Pilate governed Judea,
Herod was tetrarch of Galilee
And Philip tetrarch of Iturea,

Lysanias was tetrarch of Abilene,
2 Annas and Caiphas were the high
priests' names.
The word of God came unto John
Who in the wilderness did proclaim.

3 He came into Jordan preaching the
Baptism of repentance
For the forgiveness of man's sin,
And not to pay a penance.

4 "Isaiah wrote, 'From the wilderness
A voice crying out will say,
Make ready for the Lord to come,
Make straight His pathway.

5 " 'Every valley shall be filled up.
Rough roads will be smoothed out.
6 All flesh shall see the salvation of God;
It soon will come about.' "

7 He said to those coming, "You
brood of vipers,
Who has warned you to flee?
8 Therefore bring forth fruit of
repentance
For all the world to see.

87

" 'We are children of Abraham,' is
A thing you should not say;
For God can raise such children up
From stones along the way.

9 "The axe has been sharpened
And lies at the root.
Therefore each tree will be cut down
If it does not bear fruit."

10 The multitudes questioned John
   and they,
Asked Him, "What should we do?"
11 John gave to all of them this answer,
An answer, O so true.

"Let the man who has two tunics
With one who has none, share,
And he who has food likewise, show
His tender loving care."

12 Some publicans came to be baptized,
They asked, "What should we do?"
13 John said, "Take no more taxes than
The law allows you to."

14 Some soldiers came and asked,
   "How shall
We show we have repented?"
John said, "Accuse none wrongfully
And with your wage be contented."

15 The people came in expectation,
"Can this the Messiah be?"
16 John said, "I'm not, the One who
   comes
Is mightier than me.

"Indeed I baptize you with water,
He will baptize with fire.
I am unworthy to loosen His sandals,
Just to serve Him is my desire.

17 "His winnowing fork is in His hands
To cleanse His threshing floor;
The chaff will be consumed by fire.
The good wheat He will store.

18 With many other words John preached
The gospel unto men.
19 Even Herod the Tetrarch was
   reproved,
John said he walked in sin.

"It's not God's law for Herod," said John,
"To take his brother's wife."
20 Herod locked John up in prison so
He'd cause no further strife.

21 Now when the people were baptized
Jesus was baptized as well,
The heavens opened and God's spirit as
A dove on Jesus fell.

22 A voice came out of heaven, "You
Are My beloved Son,
I am well pleased with you and
The things that you have done."

23 When Jesus became thirty years
   of age
His ministry was begun.
He was thought the son of Joseph.
Joseph was Heli's son.

24 Heli was the son of Matthat,
And Matthat's father was Levi,
Who was in turn the son of Melchi,
Who was born unto Jannai.

Jannai was the son of Joseph;
25 Joseph was Mattathias' heir;
Mattathius was the son of Amos,
Whom Nahum's wife did bear.

Nahum was the son of Esli;
Nagge was Esli's father.
26 Nagge had been born to Maath,
Without a lot of bother.

Maath called Mattahias, "Papa."
Mattahias was Semei's son.
Joseph was Semei's father,
Who by Judah was begun.

27 Judah was the son of Joanna
And He called Rhesa, "Pa."
Rhesa was born to Zerubbable,
Who held Shealtiel, his dad, in awe.

Shealtiel was the son of Neri;
28 Melchi was Neri's dad.
Melchi was son of Addi, making
His father, Cosam, glad.

Cosam was the son of Elmodam,
And He was born to Er.
29 And Er was born to Joshua,
The son of Eliezer.

Eliezer was the son of Jorim;
Jorim was Matthat's son;
Matthat was born to Levi, and
30 Levi's father was Simeon.

Simeon's granddad was Joseph;
Judah had been born to him.
Joseph's dad was Jonan
Whose father was Eliakim.

31 Eliakim was the son of Melea;
To Melea Menan came.
Menan was the son of Mattatha,
And Nathan his father's name.

Nathan was the son of David,
32 And David was Jesse's son;
Jesse born to Obed, son of Boaz;
Boaz was born to Salmon.

Salmon was the son of Nahshon;
33 Nahshon's father was Amminadab;
Amminadab's father was Arni,
And Arni called Hezron, "Dad."

Hezron was the son of Perez,
Perez, son of Judah by Tamar;
34 Judah was the fourth son of Jacob
Born in a land afar.

Jacob was the son of Isaac;
Isaac was Abraham's son;
It was through Abraham by which
The nation Israel was begun.

35 Abraham son of Terah, of Nahor,
Son of Serug, son of Reu;
Reu was born to Peleg,
As all the neighbors knew.

36 Peleg son of Eber, of Shelah,
He of Cainan, Son of Arphaxad;
Arphaxad son of Shem, son of Noah;
And Noah called Lamech dad.

37 Lamech was son of Methuselah,
Who lived to be very old;
Methuselah was the son of Enoch,
By records we are told.

Enoch was born unto Jared,
And Jared to Mahalaleel;
Mahalaleel was born to Cainan,
In the land where they did dwell.

38 Cainan was born to Enosh;
The son of Seth, it's stated.
Seth was born to Adam, and
Adam by God was created.

Chapter 4

1 Full of the Holy Spirit, Jesus
From Jordan returned;
Led by the Spirit He drew apart,
To the wilderness turned.

2 The devil tempted Him forty days
Amidst the rocks and heat;
He hungered in that time for He
Took not one bite to eat.

3 "If you are truly Son of God,"
The devil to Him said,
"You do not have to wait to eat;
Turn this stone to bread."

4 Jesus answered, "It is written,
That mankind shall not live
On bread alone." This was the only
Answer that He'd give.

5 The devil led Him to a peak,
All kingdoms they could see.
6 He said, "I'll give You all of this
7 If You will worship me."

8 Jesus answered, "Again, it's written,
God carved it in stone;
You shall serve the Lord your God,
And shall serve Him alone."

9 The devil took Him to the temple,
Up to the very top.
He said, "If you are Son of God,
Go ahead, let yourself drop.

10 "For it is written in God's Word;
You know His Word is true;
He will give His angels charge
To watch and guard over you.

11 "In their hands they'll bear You up.
You'll not be left alone;
They'll watch always lest your foot
Should strike upon a stone."

12 Jesus answered and said to him,
"Put God not to a test."
13 The devil then departed and
Let Jesus have some rest.

14 Jesus then returned to Galilee,
Responsive to God's call.
15 He began to teach in the
synagogues
And received the praise of all.

16 He came to Nazareth, where He
Had lived 'til He was grown;
He entered into the synagogue,
The Scripture to Him was shown.

17 The scroll of the prophet Isaiah
Was handed to Him that day;
He opened it and found the place,
Read what it had to say.

18 " 'The Spirit of the Lord's upon Me,
Anointing Me to preach,
To proclaim release for the captives and
To the poor the gospel teach.

" 'Sight will be given to the blind;
The downtrodden will be set free
19 To proclaim the favorable year of
   the Lord.'
This work God has given Me.' "

20 He closed the book and then sat
   down;
All eyes were fixed on Him;
21 "Today this scripture has been
   fulfilled,"
He began to say to them.

22 All the people spoke well of Him;
They wondered at His word.
They said, "Is this not Joseph's son?"
Surprised at what they'd heard:

23 "You'll quote, 'Physician, heal thyself.'
We've heard the people tell
The things you've done in Capernaum,
Do in your hometown as well.'

24 "I don't expect to be believed;
You'll try to put Me down;
A prophet is welcome everywhere,
Except in his hometown.

25 "There were many widows in Israel
In the prophet Elijah's day;
When no rain fell for forty-two months
Famine came their way.

26 "Yet Elijah was sent to none of them,
But to a foreign land,
And fed by a widow from
   Zarephath,
According to God's command.

27 "In the days Elisha prophesied
In Israel were leprous men,
But not one of them was cleansed,
Only Naaman, the Syrian."

28 All in the synagogue became angry;
29 They cast Him from their city.
They planned to throw Him off a cliff;
They would show Him no pity.

30 But Jesus, slipping through their
   midst,
Left, going on His way.
31 He went down to Capernaum
To teach on the Sabbath day.

32 The people were amazed, for He
Taught with authority;
33 A man possessed of a demon cried,
34 "What have I to do with Thee."

"Have you come to destroy us?"
The demon shouted out,
"You are the Holy One of God."
35 Jesus said, "Be quiet, and come out."

The demon threw the poor man down,
Then left him without harm.
36 Fear and wonder came on all
And there was some alarm.

37 The news of Him spread far and wide,
Wherever man did roam.
38 Arising, Jesus left the synagogue
And went to Simon's home.

Simon's mother-in-law was very sick,
Her fever raged quite high.
They besought Him on her behalf,
And Jesus then drew nigh.

39 He stood o'er her, rebuked the fever,
And how well she did feel.
So she arose, and went
To help prepare a meal.

40 Now when the sun was going down,
On Him the sick did call.
He laid His hands upon them and
He healed them, one and all.

41 He cast out demons, who cried out,
"We know You are God's Son."
But He'd not let them speak for they
Knew He was the Holy One.

42 He departed for a lonely place,
Leaving at the break of day;
But the multitudes sought Jesus, asking
That He not go away.

43 But He said, "I must preach good
news to others,
For this is why I was sent
So throughout the synagogues of Judea,
44 Preaching the kingdom He went.

Chapter 5

1 The multitues around Him pressed
So they could hear Him more.
He was by Lake Gennesaret and
2 Saw two boats near the shore.

3 Jesus entered into Simon's boat.
Simon pushed a short way out.
Jesus sat and taught the crowd
Of God's good news coming out.

4 When He had finished speaking, He
Said, "Simon, here's My wish:
That you push out into deep water,
And there you'll catch some fish.

5 "Master, we fished all night," he
said.
"Yet brought no fish to shore,
But if that's what you want of us,
We'll drop the nets once more."

6 When they let the nets down
For the Master's sake,
They caught so many fish
The nets began to break.

7 They signaled to their partners, who
Filled both boats to the brink.
In fact they had so many fish
The boats began to sink.

8 When Simon Peter saw the catch
He fell down on his knees;
He said, "Lord! I'm a sinful man,
So won't You leave me, please."

9 For Simon Peter was astonished,
And His companions, too.
Because of all the fish they caught,
They knew not what to do.

10 James and John were also there,
The sons of Zebedee;
They were the partners of Simon Peter
Who fished in Galilee.

And Jesus spoke to Simon Peter,
"Fear not, you will catch men;
You will go forth with my gospel
The lost of earth to win."

11 When they had brought the
boats to shore,
Their comprehension dim,
They left behind everything they had
And went to follow Him.

12 There came one day in a certain
city
A man with leprosy;
He pleaded, "Lord, if You are willing,
I know You can cleanse me."

13 So Jesus said, "Yes, I am willing."
Then He stretched out His hand.
He touched the lonely leper, who
Was cleansed at His command.

14 He ordered him to tell no one,
But go as Moses commanded,
To show himself unto the priest,
As testimony demanded.

15 The news of Him spread far and wide.
The crowds grew every day.
He healed them of diseases, then
16 He slipped away to pray.

17 One day as He was teaching,
There came from all around
Pharisees and teachers of the law,
Who sat down on the ground.

The healing power was present, as
Some of the people realized;
18 They brought a man upon a bed,
This man was paralyzed.

19 They tried to push on through
the crowd;
But this they could not do.
So they took him upon the roof,
Made a hole, and let him through.

20 Jesus saw their faith and said,
"Your sins are forgiven thee."
21 The Pharisees and scribes all said,
"This man speaks blasphemy."

"Who is this who forgives all sin?
A power of God's alone."
22 Aware of this, He said, "Why reason,
With your hearts of stone?

23 "Which is the easier thing to do,
Say thy sins be forgiven,
Or say to one, 'Rise up and walk,
New strength to you is given?'

24 "But in order that you may know
I have such authority;"
He turned unto the lame man and
Said, "I command of thee,

"Arise, pick up your bed, and then
Get up and go your way."
25 The lame man rose went to his home,
And glorified God that day.

26 Those who saw this stood amazed,
Saying, "Glory be to God;"
While filled with fear some others said,
"We've seen some things quite odd."

27 As He went out from there He met
The tax collector, Levi.
He said, to him, "Come, follow Me,"
As He was passing by.

28 So Levi rose and followed Him,
And would collect no more.
29 Then Levi gave a big reception,
Called publicans by the score.

These publicans and many others
Partook of Levi's dinner.
30 The Pharisees and scribes asked
Him,
"Why do you eat with sinners?"

31 "The well need no physician; to
The sick I have been sent.
32 I haven't come to call the righteous,
But sinners to repent."

33 They said, "John's disciples often
fast;
The Pharisees do the same;
But your disciples eat and drink;
Don't you revere God's name?"

34 Said Jesus, "While the
bridegroom's here
Friends have no cause to fast;
35 The day will come when He is
taken,
Then they will fast at last.

36 "No one tears a new garment for
The old to get a patch,
For he would tear both garments and
The new piece would not match.

37 "No person takes old wine skins and
Puts new wine in the old;
For new wine will burst the skins,
And ruined, they will not hold.

38 "Fresh wine skins, new wine
hold.
39 No man desires the new;
Once He has drank old wine, He
says,
"The old is good, it's true."

Chapter 6

1 Upon a certain Sabbath day
He crossed a field of wheat.
His disciples plucked some grain,
And then began to eat.

2 Some Pharisees were looking on,
Displeased with what they saw;
They said, "This is the Sabbath, why
Do you then break the Law?"

3 In answer Jesus said to them,
"Have you not ever read
4 How David entered the house of
God
And took the priest's showbread?

"He took it and he ate it; he
Shared it with hungry men.
It was not lawful for them to eat,
But for priests only then.

5 "Man was not made for the
Sabbath, but
The Sabbath made for man."
He said to them, "The Sabbath
Lord,
Is the Holy Son of Man."

6 It came about, another Sabbath,
He in the synagogue taught;
A man whose hand was withered to
The Lord His problem brought.

7 The scribes and Pharisees
watched Him closely
Lest He would heal that day;
In order that they might accuse Him,
"You break our law," they'd say.

8 But Jesus knew their thoughts,
and to
The one with the withered hand
He said, "Arise, and come with Me."
Before Him he did stand.

9 Jesus turned to the Pharisees and
asked,
"Is it lawful to do good
Even though it is a Sabbath day;
Should one heal if he could?

"Is it lawful to do good or evil,
To save life or refuse?
Tell me teachers of the Law?
Let me have your views."

10 He looked around at them and
then
He said, "Stretch out your hand."
The man did so; it was restored
At this the Lord's command.

11 The Pharisees were filled with
rage.
They wanted Him eliminated.
His healings on the Sabbath made
Them very much agitated.

12 At this time Jesus left, and went
Up to a mount to pray.
He prayed the entire night,
Until the break of day.

13 In the morn He called His disciples
And when these followers came;
He chose twelve as a special group
And called them apostles, by name.

14 Simon, whom He also named
Peter,
And Andrew, Peter's brother,
James and John, the sons of
Zebedee,
And Philip was another.

15 Bartholomew, Matthew, and
Thomas,
And James, Alphaeus' son;
The Zealot, Simon; James' son,
Judas;
16 And Judas Iscariot, the traitorous
one.

17 They all came down the mountain and
When they reached level ground,
A multitude of other people
Had gathered all around.

They came out to hear Him teach
And be healed of their disease;
18 Those with spirits unclean were
healed
In answer to their pleas.

19 All the multitude tried to touch
Him,
And receive His healing power
Which came forth out of Him in
virtue,
To heal them all that hour.

20 He turned His gaze on His dis-
ciples
And then began to say,
"Blessed are you who are poor;
God's kingdom comes your way.

21 "Blessed are you who hunger
now,
These of you shall be fed.
Blessed are you who weep now, for
You will have laughter instead.

22 "Blessed are you when men hate you
And try to ostracize;
When insults are thrown at you and
About you men tell lies.

"They spurn your name as evil for
You serve the Son of Man,
Forsaking earthly interests and
For Me do all you can.

23 "Let gladness fill you in that day;
Leap for joy and rejoice.
They treated the prophets just the
same,
And would not heed their voice.

24 "But woe to you who are rich;
Your riches you have abused.
Your wealth shall be your only comfort;
By God you'll be refused.

25 "Woe unto you who are well fed;
One day with hunger you'll sigh.
Woe unto you who laugh today;
Someday you'll mourn and cry.

26 "Woe unto you when all men
Speak well of your name.
For I tell you that your fathers treated
False prophets just the same

27 "But I say unto all who hear,
Love your enemies.
And to all those who hate you,
You should do good to these.

28 "Bless all those who curse you,
And revile your good name.
And to those who would mistreat you,
Offer up prayers for the same;

29 "If someone strikes you on the
cheek,
The other one let him hurt.
If someone takes your cloak away,
Do not withold your shirt.

30 "Give to all who ask, and if one
Takes what to you belongs,
Do not demand it back again;
You're not to right his wrongs.

31 "As you would have men treat
you, then,
You treat them just the same;
32 By loving only those who love you,
You will have made no gain.

33 "If you do good to others, so
Their goodwill you would earn,
What credit is that to you? E'en
Sinners good, for good return.

34 "If you lend only to those who
Can pay back their account,
Even sinners will lend money to
Those who pay back the amount.

35 "But I say love your enemies,
Do good to those who hate.
And lend, never despairing, for
Then your reward is great.

"You will be sons of the most high,
Who's kind to evil men.
36 Be merciful as your Father is,
He'll treat you likewise, then.

37 "Forgive and you will be forgiven.
Give, it will be given you,
Good measure, pressed down,
running over,
And not a scanty few.

"Judge not and you shall not be
judged.
Do not criticize or condemn;
For those who pass judgment on
others,
Judgment will be passed on then.

38 "What'er you use to measure
others
Will judge you in return;
Therefore use love as a measure,
and
This measure none will spurn."

39 He also spoke a parable,
For all their benefit;
"Blind men cannot guide the blind
Or both fall in a pit.

40 "The disciple's not above his
teacher,
I say this thing to thee,
But when he is developed, like
His teacher he will be.

41 "A speck is in your brother's eye,
But then I ask you this:
Why notice specks when the beam
In your own eye you miss?

42 "How can you say unto your
brother,
'Let me take out the stuff,'
Until you tend to your own eye
You can't see well enough.

43 "A good tree does not bear bad
fruit;
A bad not good produce.
44 For a tree is known by its fruit
Whether it's of any use.

"Men do not gather grapes from
thorns,
Nor pick figs from the briars.
45 The good man of his goodness does
The things that God desires.

"The evil from his evil heart
Goes on his evil way.
His mouth speaks all the evil things,
His heart leads him to say.

46 "Why do you call Me Lord, and yet
Don't heed my teachings true?
47 If he would act upon My words
I'll show what he must do.

48 "He's like a man who builds a
house
Laying the foundation on a rock.
He digs deep to the solid base,
Carefully laying each block.

"The rains came up, the river rose,
The flood waters they did break;
But that man's house was so well
built
It did not even shake.

49 "But he, who hearing, rejects My
word,
Has no foundation at all.
When floods come up against his
house,
Great then will be its fall."

Chapter 7

1 When He completed speaking, He
Went to Capernaum nearby.
2 A centurion's slave was there who
was
Quite sick, about to die.

3 When the centurion heard of
Jesus,
Jewish elders bore his request
To come and heal the slave, and
they
Came at the man's bequest.

4 They said to Jesus, "He is worthy;
He dearly loves our nation;
5 He built for us a synagogue;
Won't you accept his invitation?"

6 Jesus started to go with them, but
When they came near the door
The centurion sent word by his
friends,
"Lord, trouble yourself no more.

"I know that I'm unworthy
To have you 'neath my roof.
7 I felt unworthy to come to you,
Not that I was aloof.

"But if you only say the word
My servant will be healed.
8 I understand authority
For this has been my field.

"I say unto a soldier, 'Go;'
He obeys my command.
I say unto another, 'Come;'
He does as I demand.
"And to my slave I say, 'Do this;'
And it is carried out,
I know your word will hear my slave;
Of this I have no doubt."

9 When Jesus heard this man He
marveled,
And turned to the multitude:
"In all of Israel I've not seen
One with such faith endued."

10 When those who had been sent
returned,
This scene is what they found;
The slave who had been near death
was
In mind and body sound.

11 Soon after, Jesus travelled on
To a city called Nain;
His disciples and the multitude
Followed closely in His train.

12 As He approached the city gate
A funeral was passing by;
He saw the coffin bearers and
He heard a mother cry.

The dead man was her only son;
Her husband had died before.
13 Christ looked upon her with
compassion,
And He said, "Weep no more."

14 Then Jesus went and touched
the coffin.
The coffin bearers stood still.
He said, "I say to you, arise!"
15 The man rose, not even ill.

He gave the son back to his mother;
16 The crowd was filled with fear;
"A prophet is among us and
Today He is right here."

17 The report reached all Judea and
All regions 'round about.
18 John sent two of his disciples
To search this question out:

19 They asked, "Are you the One
who's coming,
20 To whom we'd bend our knees?"
21 That hour Jesus cast devils out
And healed men of disease.

He gave sight to the blind, then
said,
22 "Report what you have seen.
Tell John the blind see, and lame
walk,
And lepers are made clean.

"The deaf can hear, the dead are
raised;
To the poor the gospel's preached.
23 Blessed is he who does not
stumble
When salvation's within his reach."

24 When John's disciples had gone
away,
To the crowd these words he was
saying,
"Did you go to the wilderness to see
A reed the wind was swaying?

25 "Or did you go out there to see
One in a bright soft coat?
Those gorgeously appareled live
In palaces, you note.

26 "But what did you go out to see?
A prophet, and much more,
27 This is of whom Scripture said,
'I'll send him on before.'

28 "Of all those born of women none
Greater than John will be;
But he who's least in the kingdom
of God;
Greater than John is he."

29 Some people and some tax collectors
Who were there looking on,
Acknowledged God is just, as they
Had been baptized by John.

30 But Pharisees and lawyers had,
God's purpose thus rejected.
Although they'd heard John's
words, they had
John's baptism neglected.

31 Jesus said, "To whom shall I liken
The people of this race?
32 They're like so many children
who
Sit in the marketplace.

"They say, 'You would not dance
with us,
Even though we played the flute.
Then when we sang a funeral dirge,
You wouldn't weep; you were mute.'

33 "For John the Baptist came to
you;
He took not wine or bread.
You said, 'He surely has a demon,
Residing in his head.'

34 "The Son of Man came to you
eating,
And He comes drinking, too.
You say, 'Behold! a gluttonous man;
You friend of sinners, you.'

"If we do not do things your way
Then fault with us you find;
35 Yet wisdom's always justified
In her children's mind."

36 Came a Pharisee and said to Him,
"Sometime when you are able,
I'd like for you to dine with me."
So Jesus joined his table.

37 There was a sinner of the city,
Who hearing He was there,
Brought an alabaster jar of ointment
38 And stood behind His chair.

Her tears of joy fell on His feet,
She wiped them with her hair;
She kissed them and anointed
them;
The aroma filled the air.

39 The Pharisee thought, "If He were
A prophet He'd have known
Her for the sinner that she is,
And make her leave Him alone."

40 Jesus answered and said to him,
"I've something to say to thee."
Said Simon, "Say it, Teacher, what
Words do you have for me?"

41 "A money lender had two debtors,
One owed five hundred pence.
The other owed quite little, say
He owed but fifty cents.

42 "Neither of them could pay the debt,
For both were very poor.
So he forgave them both. Now which
Of them will love him more?"

43 Simon answered and said to Jesus,
"The one forgiven most."
"Simon, you have judged correctly,"
Jesus said unto His host.

44 Looking at the woman, He said
     to Simon,
"Do you see her today?
You brought no water for My feet
To wash the dust away.

"She wet My feet with her tears,
     and
She dried them with her hair;
45 She also kissed My feet; with Me,
A kiss you did not share.

46 "You didn't anoint My head with
     oil,;
On My feet she poured perfume;
The aroma of this vial of ointment
Now fills the entire room.

47 "Because of this I say to you
Her sins, which have been many,
Are every one forgiven her;
Now she does not have any;

"She has shown that her love is great,
In how she cared for Me;
But if your love is very little
Little is forgiven thee."

48 He said, "You are forgiven, woman;
49, 50 By your faith you are saved;
From this place go in peace because
Of how you have behaved."

Those who sat with Him at the table
Conferred with one another;
"Who is this man who pardons sin,
But a blasphemous brother?"

Chapter 8

1 It came about soon afterwards,
So people would be reached,
He went from one city to another;
God's kingdom's what He preached.

His twelve disciples went with Him;
2 Some women followed about,
Like Mary Magdalene from whom
Seven devils had gone out.

3 Joanna, the wife of Herod's steward,
The Master's call did heed;
Susanna, and also many others
Contributed to His need.

4 And the multitude came together;
The people all drew near;
He spoke to them this parable
So everyone could hear.

5 "The sower went to sow his seed;
Some fell along the way.
There it was trampled underfoot,
And birds carried it away.

6 "Some fell on rocky soil, and there
As soon as that seed grew,
It withered because it lacked moisture
Except the morning dew.

7 "Some other seed fell in the thorns,
With briars all about.
It grew for just a little while,
The thorns then choked it out.

8 "Still other seed fell on good ground.
When the harvest did appear,
It yielded forth a hundredfold.
He who has ears, then hear."

9 And His disciples asked of Him
Just what the parable meant.
10 Said Jesus, "It is granted to you
To know why I was sent.

"I speak in parables for those
Who don't heed My command,
That seeing they may yet not see,
And hearing, not understand.

11 "The seed stands for the Word of
     God;
12 Those fallen on the roadway
Are those who hear the word and yet
The devil takes it away.

"The word finds no place in their
  heart;
They still the same behave;
They will not believe in My words;
Therefore, they can't be saved.

13 "And those that fall on rocky soil
With joy hear what I say,
But they have no firm root, so that
Temptations draw them away.

14 "The ones that fell among the
  thorns
Would grow amidst earth's strife.
They bring no fruit to maturity,
It's choked by cares of life.

15 "The seeds that fell upon good
  ground
Are ones who hear the Word,
Then let it grow in their hearts
And act on what they've heard.

"They hold it fast, they bear much
  fruit,
For God they persevere;
Their fruit is plentiful because
They to My word adhere.

16 "None lights a lamp then covers it,
Nor hides it 'neath his bed;
Instead he sets it on a stand
To cast the light that's shed.

17 "In this world there is nothing
That shall not be set right,
Nor anything in secret done
That shall not come to light.

18 "Therefore, take care in how you
  listen,
He with much shall receive more
And whoever has nothing will
Lose whatever he had before."

19 His mother came to see Him, and
His brothers with her, too,
But they could not get to Him;
The crowd blocked their way
  through.

20 Someone reported this to Him,
"Your family is outside;
They much desire to talk to you;
They would take you aside."

21 He answered, "My real family
Are those who hear God's Word,
And they then follow carefully
The things that they have heard."

22 Another day He said to them
"This one request I make,
For all of us to take a boat
And go across the lake."

The disciples at the Master's word,
Launched out into the deep.
23 He lay down as they sailed along
And soon was fast asleep.

As they progressed across the lake
A fearsome gale descended.
They fell in danger of being swamped,
And therefore be upended.

24 They woke the Master up and said,
"Master our lives, please save."
And when He had been fully roused,
He rebuked the wind and wave.

25 He said to them, "Where is your
  faith?"
His actions did amaze.
They said, "Who's this that has con-
  trol
E'en over wind and wave?"

26 They landed among the
  Gerasenes,
Who live close by the sea,
Which is along the water's edge
Across from Galilee.

27 When they came out into the land
They met one from the city;
His mind was filled with demons, and
On him the Lord had pity.

This man lived there among the tombs;
He had no clothing on.
He cried all night among the graves,
From dusk to early dawn.

28 He fell at Jesus's feet, said, "What
Have I to do with you?
Son of the most high God, I say,
Will you torment me too?"

29 The evil spirit seized him often.
He had been bound with chains.
Yet he would always burst his fetters,
And flee to ease his pains.

Jesus said, "Come out of him;"
30 Then asked, "What is your name?"
He said, "My name is Legion; for
Many demons cause me shame."

31 The demons then entreated Jesus
Not to send them to the pit.
32 There was a herd of swine nearby;
They asked to enter it.

He said, "Yes, you may enter them."
33 The group of hogs they found.
The herd rushed then into the lake
And in the lake did drown.

34 The herdsmen ran into the city
And in the land about;
35 When the people heard of their
    report,
A great crowd all came out.

They came to see what had
    happened;
What did the people find?
The wild man sat at Jesus's feet
And he was of right mind.

36 They became a little frightened as
The herdsmen began to tell
How the one possessed of demons
Now stood before them well.

37 The people of that country asked
For Jesus to depart;
At first they had been anxious—now
A strong fear gripped their heart.

38 The man, who had been freed of
    demons,
Said, "I will go with you."
39 But Jesus said, "Go home,
    proclaim
What God for you did do."

He did as Jesus asked of him,
He spoke to everyone.
He testified throughout the city
The things that God had done.

40 When Jesus returned to Galilee
The multitude lined the shore.
They had seen many things He'd
    done,
And wanted to hear more.

41 A synagogue ruler, named Jairus,
There fell down at His feet.
42 His only daughter was very ill
And Jesus he did entreat.

When Jesus started to go with him,
The crowd was very thick;
43 There came a woman with a
    hemorrhage;
Yes, she was very sick.

Though she'd consulted many doctors,
Poor health she still endured.
44 She touched His garment as He
    went by;
Immediately she was cured.

45 Said Jesus, "Who touched Me
    without
First gettting My consent?"
And Peter said, "The crowd is great;
It was an accident."

46 Said Jesus, "Someone did touch Me,
Of this I'm much aware,
For power has gone out from Me,
With someone I did share."

47 The woman saw she could not hide,
And at His feet she fell.
She gave the reason for her act,
And how she'd been made well.

48 He said to her, "Daughter go in
    peace,
Your faith has made you well."
She joyfully went back to her home;
Her story she oft did tell.

49 Someone came from the
    synagogue
While this was being said,
He said, "Don't trouble the Master, for
Your daughter's already dead."

50 Then Jesus said to Jairus, "Don't
Fear but only believe;
Your daughter will be made well, and
Her health she will receive.

51 When Jesus came into the house
With both the father and mother,
He also took Peter, James, and John,
But with Him took no other.

52 And Jesus said to those who wept,
"She's not dead, but asleep.
You need not look so very sad
Nor do you need to weep."

53 But they all knew that she was dead;
They laughed while they did cry,
54 But Jesus took her by the hand
And said to her, "Arise."

55 The child arose immediately.
He ordered she be fed.
56 Her parents were amazed but Jesus
Charged nothing should be said.

Chapter 9

1 He called the twelve to Him, and
Gave them power to deal
With demons and evil spirits,
And also power to heal.

2 He sent all His disciples forth
God's kingdom to proclaim,
To heal the sick and crippled, all
This in the Master's name.

3 He said, "Take naught for your journey,
No staff, nor bag, nor bread,
No money take or extra clothes,
For either body or head.

4 "Whatever house you enter, stay
Until you leave from there;
For they will then receive a blessing
As in your work they share.

5 "But those who don't receive you, who
Share not of bread or meat;
As testimony against them, strike
The dust from off your feet.

6 The disciples went to many villages,
Preached and healed everywhere;
7 When Herod heard what was happening
He did receive a scare.

For it was said by some that John
Had risen from the dead.
Herod said, "This can't be true
For I cut off his head."

8 Some others said, "He's Elijah,
Preparing the Messiah's way,
Or another prophet has arisen,"
Is what they had to say.

9 Said Herod, "I would see this man
About whom all this I hear.
Perhaps someone would bring Him
And at my court would appear."

10 The apostles returned from their mission.
Told Him the things they'd done.
They went to Bethsaida to be alone
And talk of victories won.

11 The multitudes discovered Him,
And followed to a field.
He talked to them of God's kingdom;
Those who were sick He healed.

12 The day came to a close,
And as the sun went down,
The disciples said, "Send them away
To find lodging in the town.

"For we are in a barren place,
And have no bread or meat."
13 Said Jesus, "E're I send them away
You give them food to eat."

"We have no more than two small fish
And just five loaves of bread;
Unless we go and buy much more
These people can't be fed.

14 "There were about five thousand men
15 Sitting upon the ground;
16 Once Jesus blessed the fish and bread,
It was passed all around.

17 They all ate until satisfied.
They gathered that left o'er,
Which was twelve baskets full, much more
Than there had been before.

18 Jesus and His disciples slipped away,
And while they paused to pray,
He asked, "Who do they say I am?
What do the people say?"

19 "Some say you're John the
Baptist; others
Say Elijah's here again.
Still others say one of the prophets
Returned to walk with men."

20 And Jesus turned to His
disciples,
Said, "You who with Me trod,
Who do you say I am?" Peter
answered,
"You are the Christ of God."

21 He warned them all to tell no one,
22 "The Son of Man must suffer
many things,
Rejected by the elders, chief
priests, and scribes,
Be killed and raised to life again.

23 "If anyone would follow Me
He must himself deny,
And daily gather up his cross,
And follow Me close by.

24 "Whoever would save his life, it's
lost,
But if it's for My sake,
Then he will truly save it and
A disciple I will make.

25 "What profit comes to any man
If all the world he gains
And thereby lose and forfeit self?
All he will have is pains.

26 "If you would be ashamed of Me
And of My teaching, too,
Then when I come in glory I
Will be ashamed of you.

27 "I tell you, some are standing
here
Who of death will not taste
Until they've seen God's kingdom
and
His glory they have faced."

28 It happened eight days after this,
Upon a bright, clear day;
He gathered Peter, James, and
John
And climbed a mount to pray.

29 While He was praying there, His
clothes
Became a gleaming white.
His very countenance was changed,
And Jesus shone so bright.

30 Moses and Elijah came to Him,
31 In glory did appear;
They talked to him of His death
Which now was very near.

32 Peter and the others were asleep,
But when they came awake,
On seeing Jesus with the prophets
With fear they all did shake.

33 The prophets were departing,
Peter
Said, "It is good up here;
So let us build three tabernacles
And keep them always near."

34 A cloud came overshadowing them
And made all things quite dim;
35 To them a voice spoke from the
cloud,
"This is My Son, hear Him."

36 When the voice had finished
speaking
Jesus was found alone.
They held their peace and spoke
not of
The things they had been shown.

37 Once they had come down from
the mount,
They were met by a crowd.
38 A man amidst the multitude
Cried out to Him aloud:

"Please, Teacher, look upon my boy,
He is my only child;
39 An evil spirit seizes him
And makes him act so wild.

40 "I asked your disciples to cast it out,
But nothing they could do."
41 "Oh unbelieving generation,
How long shall I be with you?"

Said Jesus, "Bring your son to Me."
42 As the boy came he fell down,
Was dashed about by the demon and
Convulsed upon the ground.

But Jesus rebuked the unclean
    spirit,
He spoke and healed the boy.
He gave him back to his father
Who cried with tears of joy.

43 They were awed by God's majesty;
Said Jesus to them then,
44 "In spite of what you saw, I'll be
Delivered unto men."

45 They did not understand this
    statement;
The meaning was concealed.
They were afraid to ask, therefore
The meaning was not revealed.

46 Instead, an argument arose,
Among the disciples then,
Of which would be the greatest
Among these twelve men.

47 He knew their hearts and took a
    child,
Said to them, "Look and see
48 If you receive him in My name
You are also receiving Me.

And anyone who shall receive Me
To him I surely state,
Receives the one who sent Me, and
The least one will be great."

49 John said to Him, "We saw one cast
Out demons in your name;
And since he does not follow us
We put the man to shame."

50 But Jesus said, "Don't hinder him,
You will find that this is true,
If one is working in your name
He'll not speak ill of you."

51 The time of His receiving up
Was drawing very near.
He resolved to go to Jerusalem
In spite of all their fear.

52 He sent some messengers ahead,
Who would prepare the way,
But when they came to Samaria
They found no place to stay.

53 The Samaritans did not receive
    them,
For Jerusalem they did face,
Because to the Samaritans
Jews were a hated race.

54 Both James and John asked
    Jesus, "Shall
We call down heaven's fire,
To come down and destroy their village
With consequences dire."

55 But Jesus turned and He
    rebuked them.
56 They went to another place
Where villagers received them with
A spirit of good grace.

57 Along the road they met a man
    who would follow Jesus;
Jesus looked at him and then replied,
58 "Foxes have holes, birds have nests,
But I have no place to reside."

59 To another He said, "Follow Me."
But to Jesus the man did say,
"I must bury my dear father,
Then follow You I may."

60 Said Jesus to him, "I say let
The dead care for their dead;
Go forth and proclaim my message
Wherever you are led."

61 Another said, "I'll follow, but
Will first tell those at home."
62 "To look back from the plow," He
    said,
"Means you'll not see God's throne."

Chapter 10

1 The Lord appointed seventy men
And sent them out two by two.
2 He said, "The harvest is very great,
But the laborers are few.

"Because the harvest is so vast,
Therefore all should pray;
Beseech the Lord of the harvest to
Add workers every day.

3 "I send you forth as many lambs
Amidst a great wolf pack;
4 Take no bag, purse, or extra shoes
And greet no person back.

5 "You are to say, 'Peace to this house,'
Before you go inside;
6 If a peaceful man dwells there it'll stay,
If not, your peace won't abide.

7 "Stay in that house, eat and drink
Whatever is given you.
For a laborer is worthy of his wage,
So you are worthy, too.

"Do not move from house to house.
8 When you enter a town,
And are welcomed, eat whatever
Before you is set down.

9 "Heal the sick who are there;
Then to the people say,
'God's kingdom has come nigh to you,
So hear His words today,'

10 "But if a city receives you not,
Then go out in the street;
11 Say, 'The Kingdom of God came
near to you;
We wipe your dust from our feet.'

12 "I say when the day of judgment
comes
The Lord will have no pity;
It will be more tolerable for Sodom than
It will be for that city.

13 "Woe to you people of Chorazin,
Woe to Bethsaida, too.
If the miracles had been done in Tyre
Which have occurred in you,

"They would have repented long ago,
In ashes and sackcloth.
14 It will be easier for them in
judgment, but
With you God will be wroth.

15 "And as for you, city of Capernaum,
Who'd rise for all to see;
You'll be brought down to Hades, for
You have rejected Me.

16 "The one who listens unto God
Then also hears Me, too;
The one who rejects Me, rejects the One
Who has sent Me to you.

17 The seventy returned with joy,
Gave Jesus this report,
"In your name demons have obeyed,
And thus your power support."

18 He said, "I saw Satan fall from heaven
Like lightning in a storm.
19 I give you power to tread on serpents,
And foes in any form.

20 "Nevertheless do not be glad
That demons heed your voice,
But that your name's on heaven's
roll,
In this you should rejoice."

21 At that time He rejoiced in spirit,:
"I thank you, Lord of heaven,
You've hidden these things from
the wise
And to babes the meaning given.

22 "By My Father all things are
given Me;
But for the Father I'm known by none;
And no one knows the Father unless
He is revealed by the Son."

23 And He said unto His disciples,
"I say, blessed are the eyes
Which have seen things that you
have seen
Both on earth and in the skies.

24 "Both kings and prophets desired
to see
Those things you've seen revealed,
And hear the things which you
have heard,
Which from them was concealed."

25 Behold a lawyer came up to Him,
To put Him to a test;
Said, "How can I find eternal life?
For this is now my quest."

26 Jesus said, "What's written in
the Law?
What does it mean to you?
How do you interpret Holy writ?
You know God's Law is true."

27 "That you shall love the Lord
your God
With all your soul and mind;
Love Him with all your heart and love
Your neighbor, is what I find."

28 Jesus looked him in the eyes,
and said,
"The answer you did give,
If you will do all of these things
Then you will really live."

29 To justify himself, the lawyer
Asked so that all could hear,
"Tell me who is my neighbor, is
It someone far or near?"

30 He answered him, "A man went
from
Jerusalem to Jericho;
It was a very dangerous journey,
But there he had to go.

"Along the way he met some robbers
Who beat him on the head;
They stripped the man of everything,
And left him there half dead.

31 "By chance a certain priest came by,
Passed on the other side;
He saw the man but journeyed on,
Pretending he had died.

32 "A Levite also came that way,
And saw him lying there;
He too passed on the other side,
He had no time to share.

33 "Then a Samaritan came along,
And saw Him on the ground.
He was not worried by the fact
That thieves might be around.

34 "He came and touched him
where he lay,
And when he heard his groans,
He poured oil and wine on his
wounds;
Bound up his broken bones.

"He put the man on his own beast
And took him to an inn.
He watched o'er him throughout
the night,
Until healing did begin.

35 "The next day he spoke to the
inn-keeper, when
His bill he went to pay;
'Here is some money, take care of him,
If more, I will repay.'

36 "Which of these three was a
neighbor to
The man whom to thieves fell?"
37 He replied, "The one who showed
Him mercy."
Jesus said, "Go, do as well."

38 They entered a house in a certain
village;
Martha asked Him, "Come and eat."
39 She had a sister named Mary
who
Then sat at Jesus' feet.

40 Since Martha was distracted by
The things she had to do,
She did not think it fair alone
To cook and serve them too.

"My sister lets me serve alone;
"For me she does not care.
Tell her to come into the kitchen
And together this meal prepare."

41 "Don't worry, Martha," Jesus said,
"Of how this food is done.
You're anxious over many things;
42 There really is but one.

"Mary has chosen the best, which is
To sit at my feet today
And hear the words of God, for this
Men shall not take away."

Chapter 11

1 It came about when He ceased
praying,
In a certain place one day,
One of His disciples said to Him,
"Lord teach us how to pray."

2 "Pray, 'Our Father which art in
heaven,
Hollowed be thy name,' he said;
Thy kingdom come; Thy will be done,;
3 Give us our daily bread.

4 " 'We ask you to forgive our sins,
As our brothers we're forgiving.
Lead us not into temptation,
From evil deliver us in living.' "

5 He spoke these words to them,
"Suppose
One of you has a friend.
You go to him at midnight and say,
'Three loaves to me please lend.

6 " 'For a friend of mine has come to
   visit,
And of food has a need.
I've nothing in my house, therefore,
My friend I cannot feed.'

7 "From in the house he shall reply,
'I'm sorry for your plight,
But everyone has gone to bed;
I cannot help tonight.'

8 "He may not give you anything
Although he is your friend,
But if you keep on knocking, he
Will help you in the end.

9 "I say ask, and it shall be given;
Seek and you will receive.
Knock and it will be opened up
If only you believe.

10 "You will receive if you ask.
By seeking you will find.
To him who knocks it will be opened;
He will have peace of mind.

11 "If a son should ask his father
To give him a piece of fish,
He will not take a snake instead
And serve it on a dish.

12 "Or if the son asks for an egg,
A scorpion will not feed;
He will provide appropriately
To answer his son's need.

13 "If you then, being evil, for
Your children take good care,
How much more will your heavenly
   Father
The Holy Spirit share."

14 He cast a demon out; it left;
And then the dumb man spoke.
The multitudes marveled greatly, but
Their jealousies awoke.

15 Some said, "It is the demon's ruler
By whom His power's given."
16 Still others said, just to test Him,
"Show us a sign from heaven."

17 But Jesus knew their thoughts
   and said,
"A kingdom's like a house or wall,
When it is divided against itself
It's surely going to fall.

18 "If Satan's divided against himself,
How shall his kingdom stand
If I cast out demons by Beelzebub,
And drive Satan from our land?

19 "If I by Beelzebub cast demons out,
As you have said of me,
By whom do your sons cast them
   forth?
Your judges they shall be.

20 "But if I by God's finger cast
Them out, then it is true
That God's great holy kingdom has
Come nigh to each of you.

21 "When a strong man guards his
   palace
And He is fully armed,
No one disturbs his possessions, and
His goods will not be harmed.

22 "Until a stronger man arrives
And takes his armor away,
Then takes the plunder for himself
And holds the man at bay.

"He takes the weaker man's
   possessions
And gives them out to others.
23 The one not with Me is against Me
And scatters evil 'midst his brothers.

24 "When an evil spirit leaves a man
It travels seeking rest
Out in the desert. Finding none,
He says, 'My old house was best.

" 'I will return to my old home,
The place from which I came,'
But when he gets back to the place,
He finds things not the same.

25 "He finds it swept and put in order;
26 He finds seven devils more.
And so the state of that poor man
Is worse than it was before."

27 And while He said these things,
   a woman
Cried for all she was worth:
"Blessed is the mother who nursed
   You
And to You she did give birth."

28 Jesus said, "Look and you will find
The ones who are most blessed
Are those who keep God's word,
and these
By whom I am confessed."

29 As the crowds grew, Jesus said,
"A sign this generation would see;
No sign except the sign of Jonah
Will be given them by Me.

30 "As Jonah was a sign to Ninevites,
So shall the Son of Man
Be a sign to this generation;
This shall be the plan:

31 "The Queen of the South shall
arise in judgment
And condemn this generation;
To hear the wisdom of Solomon
She travelled from her nation.

"Yet I say to you who stand here;
Yes, this I do avow:
A greater one than Solomon
Is here with you right now.

32 "The men of Ninevah will
condemn you,
For when Jonah did appear,
At his preaching they repented.
One greater now is here.

33 "A lighted lamp is not put in a
cellar,
Or hidden out of sight,
But it is put upon a stand
So that all will see its light.

34 "The lamp of your body is your eye
And when your eye is clear,
Your whole body is full of light;
You can walk and have no fear.

"But if your eye should become bad,
In darkness you roam about,
35 Watch that the light that's in you
Shall never be put out.

36 "Now if your body's full of light
With no dark spots at all,
Then you shall shine as brightly as
When lamp rays on you fall.

37 When He finished speaking, a
Pharisee
Invited Him to sup.
38 The Pharisee was much surprised
When He did not wash up.

39 But Jesus said, "You Pharisees,
The outer cup you clean,
But inside there is wickedness,
You think it isn't seen.

40 "Did not He who the outside made
Then make the inside too?
41 Give alms for those things found
within,
Then all is clean for you.

42 "But woe unto you Pharisees,
Who tithe of mint and rue,
But disregard God's love and justice
In all the things you do.

"You ought to do all of these things,
But others not neglect;
43 You love front seats in the
synagogue,
From men you want respect.

44 "Woe to you, you are hidden graves
Which men trod unaware."
45 A lawyer said, "You insult us, too,
And that is not quite fair."

46 "Woe to you lawyers," Jesus said,
"You give men loads to bear;
Yet you'll not lift a finger and
Their burdens you'll not share.

47 "Woe to all of you lawyers, who
Tombs for prophets build.
You say, 'Our fathers killed them,' but
You approve what they did wield.

48 "For you build tombs unto those whom
Your fathers have rejected.
You do so to show honor, but
Their teachings you've neglected.

49 "God in His wisdom said, 'I'll send
Some prophets to their nation;
50 Some they will kill and their blood
will
Be charged against your generation.

51 "From Abel's blood to Zechariah's,
Who perished at his station,
Between the altar and the sanctuary,
All cry against your generation.

52 "Woe to you lawyers, for you
   have thrown
The key of knowledge away;
You have not entered the kingdom,
   yet
For others you block the way."

53 After saying this He went outside
Where the scribes and Pharisees came
'Round him angrily and cross-
   examining
54 Trying to trick and sully His name.

Chapter 12

1 The crowd around Him grew so
   large,
Stretched far as one could see.
He said to His disciples, "Beware
The hypocrisy of the Pharisee.

2 "There's nothing that is covered up;
None of the things you've sown,
But it will be revealed and know
What's hidden will be known.

3 "What you have uttered in the dark,
Things whispered in the night,
Will be proclaimed from house tops,
   they
Will all be brought to light.

4 "Fear not those who can kill the body,
There's no more they can do.
5 But fear Him who can kill the body
And cast the soul into hell, too.

6 "Five sparrows are sold for two
   pennies,
Yet for each God does care.
7 Or reach up and touch your head;
God has numbered every hair.

"You are worth more than many
   sparrows.
8 If My name you confess to men,
I'll confess yours to the angels of
   God.
My glory you can enter in.

9 "But if you don't confess My name,
Before men I am denied,
Before God, angels, and My glory
You will be left outside.

10 "And everyone who speaks a word
Against the Son of Man,
It shall then be forgiven him
According to God's plan.

"But anyone who speaks against, and
Blasphemes the Holy Spirit,
It shall not be forgiven him.
His plea God will not hear it.

11 "When brought before courts and
   rulers,
Don't worry what to say;
12 The Holy Spirit, in that hour
Will lead you all the way."

13 One in the crowd said, "Have my
   brother
Divide his wealth with me."
14 But Jesus said, "I've not been
   appointed
To arbitrate for thee."

15 Then He said, "Always be on guard;
Shun every kind of greed.
Not even in great abundance have
You found life's every need."

16 He told this parable to them,
"A rich man's land bore a lot;
17 He reasoned with himself, 'What
   shall
I do with what I've got?

18 " 'This is what I will do,' he said,
'I'll tear my old barns down;
Then I will build even bigger ones
And store goods all aroun'.

19 " 'And I will say unto my soul
You've goods for many years,
So eat and drink and merry be,
You now are free from fears.'

20 "But God said, 'Fool, this very night
Your soul will go from thee,
Then who will get what you prepared,
For wealth from you will flee.

21 "So is the man who lays up treasure,
For himself keeps everything;
If toward God you're not rich, therefore,
Wealth will no pleasure bring."

22 He said unto His disciples, Don't
Be anxious for your life,
Or what you eat or what you'll wear;
Let no thought cause you strife.

23 "For life is more than food, the body
Is also more than clothes.
24 The raven neither sows nor reaps;
God feeds it where e'er it goes.

"You are more valuable than birds;
I say to every man.
25 Which one of you, by being anxious,
Can add to his life span?

26 "If you cannot do this little thing,
About the rest, why worry?
27 Consider the lilies how they grow,
They neither toil nor spin nor hurry.

"Yet as you look upon the lily,
So lovely and so tender,
Solomon like these was never
  arrayed
In all his wealthy splendor.

28 "If God so clothes grass of the field,
Now here but gone tomorrow,
Will He not clothe you of little faith
So you'll not have to borrow?

29 "Don't seek what you shall eat, or be
Concerned about your drink;
Put all your worries behind your back,
And do not doubtful think.

30 "For all these things the nations
  seek,
But your Father knows your needs.
31 He will provide, put His kingdom
  first,
And follow where He leads.

32 "Don't be afraid, My little flock,
Stay by your Father's side;
To you His kingdom He will give
If in Him you abide.

33 "Sell all and give to charity,
Make bags which wax not old;
The treasure which you store in
  heaven
No thief can steal or moth corrode.

34 "Your heart is where your
  treasure is.
35 In your lamps keep a light,
36 Like those who await their
  master if
He should return tonight.

"And when he knocks upon the door
The door will open wide.
37 Blessed are those who are watching,
  and
Can let the Lord inside.

"Those who are ready when He
  comes
The girded Master will serve.
They will sit at His banquet table
And get what they deserve.

38 "Whether He comes in the middle of
  the night, or
Toward morning should appear,
He will bless those awaiting Him,
Will bring them joy and cheer.

39 "And of this you can be quite sure;
I know you are aware,
If you knew when the thief would
  come
For him you would prepare.

40 "Therefore, be ready, I repeat,
So you won't be rejected,
For the Son of Man is coming at
An hour He's not expected."

41 Peter said, "Lord is this just for us,
Or everyone as well?"
42 "It's for the faithful," Jesus said,
"Who in My Spirit dwell.

"It's like a wise and faithful servant
Put in charge of a household
To give food at the appointed time,
Not having to be told.

43 "Blessed is that servant who is
True to his lord's request;
44 The master will put him in charge
Of all he has possessed.

45 "But if that slave says to himself
'My master won't come soon.'
He eats and drinks, and beats the
  young,
And stays in bed 'til noon,

46 "The master of that slave will come
At an hour he does not know.
He'll cut him up and cast him out,
With unbelievers go.

47 "The slave who knew his
    master's will
But did not do his work
Will then be given many lashes,
Because he chose to shirk.

48 "The one who didn't know his
    master's will,
And his will did not do,
He might deserve many lashes, but
He will receive very few.

"From all who have been given much,
Of much will be required;
To him whom much has been entrusted,
Much more will be desired.

49 "I came to cast a fire on earth,
I wish it were already burning.
50 I have a baptism to undergo
To accomplish what I'm yearning.

51 "I come not to bring peace to earth,
But divisions you will see.
52 Five household members will be
    divided;
Two will stand up to three.

53 "A father will stand against his son,
A daughter against her mother.
The in-laws will be divided; they
Will not love one another.

54 "When you see a cloud in the west,
'It's going to rain,' you say.
55 And when the south wind blows,
    you state,
'It will be hot today.'

56 "You hypocrites, you analyze
The earth and sky with your sight;
Why know you not the present time
57 And give judgment that is right?

58 "For as you go with an adversary
Before a magistrate,
Try settling out of court before
The judge sets a trial date.

"For the judge may rule against you
To jail perhaps you go;
59 You'll not get out of there until
You pay all that you owe."

Chapter 13

1 Some present there told Jesus of
Some things they thought weren't nice.
How Pilate had killed Galileans and
Mingled blood with their sacrifice.

2 He said, "Do you suppose these
    Galileans
Sinned more than those you know?
3 I say they are no worse than others
Just because they suffered so.

"It really makes no difference whether
A sin is great or small;
Unless you repent and turn from it
You'll perish, one and all.

4 "Do you suppose those eighteen men
On whom the tower of Siloam fell,
Were worse than any other sinners
Who in Jerusalem dwell?

5 "Again, it makes no difference if
A sin be great or small;
You must repent and turn from it
Or perish, one and all."

6 He then began to tell a parable:
"A certain man had a fig tree
Planted in his vineyard where
Its branches he could see.

"One day he came to gather fruit,
But no fruit did he find.
7 He called his gardener to him to
Tell what he had in mind.

" ' For three years I've come to this tree.
No fruit here have I found.
So cut it down, throw it away!
Why should it take up ground?'

8 "The gardener said, 'Let it alone
For just another season;
I'll dig around, I'll fertilize.
Perhaps poor soil's the reason.

9 " 'But if I dig and fertilize
And next year there's no fruit,
Then I will cut this tree down and
I will dig up its root.' "

10 As He was teaching in the synagogue
On one of the sabbath days,
11 A woman, sick for eighteen years,
Had sought to give Jesus praise.

An evil spirit had bent her double;
She could not stand up straight;
She could but raise her eyes;
This was a dreadful fate.

12 Said Jesus, "You are free from
Your sickness and your sin."
13 He laid His hands upon her and
She stood erect again.

The woman said, "To God be glory
For I was healed today."
14 The synagogue ruler was angry,
for
This was the Sabbath day.

He said, "Six other days you have
To work—go on your way,
But on the Sabbath do no work.
It is God's holy day."

15 But Jesus said, "You hypocrites,
To meet your livestock's need,
Do you not loose them on the Sabbath
To give them water and feed?

16 "This woman, a daughter of
Abraham,
Whom Satan bound for years,
Should she not be released today,
Be freed from pain and fears?"

17 His adversaries were shamed but
The multitudes were pleased,
Because of all the things He'd done
Their troubles were being eased.

18 "What is God's kingdom like?"
He asked,
"You say you'd like to know.
19 It's like a grain of mustard seed,
In a garden it will grow.

"It grows and then becomes a tree;
The garden it enhances;
The birds come to the tree and build
Their nests upon its branches."

20 Again He said, "And it is like
21 The leaven put in dough;
It's hidden under meal so it
Will make it rise, you know."

22 Jesus went through towns and villages
Teaching as He went.
On His way to Jerusalem
23 Someone asked what He meant:

"Lord, the people who will be saved,
Are there only a few?"
Jesus answered and said,
"This I say to you:

24 "Enter by the narrow door,
Many strive to enter in,
But they will find the door is locked
Because they're full of sin.

25 "When once the master shuts the
door
You'll stand outside and knock;
You'll cry, 'Lord open the door to us,"
But the door He'll not unlock.

"From somewhere in the house, the
sound
Of the Master's voice will come,
'Depart from here, I know you not,
Nor know where you are from.'

26 "You'll say, 'We ate and drank
with you,
And you taught on our street.'
27 He'll say, 'Depart, I know you not,
This message I repeat.'

28 "Some there will weep and gnash
their teeth
When these things come about,
You'll see the prophets in the
kingdom,
But you will be cast out.

29 "They will come from all
directions,
And at God's table dine.
30 Some of those you thought last
will be
The very first in line."

31 Some Pharisees came up to Him,
And they drew Him apart.
Said, "Herod wants to kill you, so
From here you'd best depart."

32 "Go tell that old fox," Jesus said,
"Today I've made some whole,
Tomorrow cast out demons, and
The third day reach My goal.

33 "But I must go along My way,
The mission must be fulfilled,
For outside of Jerusalem
No prophet should be killed.

34 "Oh Jerusalem—Jerusalem,
The prophets you have stoned,
You have killed those sent to you, for
You I would have atoned.

"As a hen gathers all her chicks around
And guards them with her wings,
But you would not come unto Me;
Your action judgment brings.

35 "Behold! your house is desolate
And I say this to you,
You'll not see Me again until
You accept My word as true.

"And when that time has come, you will
Declare in one accord,
'Blessed is He that cometh
In the name of the Lord.' "

Chapter 14

1 He went to the house of a Pharisee
To dine on a Sabbath day,
Where they were closely watching Him
To hear what He would say.

2 A man with dropsy sat in front
Of Jesus at the meal;
3 Jesus said to the Pharisee,
"Today, is it right to heal?"

4 They would not answer Jesus, they
Had not a word to say.
Jesus took the man and healed him and
Sent him on his way.

5 "Which of you with an ox," he said
"If it falls into a pit,
Even though it were the Sabbath,
Would not take care of it?

"And would you not do this
Even on a Sabbath day?"
6 To this they had no answer,
They had nothing else to say.

7 Then Jesus looked around,
And He noticed that each guest
Picked a place of honor at the table,
One they each thought was best.

8 Said Jesus, "If you are invited
To go to a wedding feast,
Do not seek out the seats of honor,
Instead seek out the least.

"For if you take the place of honor,
It later may be found
It's for a more distinguished guest.
9 They'll ask you to step down.

"You will then be embarrassed, you
Will feel you've been disgraced,
When you leave the head table
To step down to last place.

10 "But when you are invited, take
The lowest seat you see,
Then should your host invite you higher,
Honor then will come to thee.

11 "For everyone who exalts himself
Will find himself put down,
But the one who shows humility
In him honor will be found."

12 Then Jesus turned and spoke unto
The one who gave the invitation,
"When you would give a dinner, don't
Invite only those of close association.

"Do not invite your brothers or
Invite rich neighbors, too,
For they will return the favor and
Repayment will come to you.

13 "But when you give a dinner, bring
The poor, the blind, and lame,
14 And you'll be blessed by heaven for
They can't return the same."

15 One reclining at the table said,
When he heard Jesus speak,
"Blessed are those who eat at God's table,
A thing we all should seek."

16 Jesus said, "A man gave a big dinner,
Invited many to dine on meat.
17 When it was prepared he sent a servant
To call them to come and eat.

18 "They all said to the servant, 'I'm sorry,
But I must be excused.'
One said, 'I've bought a piece of land,
And must see how it's being used.'

19 "Another said, 'I've bought some oxen,
I must go try them out.
Your master will surely understand,
Of this I have no doubt.'

20 "Another said unto the servant
'I have just taken a wife;
Your master knows if I leave tonight
It might cause me strife.'

21 "The servant reported to his master
Who very angry became.
He said, 'Go out into the streets,
Bring in the poor and lame.'

22 "The servant went out, then
        reported back,
'We have followed your command,
Yet there is space remaining and
No one will have to stand.'

23 "The master said, 'Go to the highways
And go along the hedge rows;
Compel them to the banquet so
The dining room overflows.

24 "'I tell you none of those invited
Shall of my dinner taste.
It shall be fed to others, we
Can't let it go to waste.' "

25 Great multitudes were going
        with Him,
He turned to them and stated,
26 "If anyone would my disciple be
All else must then be hated.

"You must by comparison hate your
        parents,
Your children, and your wife,
Your sisters and your brothers, and
Must even hate your life.

27 "You must carry your own cross
If you would follow Me.
You must be strong in duty if
My disciple you would be.

28 "Before you build a tower, do
You not first count the cost?
For if you cannot finish it
Fulfillment will be lost.

29 "If you laid only the foundation
The public would ridicule.
30 They'd say, 'He started but
        couldn't finish,
Oh! he is such a fool.'

31 "Or what king sets out for battle
Without counsel so he'll know,
Can he with but ten thousand men
Face twenty thousand foe?

32 "If he thinks he's not able, while
His foe is far away,
He'll ask for terms of peace and will
Not enter into the fray.

33 "So, therefore, whosoever would
Desire to follow Me
Must shun possessions, or else he
Cannot my disciple be.

34 "Salt is good, and it is useful,
Unless it loses its flavor,
For if it becomes contaminated
Then it will have no savor.

35 "It is useless for the soil, I say,
And for the dunghill here,
So throw it out, it has no use,
He with ears let him hear."

Chapter 15

1 Tax gatherers and sinners came to
        Him.
They sat down at His feet.
2 The Pharisess and scribes
        complained,
"With sinners He does eat."

3, 4 "If one has a hundred sheep," he
        said.
And one sheep goes astray,
Will he not leave the ninety and nine
In the wilderness today?

5 "He'll seek until he finds it, and
When that lost sheep is found,
He will bend down beside it; He
Will lift it from the ground.

"The lost sheep He will carry home,;
He will not count the cost,
6 Will call unto the neighbors, 'Rejoice,
I've found the one I lost.'

7 "I tell you it's the same in heaven.
When one sinner God's word heeds
There's more joy than for ninety-
        nine righteous,
Who no repentance needs.

8 "If a woman lose one of ten
   silver coins,
She then will sweep with care,
And will go o'er each room of the
   house.
She will look everywhere.

9 "And when she finds the coin she'd
   lost
She'll jump and shout with glee.
She will call friends and neighbors,
'Come and rejoice with me.'

10 "In the same way I tell you
God's angels all rejoice
Over one sinner who repents,
In praise lifts up his voice.

11 "A father had two sons; to Him
12 The younger said, 'Why wait?
Please give me my inheritance.'
The father divided his estate.

13 "A few days later the younger son
Gathered everything he had.
He went away and squandered it,
A good time awhile, he had.

14 "And when he had spent every-
   thing
And all his money was gone,
A famine came to that country and
He had nothing to live on.

15 "He attached himself to a farmer,
Whose pigs' husks he did eat.
16 This young man was so hungry that
Those husks looked like a treat.

17 Finally he came to his senses, saying,
'My father has hired men
Who have more than enough to eat.
I'll die in this pig pen.

18 " 'I will arise and go to my father,
And will confess all my sin;
19 I'll say, I'm not fit to be your son,
Make me one of your hired men.'

20 "He got up and started home,
Still a short distance to go,
The father, looking down the road,
Said, 'That's someone I know.'

"As the boy drew closer to the father
He recognized his son.
He ran and kissed his son in spite
Of the evil he had done.

21 "The son said, 'I've sinned
   against heaven,
As well as in your sight;
For me to be considered your son
No longer would be right.'

22 His father called, 'Bring the best
   robe,
Put sandals on his feet,
A ring upon his finger, kill
23 The fatted calf to eat.

24 "'This son of mine was dead, and he
Has come to life again.
He was lost but he now is found,'
And they rejoiced within.

25 "The older son came from the field,
And to the house drew near;
26 He heard the sound of music, and
He asked, 'What's happened here?'

27 "A slave said, 'Your brother has
   returned,
Your father's killed the calf,
Because he's received his son again
He can rejoice and laugh.'

28 "The older son would not go in
And join the merry making;
He was so angry at this event
That he was even shaking.

"His father came to talk with him;
He said, 'My son come in;
Join with us in rejoicing, for
Our family's complete again.'

29 "The son said, 'I've served many
   years;
Your commands I've not neglected.
You've never given me a party;
You I have always respected.

30 " 'But this wicked son of yours,
Who devoured your wealth in sin,
For him you killed the fatted calf
When he came home again.'

31 "The father said, 'My child it's true
You never left my doors;
You always have been with me, and
Everything I have is yours.

32 " 'But we had to have a celebration
And spread the word around,
Your brother who was dead, is alive;
Was lost and has been found.'"

Chapter 16

1 He said, "A rich man had a steward
Who squandered large amounts.
2 He called his servant and said to him,
'We must check your accounts.'

"He also said unto his steward,
'If what I hear is true,
You can no longer be my steward;
The post I'll take from you.'

3 "The steward said unto himself,
'Now just what will I do,
If he takes back the stewardship
I can't learn something new.

" 'I am not strong enough to dig;
To beg would cause me shame.
There is no excuse that I can make
My master knows I'm to blame.

4 " 'I'll call on those who owe my
master
And will reduce their bill,
So that when I am no longer steward
I will have their goodwill.'

5 "He called the master's debtors in.
He said, 'What do you owe?'
6 One said, 'Of oil one hundred
measures.'
'Write fifty, then and go.'

7 "Another debtor then he called,
'How much is owed today?'
'Of wheat one hundred measures.'
'Write eighty, be on your way.'

8 "The master praised the steward's
action,
Though he had not done right.
But the sons of this age are shrewder
Than are the sons of light.

9 "But shall I tell you to live like that
With injustice friends to make;
Will this guarantee you a place in
Heaven,
With righteous men to take?

10 "He who's unfaithful with little
Will be so with a lot.
But he who's faithful with a little
You can trust with all you've got.

11 "If in the use of worldy goods
You have not been found true,
When truer riches come along
No one will then trust you.

12 "If in the use of another's goods
Faithfulness you have not shown,
You will find they will not trust you
With what should be your own.

13 "You cannot serve two masters, no
This thing cannot be done,
For you will hate one master and
Will love the other one.

"Or else you will hold to one,
And then despise the other.
You cannot serve both God and
mammon,
I say to you, my brother."

14 The Pharisees, lovers of money,
Were listening to His word.
They all scoffed and laughed at Him
At those things they had heard.

15 "You justify yourselves," He said,
"Before the sight of men.
God knows what is within your heart;
He knows you're full of sin.

16 "The law and prophets were
proclaimed
'Til God's kingdom would begin,
Since then we've preached God's
kingdom and
Many strive to get in.

17 "If you try to get in by the Law,
You'll find you will never prevail.
It's easier for heaven and earth to
pass
Than for one dot of the Law to fail.

18 "Should you divorce and marry
another,
An adulterer this will make of you,
And the man who marries a
divorced woman
Will live in adultery too.

19 "There was a rich man, finely
dressed,
Who each day lived in splendor.
20 Poor Lazarus lay before his gate,
With open sores so tender.

21 "Longing to be fed from crumbs
From in the rich man's stores,
He was so weak, as days went by
Dogs licked the poor man's sores.

22 "It came to pass the poor man
   died,
He was no longer harried;
In Abraham's bosom he reclined.
The rich man died and was buried.

23 "From hell the rich man raised
   his eyes,
Saw Abraham far away,
He also saw the beggar, Lazarus,
Who in Abraham's bosom lay.

24 "He cried out, 'Father Abraham,
Have mercy, I'm in agony;
Send Lazarus with a drop of water
To cool my tongue for me.'

25 "'Your life was prosperous,'
   Abraham said,
'While Lazarus received the bad.
Now Lazarus is in comfort here
And you are in torment sad.

26 " 'And there's a gulf between us,
   though
You want, you can't come here,
And neither can we cross to you
And bring you any cheer.'

27 "He said, 'Then Father Abraham
I would beg this of you,
Please send someone to warn my
   brothers,
28 Or they will come here too.'

29 " 'They have both Moses and the
   prophets,'
To the rich man Abraham said.
30 He replied, 'They pay no heed,
   but would
Heed someone from the dead.'

31 " 'If they don't listen,' Abraham
   noted,
'To what Moses and the prophets
   said,
Then neither will they be persuaded
Though one rise from the dead.' "

Chapter 17

1 He said, "Stumbling blocks are
   sure to come,
And be placed in the path,
But woe to him by whom they come,
For he will face God's wrath.

2 "It would be better if a millstone
Were hung about his neck
And he were thrown into the sea,
Than these little ones to wreck.

3 "Be on your guard, I say to you,
Rebuke your brother's sin;
If he repents forgive him, do
It o'er and o'er again.

4 "If he sins against you seven
   times a day,
And when he does return
Forgive him each time he repents.
Do not your brother spurn."

5 His disciples said to Jesus, "What
You ask is hard to do;
Oh, Lord increase our faith so that
We may then live anew."

6 He said, "With faith like a
   mustard seed
To this tree you could say,
Uproot; be planted in the sea;
This tree would then obey.

7 "If your servant works in the field
And it comes time to eat,
Do you call your servant from his work,
And say come and take a seat?

8 "Will you not say, prepare my
   meal,
And when my meal is o'er,
Then you can go and eat and drink
From what is left in store?

9 "And you don't thank your servant for
Doing what he is commanded,
Because he only did the things
His master had demanded.

10 "So when you do the many things
The Lord demands of you,
Say, 'We're unworthy servants doing
Only what we ought to do.' "

11 As He was going to Jerusalem,
Between Samaria and Galilee,
12 He met ten leprous men, who said,
13 "Lord on us have great mercy."

14 When He saw them, He said,
"Go, by the priests be seen."
And as they went along the way
These lepers were made clean.

15 When one saw he was healed, he then
Turned and to Jesus ran.
16 At Jesus's feet he gave his thanks,
This healed Samaritan.

17 Jesus answered and said to all,
"Were not ten cleansed today?
Of ten but one has given thanks.
The others, where are they?

18 "Did not any of them come back,
Except this foreign one?
Did none give God glory except this man
At the feet of God's Son?

19 Unto the one who had returned,
And at His feet still lay,
He said, "Your faith has made you well;
Rise up, go on your way."

20 The Pharisees asked Jesus when
God's kingdom would appear.
He said, "God's kingdom is not coming
With signs you can see and hear.

21 "Nor will they say, look, here it is!
Or no, it's over there.
The kingdom of God is in your midst,
Of this you should be aware.

22 "Someday you surely will want to see
The days of the Son of Man;
You'll never see those days except
According to God's plan.

23 "Some will say unto you, 'Look here,'
While others say, 'Look there.'
Do not run after them, and of
False teachers be aware.

24 "For as the lightning streaks the sky,
From one end to the other,
So will the Son of Man in that day.
Therefore, be alert my brother.

25 "But first He must suffer many things,
And by men be rejected;
26 As happened in the days of Noah
All warnings will be neglected.

27 "They ate and drank and married, for
These things did them enthrall.
The day Noah entered the ark,
The flood destroyed them all.

28 "Likewise it was in days of Lot,
They were eating and drinking;
As they were buying, selling, building,
Of God they were not thinking.

29 "The day Lot went from Sodom, they
Saw fire and brimstone fall.
30 On that day it will be the same,
The Son of Man seen by all.

31 "If one is on the housetop and
His goods are down inside,
Let him not take time to get them,
But let him run and hide.

"Or if he's working in the field
Let him flee for his life,
Not looking back for anything.
32 Remember about Lot's wife.

33 "Who seeks to gain his life will lose it,
Or lose it, life will gain.
34 Two men will be in bed, one
Will go and one remain.

35 "Two women will be grinding meal
Together at the grindstone;
That day one will be taken and
The other left alone."

36 "Two men shall be working in the field,
Working side by side.
One shall be taken, the other left
With no place to abide."

37 Then His disciples asked of Him,
"Where, Lord will these things be?"
He said, "Where'er the body is
The vultures you will see."

Chapter 18

1 He told to them a parable,
That they should always pray,
And should not be discouraged if
Not answered right away.

2 He said, "There was an unjust judge,
Living in a certain city;
This judge possessed no fear of God,
And on man had no pity.

3 "There was a widow in that town
Who to the judge each day,
Said, 'Avenge me of my enemy,
He who has gone astray.'

4 "At first the judge ignored her, but
At last the judge got tired,
Said, 'Though I fear not God or man
5 I'll give her what's desired.

" 'For because this widow bothers me,
She's constantly about,
I will judge in her favor, or
She'll surely wear me out.'

6 "Hear what this judge said, one
     who did
Not know his wrong from right.
7 Won't God avenge all those who call
Upon Him day and night?

"Will He delay long over them?
He will avenge with speed.
8 When the Son of Man returns to
     earth,
Will He find faith indeed?"

9 He told another parable,
"Some thought they were exempt,
Because they were so righteous and
Held others in contempt.

10 "Two men went up into the temple;
They went there the same day.
A Pharisee and a tax collector,
They both went there to pray.

11 "The Pharisee prayed to himself,
'God, I give thanks to Thee,
That I'm not like the others who
Are praying alongside me.

I know I'm no extortioner.
I neither cheat nor rob,
Nor do I commit adultery,
Or do this publican's job.

12 " 'Lord you know I fast twice a week,
And tithe all I get;
I keep each letter of the law;
I know you'll not forget.'

13 "But the publican there stood apart,
Head bowed and beat his breast.
Said, 'Lord be merciful to me a sinner;
This is my sole request.'

14 "This one returned home justified,
By God no longer faulted.
He who exalts himself will fall,
The humble will be exalted."

15 Some mothers brought their
     children to Him.
"Please bless them," they would say.
The disciples rebuked them, saying,
"These children take away."

16 But Jesus said, "Don't hinder
     them,
But bring them to me, please,
For I tell you God's kingdom will
Belong to those like these.

17 "Unless you're like a little child
When at God's door you call,
You'll not receive the kingdom, you
Can't enter it at all."

18 A certain ruler said to Him,
"Good teacher, I ask of you,
How can I gain eternal life.
What is it I must do?"

19 He said, "Why do you call Me good?
None's good but God alone.
20 You have been taught the
     commandments
At school and in your home.

"Do not commit adultery;
Don't steal and do not lie;
Honor your father and your mother,
And cause no one to die."

21 The ruler said, "These things I've
     done;
I've kept them from my youth,
Yet I feel something's missing and
I seek from you the truth."

22 Said Jesus, "One thing you still lack.
Go sell all you possess,
Then give the proceeds to the poor
And then, My name confess.

"Heavenly treasures you will have,
Eternal life this brings."
23 The young ruler, who was very rich,
Was sad to hear these things.

24 Jesus looked at him and said,
Words which to some seemed odd,
"It is hard for the rich to enter
The holy kingdom of God.

25 "It is easier for a camel to
Go through a needle's eye
Than for the rich to enter the
kingdom,
No matter how they try.

26 Those that heard Jesus' words,
Turned to him and pled,
"Tell us, who then can be saved?"
27 Jesus answered them, and said:

"Things which are impossible
For any man to do
Are only possible with God."
Then Peter questioned, too:

28 "Lord we have left all,
That we might follow you.
We've given up everything
To help in all you do."

29 Jesus said to all of them,
"No service can you make,
Unless leaving house and family
It's for God's kingdom's sake.

30 "I say you will receive much more
Than in this world of strife,
And in the heavenly world to come
You'll have eternal life."

31 He took the twelve aside and said,
"To Jerusalem we go;
All of the writings of the prophets
Must come to pass you know.

32 "The Son of Man will be delivered,
And mocked by spiteful men.
33 He will be scourged and killed, but on
The third day rise again."

34 They did not comprehend His
saying;
To them His truth was hidden,
They could not understand His words,
But did as they were bidden.

35 As He was approaching Jericho
A beggar, who could not see,
36 Could hear the multitude passing
by,
And asked what this might be.

37 They told him Jesus was close by.
To be heard above the crowd,
38 He cried to Jesus, "Please have
mercy!"
He cried out very loud.

39 Those going before rebuked him, but
He called out all the more.
"Have mercy, Son of David! Please!"
He called out as before.

40 And Jesus stopped right where He was
And said, "Bring him to Me."
41 He asked then, "What do you want?"
The man said, "I would see."

42 Said Jesus, "Then receive your sight,
Your faith has made you well."
43 Immediately his eyes did open,
"Praise God!" The crowd did yell.

Chapter 19

1 He entered the city of Jericho;
As He was passing through,
2 A rich publican named Zacchaeus
3 Wanted to see Him too.

He was a short man, so above
The crowd he could not see;
4 Therefore he ran before the throng
And climbed up a sycamore tree.

5 When Jesus came up to that place
He looked into the tree.
"Zacchaeus, hurry and come down.
"I'll spend the day with thee."

6 Zaccheus climbed down from the tree,
And received Him very gladly.
7 But there were many in the crowd
Who thought He acted badly.

They said, "He's gone to a sinner's house.
And there to be his guest,
And to make matters even worse,
It's at His own request."

8 Zaccheus stood and said to the Lord,
"I give half to the poor;
If I've defrauded any man
I'll give back four times more."

9 "Salvation has come to this man;
10 For him I'll pay the cost.
The Son of Man has come to seek
And save those who are lost."

11 He told the crowd this parable,
When Jerusalem they drew near,
They all supposed God's kingdom would
Immediately appear.

12 "A nobleman sought a distant country
For a kingdom, and to return.
13 He gave ten servants one pound each
And said, 'See what you earn.'

14 "Some citizens, though, hated him,
And sent a delegation,
Saying, 'We don't want him to be king,
To reign over our nation.'

15 "It happened after he returned
And the kingdom he had won,
He called those he had given money
To see how they had done.

16 "The first appeared before him saying,
'I turned your money o'er.
The single pound you gave me has
Now yielded ten pounds more.'

17 " 'Well done, good servant,' the master said,
'Before me you stand tall.
You'll have authority o'er ten cities;
You're faithful in things small.'

18 "The second came saying, 'Lord,
Thy pound has gained five more.'
19 He said to him approvingly,
'Over five cities you'll rule o'er.'

20 "Another said, 'Here is your pound,
Which I wrapped and put away.
I've carefully kept it laid up
To return to you today.

21 " 'I was afraid to trade with it,
You are demanding I know,
You take what you did not lay down,
Reap where you did not sow.'

22 " 'By your own words will I judge you.
Where I don't sow I reap.
I am an exacting man you know
And not one pound you'll keep.

23 " 'Why didn't you put it in the bank,
Let interest be collected?
Because you balk at little things,
For great things you're rejected.

24 " 'So take the pound away,' he said.
To those who stood about.
'And give it to the one with ten
And throw this rascal out.'

25 "They said, 'But he has ten already.'
26 Their words He did ignore,
Except to say, 'I tell you, he
Who has is given more.'

" 'But he who very little has
And does not use it right,
Shall lose the little that he has,
Be banished from my sight.

27 " 'Now bring in all mine enemies,
Who strove against my crown,
Slay them in my presence, so
Rebellion be put down.' "

28 Once He had spoken of these things
He proceeded on His way,
Ascending to Jerusalem,
Which He would reach that day.

29 He approached Bethpage and Bethany,
Near the mount called Olivet;
He sent two of His disciples, saying
30 "There's something you must get.

"Go to the village opposite,
Within it you will see
A donkey colt tied to a post;
Loose it and bring to Me.

31 "If you're asked why you take the colt
To them you are to say,
The Lord has need for it, for He
Will ride this colt today."

32 Those sent there found the colt,
The donkey they untied.
33 The owners said, "Why do you do
this?"
34 "The Lord needs it to ride."

35 They brought the colt to Jesus, and
They threw their coats on it.
And Jesus climbed upon the colt
And on its back did sit.

36 Jesus then picked up the reins
And on that colt He rode.
And as they went, the people spread
Their garments on the road.

37 As He came down Mount Olivet,
The crowd before Him bowed.
Then they began to praise the Lord
With voices clear and loud.

38 "Blessed is the king who comes
In the name of the Lord most high;
Peace in God's heaven and on earth;
God's glory here draws nigh."

39 Some Pharisees in the multitude,
Self righteous and quite proud,
Said, "Teacher rebuke your
disciples,
Not to say that aloud."

40 Jesus turned and answered them,
He said, "I have no doubt
If these people should be silent then
The stones would all cry out."

41 And when he approached Jerusalem
He paused and wept o'er it.
42 Saying, "The days are coming on you
Which you will soon regret.

"If you had known this day things
which
Are hidden from your eyes,
You would have sought to know
true peace
And listened to My cries.

43 "The day will come when enemies
Hem in on every side.
44 They will dash you upon the
ground;
You'll have no place to hide."

"They'll crush your children and
your walls;
No stone will thereon stand,
For you knew not the time God came
To show you the kingdom land.

45 He entered the temple, casting out
All those who bought and sold.
46 Saying, "My house is a house of
prayer,
And not a robber's hold."

47 He taught in the temple daily,
The chief priests were annoyed.
The people listened to Him, but
The priests wanted Him destroyed.

The leaders and the scribes also
Wanted to have Him killed.
But they did not dare try anything,
With Him the crowd was thrilled.

Chapter 20

1 It came to pass one day when He
Was in the temple preaching
The religious authorities
confronted Him
And questioned all His teaching.

2 They spoke to Jesus and they said,
"We would ask this of Thee,
By what right do you do these things?
Who gave authority?"

3 He answered and said unto them,
"A question I ask of thee.
I'll answer yours for you if you
Will answer mine for Me.

4 "When John came to the Jordan,
preaching
Repent and be baptized,
Did his authority come from heaven,
Or from the worldly wise?"

5 They reasoned thus: "If we say
From heaven it was received,
Then He will say to all of us,
'Why have you not believed?'

6 "But if we say, it came from men,
This we do believe,
By people we'll be stoned, he was
A prophet they perceive."

7 So they said, "We know not where
John got his authority."
8 "I'll then not answer," Jesus said,
"Since you didn't answer Me."

9 He began to tell this parable:
"A man who owned some ground,
Started a vineyard, rented it out,
Then traveled out of town.

10 "At harvest time he sent a servant,
Part of the crop demanded,
But the tenants beat the servant and
Sent him back empty handed.

11 "The owner sent another servant.
They treated him with shame.
They also left him empty handed.
He returned as he came.

12 "The owner sent a third servant, who
They wounded and cast out.
They didn't intend to pay the rent,
It seemed there was no doubt.

13 "The owner said, 'What shall I do?
My servants have been rejected.
I'll send to them my beloved son,
Perhaps he'll be respected.'

14 "But when the vine growers saw
him
They reasoned, 'He's the heir,
Let us kill him and throw him out,
Then we can seize his share.'

15 "They threw the heir out of the
vineyard,
Then they killed him, too.
When the owner returns to his land
What will the owner do?

16 "He will come and destroy the
renters,
I am sure this you agree.
He will find other renters who
To him will pay the fee."

Hearing this, they shook their heads:
'God forbid that this should be,
That wicked men should kill the son
Of the owner of the property."

17 He looked at them and He said,
God's word has been made known;
The stone the builders rejected has
Become the cornerstone.

18 "All who fall on that stone will be
There broken and be battered.
And on whomever that stone falls
Like dust he will be scattered."

19 The scribes and priests then
tried to seize Him,
To arrest Jesus that hour,
For they knew Jesus spoke of them,
But feared the people's power.

20 They sent spies to watch Jesus, who
Feigned to be righteous men,
To catch Him in something He'd say,
And thereby turn Him in.

21 They said, "Teacher you teach
correctly;
You're not partial, or lax.
You teach the way of God in truth.
22 Is it lawful to pay the tax?"

23 He knew they meant to trick
Him. He
24 Said, "Show a coin to Me.
What is stamped on its face, and whose
Inscription do you see?"

They said, "The coin has Caesar's
mark;
That makes it legal tender."
25 Said Jesus, "What belongs to Caesar,
To Caesar you must render.

"But whatever belongs to God
You are to give to Him.
To serve both God and government,"
Thus Jesus answered them.

26 And so they could not trap Him, no
Not even with one word.
They marveled and were silent, then,
Because of what they heard.

27 There came to Him some
Sadducees,
Who sneer at resurrection,
And they began to question him,
Pretending to seek direction.

28 They asked Him, "Should a husband
die,
To whom no children came
His brother shall take that wife, and
Raise children in his name.

29 "Now there were seven brothers; and
The first one took a wife,
But none were born to them before
He departed from this life.

30 "Therefore, the second brother
    took her,
31 Then also by the third,
All seven brothers had her to wife,
Still no babes' cries were heard.

32 "At last the woman died herself,
All had passed from this life.
33 Now when the resurrection comes
Who'll have her for his wife?"

34 "The sons of this age marry, and
In marriage they are given,
35 But marriage is not given for those
Who reach God's holy heaven.

36 "For they do not die anymore.
They're sons of the resurrection.
Like angels they are sons of God
And follow His direction.

37 "In the passage of the burning bush
Moses showed these words to you,
'God is the God of Abraham,
Of Isaac and Jacob, too.'

38 "Now God is not God of the dead,
The living in God do dwell."
39 Some standing among the scribes
    said,
"Teacher you have answered well."

40 They no longer had the courage
To question what He'd done.
41 He asked, "How is it that they say
The Christ is David's son?

42 "Said David, 'The Lord said to
    my Lord,
At My right hand take Thy seat
43 Until I make thine enemies
A footstool for Thy feet.'

44 "So David therefore calls Him, 'Lord,'
How can He be His son?"
45 No one answered Him anything,
No, not a single one.

While people listened, He said to
The disciples in the throng,
46 "Beware of the scribes who like
    to walk
While wearing garments long.

"They love salutations in the market,
Chief seats in the synagogue take,
Places of honor at banquet tables,
All for appearances sake.

47 "Yet they devour widows' houses,
And make a show of prayer.
Their condemnation will be greater,
For burdens they won't share.

Chapter 21

1 He looked and saw rich men putting
Gifts in the treasury chest.
2 He also saw a poor widow who
Gave her very best.

She put in two small copper coins.
3 Then Jesus He did say,
Of a truth this widow in her poverty
Put in more than these today.

4 "For they out of their surplus put
Coins in the treasury,
But she gave everything she had,
Out of her penury."

5 Some were talking about the temple,
With precious stones all around.
6 He said, "The stones you're
    looking at
Will some day be torn down."

7 And hearing this they questioned Him,
"When will all these things be?
And when will they all take place?
What will the warnings be?"

8 He said, "Take heed, go not astray;
In My name some will say,
'I am the one, come follow me.'
From that one turn away.

9 "And when you hear of wars and
    riots,
Don't fear and don't forget,
These things must first take place,
    however
The end is not here yet."

10 And He continued saying to them,
"Nations war with one another.
Kingdom will rise against kingdom,
Setting brother against brother.

11 "There will be earthquakes in the
land,
And plagues in many places.
Famines and hardships will surely come,
And terror on people's faces.

12 "But before these things will
come about
They will lay hands on you,
You'll be delivered to the synagogues
And put in prison, too.

"You'll stand before kings and
governors,
Your defense you will make;
13 It will be a good chance for you
To speak for My name's sake.

14 "Therefore, do not spend time in
worry,
Preparing your defense,
15 None will refute your words, for I
Will give you utterance.

16 "But you will be delivered up
By parents and your brothers.
You'll be loathed by your relatives,
Your friends and many others.

"They will put some of you to death
If My name you would cherish.
17 You will be hated on My account,
18 Yet none of you will perish.

19 "Here's something else you need
to know
When this trouble comes to be,
Be patient and endure it all;
You will gain your souls, you'll see

20 "When you see Jerusalem
surrounded
Desolation is at hand;
21 Let those in Judea flee to the
mountains
Or be wiped from the land.

"Let those who are within the city
From the city quickly flee.
Those outside must not return or
Destruction they will see.

2 "These are days of vengeance, as
God through His prophets willed,
That all things which are written in
These times will be fulfilled.

23 "Woe unto those who are with child
And those who babies nurse.
Wrath will be upon the land.
You'll hear the people curse.

24 "Some will fall by the sword, and
others
Held captive by the score.
Jerusalem will be trodden down
Til the Gentiles' times are o'er.

25 "There will be signs in sun and stars,
And how the moon behaves;
There will be dismay upon the earth
And roaring of the waves.

26 "Strong men will faint from
expectation
And fear of things to come.
The powers of heaven will be shaken
And men will be struck dumb.

27 "And they will see the Son of Man
Coming to earth in a cloud.
They will see his power and glory
And people will cry aloud.

28 "But when these things begin to
happen,
Stand up, lift your head high,
Because redemption is drawing near,
Your salvation is nigh."

29 Then Jesus told this parable,
30 "When fig trees' leaves appear,
You see it and know for yourselves
That summer soon draws near.

31 "Therefore, when you see these
things come,
Then you will recognize
And know God's kingdom is at hand;
It will be no surprise.

32 "Truly I say this generation
Will not all pass away
Until all this has taken place.
Listen to what I say."

33 "Though heaven and earth will
not remain,
My words won't pass away.
These things that I have spoken, all
Will come to pass some day.

34 "Therefore, be always on your guard
And keep your mind alert.
Don't dissipate or worry or
In that day you'll be hurt.

35 That day a snare will come on all,
36 Be sure to watch and pray,
That you may escape these things
And stand before me that day."

37 He taught in the temple every day,
But He would spend each night
Upon the mount called Olivet
Beneath the stars so bright.

38 All of the people would rise early
And in the temple hear
The words that Jesus had to say,
And unto Him draw near.

Chapter 22

1 The feast of unleavened bread
approached.
2 Priests wanted Him waylaid.
They'd put Jesus to death but of
The people were afraid.

3 Now Satan entered into Judas,
Iscariot by name,
He was one of the twelve, but He
Forsook Him just the same.

4 He went and discussed with the priests
How Christ could be betrayed;
5 They were delighted and agreed
That Judas would be paid.

6 So Judas sought opportunity
To carry out their plan.
Away from the multitudes, they
could
Then seize the Son of Man.

7 Then came the day of unleavened
bread
And of the sacrifice.
8 He said, "Prepare the Passover.
We'll eat; it will suffice."

9 Peter and John said, "Where will
we go?
Where shall we go prepare?
We need a room that's large enough
For us to meet and share."

10 "When you enter into the city,"
The Lord said unto them,
"You'll see a man with a water pitcher,
Go you and follow him

"Into the house to which he goes
11 And to the owner say,
'The Master asks where's the guest
room
That we'd prepare today.'

12 "He will show you a furnished room,
The Passover you'll prepare.
It will be a large upper room
And there the feast we'll share."

13 They went and they found every-
thing
Just as the Lord had said.
Then they prepared the feast so that
All of them could be fed.

14 And when time came, the apostles
sat
Reclining at the table.
15 He said, "I long to share with you;
I'm so glad we are able.

"For soon I will be made to suffer,
16 I shall not eat again
Until it be fulfilled within
God's kingdom—only then.

17 He took a cup, gave thanks and said,
This to you I declare,
Take the cup and pass it so
That all of you can share.

18 "For I now say this to you,
I will drink no more wine
Until God's kingdom comes to pass
And I with God shall dine."

19 Then Jesus broke some of the
bread
And He gave thanks for it.
He said, "Share this among
yourselves,
And eat you all of it.

"This bread is my body, I say,
Which is given for thee;
In the future times when you do this,
You'll then remember Me."

20 In the same way He took the cup,
Gave thanks and passed it around.
He said, "This is My blood which is
Poured out upon the ground.

21 "Behold, however, the hand of one
Who would betray Me tonight
Is with Me at this table, and
Determined is his plight.

22 "The Son of Man indeed will go,
As prophecy portrayed,
But woe be it unto that one
By whom He is betrayed.

23 They began to discuss among
themselves
Who would do this thing;
24 They also argued who'd be greatest,
When Christ became their King.

25 He answered them, "The Gentile
kings,
Those in authority,
Are called your benefactors, but
26 It's not to be so with thee.

"Let him who'd be greatest become
As the youngest one of all,
And let the leader be a servant
Who waits upon your call.

27 "Who is the greater one, he who
At banquets does recline,
Or he who serves the guests, and those
Who have come there to dine?

"Is it not he who sits at the table
And of the feast partakes?
But I am as the one who serves,
And serves for all your sakes.

28 "You are the ones who stood by Me
In trials and troubles too,
29 As God gave Me a kingdom, so
I grant such things to you.

30 "You'll surely join Me at My table
And on thrones you will sit.
You will judge Israel's twelve tribes
And justice they will get.

31 "Simon, Satan asks to have you, that
He might sift you like wheat.
32 I have prayed that your faith fail
not
When trials you will meet.

"Although you might still slip and fall,
When you once turn again,
Give strength unto your brothers and
Lead all the lost from sin."

33 "You know I'm ready," Peter said,
And as long as I have breath
I will go everywhere with you
To prison and to death."

34 And Jesus said, "I tell you Peter
From Me you'll turn away;
Three times you'll deny Me ere
The cock has crowed today."

35 And Jesus said to His disciples,
"Did you have any lack
When I sent you with nothing but
The clothes upon your back?"

They said, "We lacked for nothing,
Lord,
In places where we preached.
Everything was provided for us
By people that we reached."

36 And Jesus said to them again,
"Now let him with a purse
Be sure to take it with him for
Things will get much worse.

"You then should also pack a bag
And when your packing's done,
If you do not possess a sword
Then sell your robe for one.

37 "For that which has been written
Is fulfilled in Me, I say,
'He was counted with transgressors;'
Will come about some day."

38 They said, "Lord, we have two swords
Here with our other stuff."
Said Jesus unto His disciples,
"For now, that is enough."

39 Then He, as was His custom, went
To Olivet to pray,
And His disciples followed Him
As Jesus led the way.

40 When He had reached that
certain place,
He said to one and all,
"I'd have you also pray, that in
Temptation you'd not fall."

125

41 And he withdrew from them, about
A stone's cast away;
In the garden He knelt down
And there began to pray.

42 He prayed, "If Thou be willing,
   Father,
Take this cup from Me,
Yet not my will but Thine be done,
Whatever that might be."

43 An angel came and strengthened Him;
44 Still bloody sweat dropped down
Which fell around His feet as
He knelt there on the ground.

45 All His disciples were sleeping
When He arose from prayer;
These moments of His sorrow, it
Seemed they could not share.

46 He said, "Why are you sleeping?
You should rise up and pray
That you not in temptation fall
When evil comes your way."

47 While He was speaking thus,
   behold,
A crowd of enemies came,
Led by one of the twelve apostles,
Judas was his name.

He came to Jesus and kissed Him,
According to his plan.
48 Said Jesus, "Judas, with a kiss,
You betray the Son of Man?"

49 The disciples who were with Him, and
Those who stood very near,
Said, "Shall we smite them with a
   sword?"
50 One cut off a servant's ear.

51 But Jesus said, "No more of this
Do on behalf of Me;
I came to give My life for men
And this is what shall be."

He touched and healed the
   servant, so
This ear was good as new;
52 Then He said to the religious
   rulers, "I
Have this to say to you,

"You have come with your swords
   and clubs
As if I were a thief.
53 I was in the temple daily, where
Oft I expressed My belief.

"In the light of day I taught.
Why didn't you seize Me then?
But this is the time when
   darkness rules;
It is preferred by men."

54 The officers then seized Him, and
His hands they yet did bind.
They took Him to the high priest's house;
Peter followed far behind.

55 In the middle of the courtyard they
Built a fire to be warmed,
And Peter sat down hoping
That he would not be harmed.

56 A certain maid saw Peter there
Before the firelight;
She said, "He was with Jesus, he
Was following Him tonight."

57 But Peter, fearing for his life,
Said, "Him I do not know;
I have not heard of Him before,
I declare that this is so."

58 And later on another said,
"You are one of them, too."
But Peter said, "No, I'm not,
Again I say to you."

59 In about an hour another said,
"We all can plainly see
That you must be one of them for
You are from Galilee."

60 Said Peter, "I declared before
This man I do not know."
As these words fell from Peter's
   mouth
Out there the cock did crow.

61 The Lord turned, and looked at Peter
Who recalled what He'd had to say,
"Three times you will deny Me ere
The cock has crowed today."

62 As these words came to Peter's ears,
He thought, "Him I've denied."
He then got up and left the crowd
And slipped outside and cried.

63 Those who arrested Jesus mocked
The Lord and beat Him, too,
64 They put a blindfold on Him and
said,
Prophesy: Who did strike you?"

65 They kept heaping insults on Him,
More than most could remember;
66 When daylight came that morn,
they led Him
Off to the council chamber.

67 They said, "If You are truly Christ
Say so, and don't deceive."
But Jesus said, "If I tell you
You still will not believe.

68 "And if I ask of you a question
You'll not reply this hour,
69 But you will see the Son of Man
At God's right hand of power."

70 They said, "One thing we ask of
You,
To us confess today,
Are You then the Son of God?"
He said, "It's as you say."

71 They said, "Give no more
testimony,
We all have heard Him speak;
He has blasphemed the Holy God;
A sentence we should seek."

Chapter 23

1 The multitude arose as one body,
To Pilate they brought the Lord,
Declaring Jesus to be a seditionist,
In this they were of one accord.

2 They said, "This man misleads
our nation,
To pay taxes He did refuse.
He says he is the Christ, and claims
He is King of the Jews."

3 Pilate asked, "Are you the Jewish
king?
Tell me the truth this day."
And Jesus answered him and said,
It is just as you say."

4 Said Pilate to the chief priests and
To those who stood around,
"I have examined this man and
No guilt in Him I've found."

5 But they said, "He stirs up the
people
As you should plainly see,
Teaching all over Judea,
Starting from Galilee."

6 When Pilate learned that Jesus was
A man from Galilee,
7 He passed Him on to Herod as
His responsibility.

8 Herod had longed to see Jesus,
Of Him he'd been informed;
He hoped that in his presence a
Great miracle would be performed.

9 Herod asked Jesus many questions,
But Jesus gave no reply.
10 While the priests and scribes kept
saying,
"This man deserves to die."

11 "When Jesus would perform no
miracles
To entertain the court,
Then Herod and his soldiers
mocked Him,
And of the Lord made sport.

They dressed Him in a gorgeous
robe,
And then their knees they bent.
When they were tired of mocking
Him,
To Pilate He was sent.

12 So Herod and Pilate became friends,
Forgetting their enmity,
They'd envied each other's power
And knew great jealousy.

13 Pilate called Jesus' accusers and
said,
14 "You brought this man to me;
You said He incites rebellion, but
No wrong in Him I see.

15 "Neither has Herod faulted Him,
He sent Him back to me,
Saying, 'There is nothing deserving
death
In the charges that I see.'

16 "But I will scourge Him anyway,
Though no guilt do I find,
Then I will grant to Him release,
And hope this calms your mind."

17 Now it was the custom at that
feast
For the authorities to release
A man accused of criminal acts
Against the people's peace.

18 But all of them cried out together,
Saying, "Put this man away.
Release for us Barabbas, and
We want it done today."

19 Barabbas had been thrown in jail
For insurrections made.
He also had committed murder,
And penalty would be paid.

20 But Pilate desired to loose Jesus
And made another try,
21 But the multitude kept calling out,
"Crucify! Crucify!"

22 He said to them yet a third time,
"Why, what has Jesus done?
I've found no cause for death in
Him,
We'll scourge Him and be done."

23 But they continued to demand
That He be crucified;
Their voices so insistent
Were not to be denied.

24 Pilate pronounced the sentence.
He yielded to their demand.
25 He released to them Barabbas,
One of a murderous band.

26 They seized Simon of Cyrene,
As they led the Lord away;
From His country He had come
To Jerusalem on that day.

They laid the cross on Simon and
Behind Jesus 'twas carried.
27 There followed Him a multitude,
Some woeful and much harried.

Some women were lamenting, but
He turned to them and said,
"Daughters, weep not for Me, weep
For you and yours instead.

29 "The days are coming when
they'll say,
The barren are the blest,
And wombs that never bore and no
Child ever nursed their breast.

30 "They'll say to mountains, 'Fall
on us,
And cover us,' they will cry.
31 If they do this with a green tree
What will they do with a dry?"

32 Two others, who were criminals,
Were also marked for death,
33 One crucified on His right hand,
The other on His left.

34 Jesus prayed, "Father forgive
them,
Their acts they know not what."
The soldiers who guarded Him for
His clothes cast their lot.

35 Many people stood by looking on,
And the rulers even sneered,
"He saved others, let Him save
Himself,
If He's God's Son," they jeered.

36 The soldiers also mocked Him,
and
They gave Him sour wine,
37 Saying, "If you are King of the Jews,
Save yourself, king divine."

38 They placed an inscription on the
cross,
By many it was read;
"This is the King of the Jews," is
What the inscription said.

39 One of the criminals hanging there
Said, "If it's really true
That you are Christ, then save yourself
And also save us, too."

40 The other thief rebuked him, saying,
"Don't God you even fear?
We're under the same condemnation,
And death is very near.

41 "We are being justly punished. We
Are getting what we deserved;
But that this man did nothing wrong
Is something I observed."

42 Then turning unto Jesus, he said,
"Lord, this is my one plea,
When you are in your kingdom, won't
You please remember me?"

43 And Jesus spoke unto the thief,
"Although you're suffering now
You'll be with Me in paradise;
To you I make this vow."

44 Darkness fell from the sixth hour
Until the ninth hour of the day.
God would not look on this vile
    scene;
He turned His face away.

45 The sunlight was obscured, the
    veil
Of the temple was torn in two.
46 Jesus cried out, "My Father,
I commend my spirit to You."

Once Jesus said these words He
    bowed
His head and breathed His last.
47 The centurion who was standing
    guard
Observed all that had passed.

He started praising God and saying,
"I've not a single doubt
That this man Jesus was innocent
Of what had come about."

48 The multitude who came together
To witness this event,
Returned beating upon their breasts,
Of the deed some did repent.

49 And all of His acquaintances,
And the women from Galilee,
Were standing at a distance but
His death they all could see.

50 Behold a man named Joseph came,
A good and righteous man,
51 A member of the council, he
Had not endorsed their plan.

Joseph lived in Arimathea,
A city of the Jews;
He was waiting for God's kingdom when
He heard the dreadful news.

2 This man went up to Pilate, said,
"It's almost Sabbath day;
May I take Jesus' body down
And carry it away?"

53 He took the body from the cross,
With linen covered it o'er,
He laid it in a tomb of rock
Where none had lain before.

54 The Sabbath was about to start,
Preparation was being made.
55 The women who had been with
    Him
Observed where He was laid.

56 They went and prepared some
    spices, and
Kept some perfume on hand,
They rested on the Sabbath day
According to God's command.

Chapter 24

1 But on the first day of the week,
Just at the break of day,
The women brought spices to the
    tomb.
2 The stone was rolled away!

3 When they entered into the tomb
His body they did not find.
4 They wondered what had
    happened and
Were perplexed in their mind.

Two men in bright apparel came
And stood there by their side.
5 The women bowed unto the ground
For they were terrified.

The men approached the women and
Kindly to them said,
"Why do you seek the Living One
In tombs among the dead?

6 "He is not here, He's risen;
Remember how He spoke to you
While He was still in Galilee?
Now you know His words are true.

7 "He said He'd be delivered into
The hands of sinful men,
By them be crucified, but on
The third day rise again."

8 They remembered the words He'd
    spoken and
9 They returned from the tomb.
They told of what had happened to them
To all those in the room

129

10 Among them Mary Magdalene,
Joanna, Mary, James' mother;
They told these things to the eleven,
Confirming one another.

11 Their words appeared as idle talk.
The eleven would not believe.
12 Peter arose, ran to the tomb,
His doubts he would relieve.

He looked into the tomb, he saw
The linen wrappings there;
He went away then to his home,
Wondering why the tomb was bare.

13 Behold! two of the disciples were
Going that very day
To a village called Emmaus,
About seven miles away.

14 They spoke of what had happened, as
To Emmaus they did walk,
15 As they were thus conversing, Jesus
Approached and joined their talk.

16 They did not recognize Him, for
They knew their Lord was dead,
And even when He spoke to them
And joined their talk and said:

17 "What are these words you're
saying in
The conversation you had,
As you walk along the road
What makes you look so sad?"

18 One of them named Cleopas,
answered,
"I really am amazed,
You have not heard what
happened in
Jerusalem these past days."

19 And Jesus to those who walked,
Asked, "What things do you mean?"
And they said unto Jesus, "Those
About the Nazarene.

"He was a mighty prophet both
In deed and in His word;
He was great in the sight of God
And everyone who heard.

20 "We were hoping He was the One
by whom
Israel is redeemed,
But now He has been put to death
Things are not as they seemed.

21 "For our rulers and chief priests
delivered
Him to be crucified,
And now it has been three days since
This mighty prophet died.

22 "And certain women have
amazed us
For right after the dawn,
23 They went unto the very tomb
And found His body gone.

"They saw angels there who said
'He's risen from the dead.'
24 Some of us sought the tomb and
found
It as the women said.

"The women's message sounded
foolish;
None of us could agree
If it was true or not, because
The Lord we did not see."

25 Said Jesus, "Oh! you foolish men,
Slow hearts who won't receive
The message all the prophets spoke,
Oh, why won't you believe?

26 "You've heard the prophets
message, you
Have often heard their story
Of how the Christ must suffer and
Then enter into glory."

27 He began with Moses, then explained
Other prophets, too,
How they said He would suffer and
Then would arise anew.

28 When they drew near the
village, He
Said that He would go on,
29 But they said, "Please stay with
us, for
The day is almost gone."

And He went in to stay with them.
30 When they sat down to meat,
He took some bread and blessed it, and
Gave it to them to eat.

31 At that, their eyes were opened and
The Lord they recognized.
Then Jesus vanished from their sight
And they were much surprised.

130

32 They said to one another, "As
He spoke upon the road
Did not our hearts burn in us as
He to us Scripture showed?"

33 They rose that very hour, and
Returned to Jerusalem,
They found the eleven disciples, and
The others were with them.

34 "The Lord is risen, and been seen
By Simon," the disciples said.
35 Then they told of their
experience
And how He had broken bread.

36 As they spoke among themselves,
Suddenly Jesus they were seeing
37 They were startled by His
appearance
They thought He was a spirit being.

38 He said, "Why are you troubled? in
Your heart why is there doubt?
39 Both see My hands and touch My
feet,
There's evidence about.

40 "A spirit has not flesh and bones,
Or walks upon its feet."
41 Still they could not believe for joy.
He said He'd like to eat.

42 They gave Jesus some broiled fish,
43 He ate and had His fill.
44 Then said, "These words I spoke
to you
While I was with you still.

"All things that were written of Me,
Which the Law and Prophets said,
They all said I would suffer and
Then be risen from the dead."

45 Then He explained to them the
Scriptures,
46 "Thus did God's Word say,
'That Christ should suffer and rise
from the dead
For you on the third day.'

47 "The Scriptures also plainly say
That repentance and remission of sin,
Should be preached of Him to every
nation
Beginning at Jerusalem.

48 You are witnesses of these things;
You've seen them come to pass.
You know that God has spoken,
And Christ has come at last.

49 "Behold! I send my Father's promise,
Which soon shall fall on you;
Stay in Jerusalem until it comes,
Power from on high is due."

50 He went with them to Bethany,
Then lifted up His hands.
51 He blessed them, parted, and
then rose
Up into heaven's land.

52 They all returned to Jerusalem
And in joy their voices raised;
53 They met continually in the temple
And gave God all their praise.

•

The Gospel According to John

Chapter 1

1 In the beginning was the Word,
The Word was God also.
The Word was also with God from
2 The beginning quite long ago.

3 Through Him all things were
   made, apart
From Him naught was created.
And through the Word all things
   have come,
As God Himself has stated.

4 In Him was, and in Him is life,
The very Light of men.
5 The Light shines in darkness; the
Darkness does not comprehend.

6 A man named John was sent from
   God,
7 As a witness to the light,
That all men might believe in Him
And do things that are right.

8 Though John himself was not the
   Light,
A witness to it he'd be.
9 The light would open each man's
   eyes,
So he might truly see.

10 He was in the world when it was
   made;
The world was made through Him;
But by the world He was not known;
Their eyes were very dim.

11 He came to live among His own,
But He was not received.
12 He gave the right to be God's
   child
To all who would believe.

13 Born not of blood, nor born
Man's pleasure to fulfill,
Nor were they born out of the flesh
But according to God's will.

14 The Word became flesh and with
   us dwelt;
We looked upon His face,
The only begotten of the Father,
Full of truth and grace.

15 John bore the Savior's witness
   when
These very words he'd cry,
"He who comes after, lived before
   me,
Of higher rank than I."

16 His fullness we have all received,
And mercy before His face.
17 The law preached us by Moses,
   through
Him will come truth and grace.

18 No man has ever seen God
   anytime;
The Son stood before His face
And in the bosom of His father
Declared Him and His grace.

19 When Jews, by priests and
   Levites sent,
Asked of John, "Who are you?
We must report to those who sent us;
Give us your answer true."

20 John said, "Pay attention to
   what I say,
Your request I'll not deny,
I tell you I am not the Christ.
You have my true reply."

21 They asked, "Are you Elijah who
Has come to earth again?"
When he said, "I am not," they
   asked,
"Another prophet, then?"

John said, "I'm not a prophet, I
Have told all of you so."
22 They said, "Who are you then?
Those who
Sent us would like to know."

23 He said, "I'm a voice crying in the
wilderness,
Crying, make the Lord's path
straight;
As the prophet Isaiah did say,
I'm he whom you await."

24 Now those sent from the
Pharisees
25 Asked, "Why do you baptize
If you are not Elijah, Christ,
Or another in disguise?"

26 John said, "I baptize with water,
But One you do not know,
Now stands out there among you,
and
The way of truth He'll show.

27 "He who comes after me, His
shoes
I'm unworthy to untie;
For Him I will prepare the way,
I ask you, heed my cry."

28 These things took place in
Bethany,
Beyond the Jordan, on the sod.
29 The next day John saw Jesus
coming,
Said, "Behold! the Lamb of God."

"He takes the world's sin away,
30 It's of Him that I testify.
He comes after, but was before me,
He's a higher rank than I.

31 "I knew not who He was before,
He was not recognized,
But to Israel He must be
manifested,
So therefore, I baptize."

32 And John bore witness saying, "I
Saw the Spirit like a dove,
Come and remain upon Him, sent
Out of heaven, from above.

33 "I did not recognize Him, but
He who had sent me said,
'When you baptize the One, My Spirit
Will alight upon His head.

34 " 'He baptizes with the Spirit,'
According to God's call;
I have record He is God's Son,
The Savior of us all."

35 The next day John and two
disciples
36 Saw Jesus pass that way,
John said, "Behold! the Lamb of
God,
Hear what He has to say."

37 The two disciples listened as
To others He did speak.
When Jesus left they followed Him;
38 He asked, "What do you seek?"

And they said to Him, "Rabbi, where
Is it you're going to stay?"
39 He said, "Come with me; you'll
see."
They abode with Him that day.

40 Andrew, Simon Peter's brother,
Was one who heard Him speak.
He was convinced He was the
Christ,
41 For Simon he did seek.

42 He brought his brother unto Jesus,
Who looked on him and said,
"You're Simon, son of Jonas; you'll be
Called Peter, a rock, instead."

43 The next day He went to Galilee,
Met Philip along the way.
Said Jesus, "Philip, follow Me,
Observe what I do and say."

44 Now Philip was from Bethsaida,
The home of Peter and Andrew.
45 Philip found Nathaniel and said
to him,
"I have good news for you.

"We've found Him of whom Moses
wrote,
Whom the prophets did proclaim,
The son of Joseph, from Nazareth,
And Jesus is His name."

46 Nathaniel said, "From Nazareth
Can there come any good?"
Said Philip, "Come and see yourself;
I really think you should."

47 Jesus saw Nathaniel coming,
And He said, with a smile,
"Behold! an Israelite indeed,
In whom there is no guile."

48 Nathaniel looked on Jesus, puz-
zled,
Said, "Just how did you know me?"
Said Jesus, "Before Philip called
I saw you 'neath the fig tree."

49 Nathaniel answered, "I believe
you,
From your words I can tell,
I know you are the Son of God,
The King of Israel."

50 Jesus replied, "Because I said
I saw you 'neath the fig tree,
You shall see even greater things
Because you do believe in Me.

51 "You'll see the heavens opened
and
See things that will astound,
Angels from heaven, traversing
with
The Son of Man, they're found."

Chapter 2

1 On the third day came a marriage,
In Cana of Galilee.
Jesus' mother was at the wedding,
The whole town seemed to be.

2 They invited Jesus for the occasion,
and
With His disciples He came.
3 When the wine ran out, the mother
Of Jesus called His name.

She said, "They don't have any wine."
4 Jesus said, "Woman what have I to
do with you?
You know My hour has not yet come."
5 She bade the servants, "Do as He
tells you to do."

6 Now there were six stone water pots
Holding twenty to thirty gallons each,
Brought for purification,
Setting within easy reach.

7 Said Jesus, "Fill the water pots."
They filled them to the brim.
8 He said, "Draw some, then see the
manager."
They did, then went to him.

9 And when the manager tasted it,
It now had become wine;
He did not know from whence it
came,
But knew it tasted fine.

He called the bridegroom to him, said,
10 "The good wine is served first,
Then when the men have freely drunk
They serve that which is worst.

"But now your servants brought
some wine,
And to you I avow,
You served the poorest first and saved
The best wine until now."

11 This first of signs Jesus did begin
In Cana of Galilee.
His disciples believed on Him,
His glory they could see.

12 Then to Capernaum He went down,
With His brothers and His mother,
And His disciples also went;
For a few days there together.

13 He went from there to Jerusalem,
For Passover was at hand.
14 He went into the Jewish temple
And there He took a stand.

He found them selling livestock there
Inside the temple gates,
And money changers seated who
Were charging excessive rates.

15 He made a lash of small cords
And drove all of them out.
He turned the changers' tables o'er
And scattered coins about.

16 To those who were selling doves
He said, "Take them away!
This house is not for merchandise,
But a place to come and pray."

17 His disciples remembered it was
written,
"Zeal for Thy house consumes Me."
18 The Jews said, "Why did you do
this? What
Is your sign of authority?"

19 Said He, "Destroy this temple,
and in three
Days I'll raise it again."
20 They said, "To build took forty-
six years,
Three days, You'd just begin."

21 But He was speaking of His body.
22 When He rose from the dead,
His disciples remembered this occasion
And believed what He'd said.

23 Now when He was in Jerusalem,
Passover had begun;
Many believed in Jesus's name
Beholding signs He'd done.

24 He did not trust Himself to them,
For Jesus on His part
25 Needed no one to tell Him of man,
For He knew each man's heart.

Chapter 3

1 A Pharisee, named Nicodemus,
Was a ruler of the Jews;
2 He came to Jesus in the night.
He desired to hear His views.

He said, "Rabbi, you come from God
Because of the signs you do;
You could not do these things un-
less
God was along with You."

3 Said Jesus, "Except a man is born
again,
God's kingdom he'll not see."
4 Nicodemus asked, "What if he's
old?
In the womb he cannot be."

5 Said He, "Unless you're born of
water
And then of Spirit, too,
You cannot enter the kingdom
gates;
There is no place for you.

6 "That which is born of flesh is
flesh,
And spirit's of Spirit born.
7 Do not marvel at what I said,
And do not look forlorn.

8 "The wind blows where it wishes and
You can hear the sound of it;
You don't know how it comes or
goes,
Like one born of the Spirit

9 Nicodemus answered and said to
Him,
"How can this come about?"
10 Said Jesus, "Are you Israel's
teacher
And still you're full of doubt?

11 "I say we speak that which we
know,
Our words you must believe;
We bear witness to what we've seen
Yet you do not receive.

12 "If I told you of earthly things
And you doubted what you heard,
Then if I told you heavenly things
Would you believe My word?

13 "None has ascended into heaven;
I tell you no one can,
Except He who came down from
heaven,
Who is the Son of Man.

14 "As Moses lifted up the serpent
When men were full of strife,
So must the Son of Man be lifted
15 That sinners might have life.

16 "For God so loved the world His
only
Begotten Son He gave,
That whosoever believes in Him
His soul will surely save.

"He who believes will never perish,
But have eternal life.
17 God did not send His Son to judge
But save from sin and strife.

18 He who believes in Him is not
judged,
But judgment has been done
For those who have no faith
In God's own holy Son.

19 "This is the judgment, I proclaim
Light has come unto men,
But men loved darkness more than
light,
Because they're deep in sin.

20 "He who does evil hates the light
And from light turns away,
Lest all his deeds should be exposed
By light's bright shining ray.

21 "But he who's truthful seeks the
light,
His deeds to be manifested;
As if wrought by a holy God,
For by God's light they're tested."

22 Jesus and His disciples left that
place
And to Judea came.
There they spent time with Him
and did
Some baptizing in His name.

23 John also baptized in Aenon,
Which is near unto Salim,
Because there was much water
there,
They'd be baptized by Him.

24 John was not yet cast in prison
when
25 There arose a discussion with
the Jews
About the means of purification
And just what John should do.

26 They came to John and said to
him,
"He with you beyond the shore,
The One to whom you gave witness
Is baptizing more and more."

27 John answered those who came to
him,
"A man naught can receive
Unless it's given him from heaven;
This truly I believe.

28 "Yourselves you bear me witness, for
Each of you heard me say,
I am not Christ the Messiah, but
The one who prepares His way.

29 "Tis the bridegroom who has the
bride,
But his friend does rejoice
When he stands near the bridegroom
and
He hears the bridegroom's voice.

30 "Therefore my joy is fulfilled,
So now He must increase.
I say to you, it has come
That I must now decrease."

31 He said, "He who comes from
above
Is placed above all things,
And He who is from the earth will
Speak of from which he springs."

32 "And so I say, of what He's seen
And that which He has heard,
He gives His testimony, yet
No man receives His word.

33 "And He who has received His
witness
Has set his seal to this,
That God is true and faithful and
In Him no prejudice.

34 "For He whom God has sent to
earth
Speaks of what God has done;
He gives the Spirit without
measure,
35 For the Father loves the Son.

"He's given all into His hands,
36 He who believes will live forever,
But he who believeth not,
God's wrath's he will not sever."

Chapter 4

1 When therefore, Jesus knew that
all
The Pharisees had heard
That daily more disciples were
Believing in His word,

2 That Jesus' disciples baptized more
Than John, it seemed to be;
3 Therefore, Jesus left Judea and
He went to Galilee.

4 He had to pass through Samaria,
5 At Sychar, near the ground
That Jacob had given unto Joseph;
6 There Jacob's well is found.

Jesus tired from travelling,
Sat down to rest and think.
7 A Samaritan woman came to the
well;
Said Jesus, "Give Me a drink."

8 The disciples had gone to the city
To buy some food to eat,
But Jesus had remained behind
And made the well His seat.

9 The woman answered, said, "You're
a Jew
This I see quite clearly,
But Jews don't deal with Samaritans
So why ask this of me?"

10 Jesus answered, "If you knew God's
gift
And He who asks of you
To give to Him a drink of water,
This is what you'd do.

"You'd say, 'give me a drink,'
And living water I would give.
Your thirst would then be
quenched and you
Would then begin to live."

11 "Sir, you have neither rope nor bucket,
The water's far from the top.
Where do you get this living water.
Does it from heaven drop?

12 "Are you greater than our father
Jacob,
Who gave to us this well?
He drew water for his family and
cattle,
Their thirst He would dispel."

13 Said Jesus, "Whoever drinks this
water
Will more water soon implore,
14 But whoever drinks the water I
give
He shall thirst no more.

"The water that I give shall be
A well springing up inside;
It will give him eternal life
And be his stay and guide."

15 The woman said, "Sir, give me
some
That I might thirst no more;
I will not have to draw each day
As I have done before."

16 He said, "Go call your husband
and
Bring him along with you."
17 The woman said, "I have no husband."
Said Jesus, "I know that's true.

18 "For you have had five husbands,
but
The one you live with now
Is not your legal husband, you've
Not made a marriage vow."

19 The woman said, "You are a
prophet,
20 Yet on this mountain space
Our fathers here did worship, yet
You say Jerusalem is the place."

21 Said Jesus, "The time is coming,
Pay attention to My word,
Neither here nor in Jerusalem
Will worship be seen or heard.

22 "You worship what you do not
know,
But I bring you good news;
We worship what we really know,
For salvation is from the Jews.

23 "But the hour is coming, and now
  is,
When believers will hear it,
Those who would truly worship God
Will worship in truth and spirit.

"This is the worship that God wants
To trust in Him each day.
24 For God is truth and spirit and
Must be worshipped in this way."

25 She said, "I know Messiah cometh,
The one who is called Christ.
He will declare all things and He
Will give us true advice."

26 Said Jesus unto the woman, "I
Who speak to you am He."
27 That moment the disciples came
And the woman they did see.

They marvelled that He spoke to her,
Yet none said, "What do you seek?"
Or, "To this woman of Samaria
Why take you time to speak?"

28 So the woman left the water spot
And 'neath the noonday sun,
Turned to go back into the city,
And broke into a run.

She said to the men of the city,
29 "Come see one who looked at me,
Then told me everything I had done.
He the Christ must surely be."

30 The men hurried out of the city,
So this man they could meet.
31 Meanwhile His disciples said,
"Rabbi, we've food to eat."

32 Said Jesus, "I have meat to eat
Which you know not about."
33 The disciples said, "Where is this
  food?"
They looked around with doubt.

34 "My food," said Jesus, "Is to do
The will of Him who sent
Me to earth to finish His work.
This is my intent.

35 "You say, 'Four months precede
  the harvest,'
But I say unto you:
Look on the fields, for they are ripe,
Ready for harvest, too.

36 "The one who reaps is gathering
  fruit,
For a life that lasts forever;
Then he who sows and he who reaps
Will all rejoice together.

37 "For herein is the saying true
'One reaps, another sows.'
38 The work was done by others, but
You reap the fruit that grows."

39 Many Samaritans believed because
Of the woman who testified,
"He told me all things I had done."
40 They said, "With us abide."

Therefore, He stayed with them two
  days.
41 Many more believed His Word.
42 They said, "Not due to what she
  said,
But we ourselves have heard.

"For we have heard Him for
  ourselves
And know He is the one
Who is the Savior of the world,
God's only begotten Son.

43 After He had been there for two
  days
He went on to Galilee,
44 For Jesus testified, "A prophet's
Not honored in His country."

45 So He came into Galilee
And there He was received;
They'd been at the feast in
  Jerusalem
And had his deeds perceived.

46 He came again to Cana, where
The water He'd made wine.
47 A certain official came and said,
"Come see a son of mine.

"For he lies sick in Capernaum
And to you I appeal,
Won't you please come and go with
  me,
My son I'd have you heal."

48 Said Jesus, "Unless you see my
     signs
You'll not believe My cry."
49 The ruler said unto Him, "Sir,
Come or my son will die."

50 To the official Jesus said,
"He lives; go on your way."
The man believed the Word of the
     Lord
And returned home right away.

51 As he was going home, his
     servants
Met him along the way;
They said, "Your son lives; he
     improved
52 The seventh hour yesterday."

53 The father knew it was that hour
By Jesus he'd been told,
"Your son lives," and he believed
     with
The members of his household.

54 This was the second sign of Jesus
So those around could see,
When He came from Judea to
The province of Galilee.

Chapter 5

1 There was a feast in Jerusalem,
He went as was His rule.
2 Now in Jerusalem by the gate
For sheep, there was a pool.

In Hebrew it is called Bethesda,
With five porches around its side;
3 In these lay multitudes of sick,
For healing each one cried.

4 They waited there believing that
When an angel stirred the pool,
The first to step in would be healed,
And not be called a fool.

5 One had been there almost forty
     years,
He was lame and often fell.
6 Jesus saw him lying there and said,
"Do you wish to get well"

7 The man said, "None will put me in;
When the water's stirred anew
I try my best to get in the pool,
But one goes before I do."

8 Said Jesus to the man, "Arise,
Take your bed and walk away."
9 The man was healed and did as
     told.
This was the Sabbath day.

10 And some Jews saw him with his
     cot
And to the healed man said,
"Don't you know it's the Sabbath day;
You should not lug your bed."

11 He answered, "He who made me
     well
Said, "Take your bed and walk."
12 They asked, "Who on the Sabbath
     day
Would make such evil talk?"

13 The healed man said he did not
     know,
For Jesus had left that place.
And there was such a crowd around,
The man found not His face.

14 Later Jesus found him in the temple,
Said, "You're well, sin no more,
Or evil will befall you and
You'll be worse than before."

15 The man went out and told the Jews
Jesus made him well that day.
16 Therefore, they sought to slay Him,
For violating the Sabbath that way.

17 Said Jesus, "My Father works 'til
     now
And I am working, too."
18 Therefore, they sought the more
     to kill Him
Because of their blinded view.

Not only had He broken the Sabbath,
But now they heard Him claim
That God was His true Father, hence
Making He and God the same.

19 Jesus answered and said to them,
"Truly, I say to you,
The Son can nothing do but what
He sees the Father do.

"He watches what the Father does;
The Son will strive to please;
20 The Father loves the Son and so
Shows greater works than these.

21 "Just as the Father raises the dead
And gives them life again,
The Son gives life to whom He will
And cleanses them from sin.

22 "For the Father judges no one, He
To the Son judgment gives;
As honor is given to the Father
Honor is given to the Son Who lives.

23 "He who gives not honor to
The Son the Father sent,
Then he does not give honor to
The Father subsequent.

24 "Truly the one who hears My word
And believes in Him who sent Me;
That one has gained eternal life
And judgment he'll not see.

25 "The hour is coming, it is now;
The dead His voice shall hear.
And those who hear will come alive
And to the Son draw near.

26 "As the Father has life in Himself
The Son has life also,
27 And He's been given authority to
    judge;
He's the Son of Man, you know.

28 "Don't marvel, for the hour comes
When entombed will hear His voice,
And shall come forth, and they that
    have
Done good things will rejoice.

29 "Those who committed evil deeds
Must face the judgment day,
Because their hearts are evil, they
From heaven are turned away.

30 "I can do nothing on My own.
I judge by what I see.
I do not seek My own will, but
The will of Him who sent Me.

31 "If I bear witness of Myself,
My witness is not true.
32 It is another who bears witness
Of Me and things I do.

33 "You have sent messengers out
    to John
Who told you who I am,
34 But the witness which I have
    received
I've not received from man.

"I say these things unto you that
You're saved if you believe.
35 He was the lamp that brightly
    shone;
You rejoiced in the light received.

36 But the witness which I have is
    greater
Than that which John told you;
For the works the Father's given
    Me,
These are the works I do.

"These works bear witness of Me, that
The Father sent Me to you;
37 He has borne witness to Me and
You know His word is true.

"You have not heard His voice, and you
His face do not perceive;
38 His word does not abide in you
And you do not believe.

39 "You search the Scriptures,
    thinking that
In doing so you'll see
How you will find eternal life;
Those scriptures point to Me.

40 "You will not come to Me for life,
41 My glory's not from men,
42 But I know each of you has not
The love of God within.

43 "I am come in My Father's name,
But Me you don't receive;
If another comes in his own name
That one you will believe.

44 "You believe when one gives you
    honor, or
When another gives you fame,
Yet you don't seek the glory which
Comes in the Father's name.

45 "I'll not accuse you to the Father,
But Moses in the Law;
In Moses you have set your hope,
Yet believe not what you saw.

46 "If you believed what Moses wrote
Then you'd believe in Me,
47 But if you doubt his writings, then
With Me you'll not agree."

Chapter 6

1 After these things Jesus went away
Across the Sea of Galilee.
2 A great crowd followed Him,
Signs from Him they would see.

3 Up a mountain side, with His
Disciples He took His seat,
4 Passover at hand, Jesus said,
5 "Where buy we food to eat?"

6 He asked this to test Philip, for
He knew what He would do;
7 Said Jesus, "Fifty dollars worth
Is for each a bite or two."

8 Andrew, Peter's brother, said,
9 "A lad has loaves and fish,
Five of the one, two of the other
If that is what you wish.

"But the people are so many, that
Much more food must be found."
10 Jesus said to His disciples, "Have
Them sit upon the ground."

They had no tables in that place,
Nor did they have a chair,
But they sat on the grassy slope
Out in the open air.

There present were five thousand men
Or somewhere there about;
11 He took the food, then gave
     thanks and
Began to pass it out.

12 When all had eaten and had
     their fill,
Jesus said to His disciples, "Rather,
Any food should be lost, go
And all the fragments gather."

13 And so they gathered up the
     pieces
From the leftovers of the bread;
They gathered up twelve baskets full
Once everyone was fed.

14 The people seeing the sign,
     remembered
What He had done before.
They said, "Of truth, this is the prophet
Who would our kingdom restore."

15 Jesus knew what they planned
     to do,
To Him their thoughts were known,
That by force they would make
     Him king;
He withdrew to be alone.

16 His disciples moved down to the
     sea
When the end of day did come,
17 They got into a boat
And started to Capernaum.

He had not come to them, although
The sun had since gone down,
18 And a strong wind was blowing, and
The waves swelled all around.

19 After rowing for several miles,
Perhaps four, maybe three,
They saw Him drawing near to them
By walking on the sea.

This frightened them, but Jesus said,
20 "It's I, be not afraid."
21 Jesus they took into the boat
And soon a landing made.

22 The next morn, all the multitude
Looked up and down the shore.
Jesus had not gone with His disciples;
They found Him there no more.

23 There came other boats from
     Tiberias,
Near where they ate the bread,
And after Jesus had given thanks,
Five thousand had been fed.

24 When they saw Jesus was not there
And no disciples were around,
They all went to Capernaum to
See if He could be found.

25 When they found Him on the
     other side,
It gave to them much cheer,
And they said unto Him, "Rabbi,
When was it that you got here?"

26 Jesus answered and said to
   them, "Truly
I say this unto you,
You don't come seeking Me because
Of signs you saw Me do.

"Instead you come because of the
   loaves
Which yesterday you ate,
Because each of you had your fill,
You thought this was just great.

27 "Do not work just for food, for you
Know that food soon will spoil,
But work for food of eternal life,
For this you should always toil.

"The Son of Man will give you this,
God placed His seal on the Son."
28 Therefore, they said unto Him,
   "Lord,
Show us the works God wants done."

29 Jesus answering said to them,
"This is the work of God,
That you believe the one He sent
And receive His approving nod."

30 Therefore they said unto the Lord,
"What is this that You do?
Can You perform a sign for us
That we'd believe in You?

31 "Our fathers ate manna in the
   wilderness;
God gave it every day;
Will you then give us bread from
   heaven
As we daily go our way?"

32 And Jesus therefore said to them,
"Truly, truly I say to you,
It was not Moses who did give
This heavenly bread to you.

"My Father gives the heavenly bread,
33 The bread which brings you life."
34 They said, "Lord give to us this
   bread,
Ending hunger and our strife."

35 Said Jesus, "I'm the bread of life;
You may think this a wonder,
But he who does believes in Me
Will never thirst or hunger.

36 "I say all of you have seen Me
Yet you are full of doubt.
37 Those who the Father gives shall
   come,
And I'll not cast them out.

38 "I came down from heaven,
Not to do My will, you see.
I came to do the will of Him who
From heaven sent Me.

39 "This is My Father's will who
   sent Me
That of all He's given Me, I may
Lose nothing, but that I should
Raise it up again at the last day.

40 "Everyone who believes in the Son
Will hear the Father say,
'You may enter into eternal life;
I'll raise you on that last day.' "

41 The Jews were grumbling because
He said, "I am the bread
Which came down out of heaven so
The hungry may be fed."

42 They said, "Is not this Joseph's son
Whose parents we all know,
How can He say He came from
   heaven?
How can He claim it's so?"

43 Jesus answering said to them, "Do
Not murmur at what I say;
44 None comes to Me unless My
   Father,
Draws him along the way.

45 "It's written in the prophets, 'And
They shall be taught of God;'
Those who learned from the Father
   come
To me and give a nod.

46 "No one has seen the Father but
His only begotten Son.
He has gazed on the Father, and
He is the only one.

47 "Truly I say he who believes
Gains life for evermore.
48 I am the bread of life, for you
I open heaven's door.

49 "Your fathers ate manna in the
  wilderness,
And there all their bones lie.
50 This bread which comes from
  heaven, if
You eat, you'll never die.

51 "I am that very living bread,
From heaven I've come down.
If anyone eats of this bread
Then in Him I'll be found.

"That one shall live forever, for
Within him I shall live,
And for new life to this world
My own flesh I will give."

52 The Jews strove among themselves,
And Jesus heard them say,
"How can this Man give His flesh
  for food?"
53 Said Jesus, "There's no other way.

"Except you eat the flesh of the Son
  of Man,
And of His blood you drink,
I say to you, you'll have no life,
No matter what you think.

54 "He that eats of my flesh and He
That drinks My blood I say,
He has been given eternal life,
And will rise that last day.

55 "My flesh is meat, My blood is
  drink;
56 The partaker abides in Me.
I will also abide in him,
A new person he will be.

57 "As the Father sent me,
Because of Him I Live;
To him that eats of Me,
Eternal life I'll give.

58 "This is the bread from heaven, not
As the fathers ate and died;
He who eats shall forever live
In him I will abide."

59 He said this in Capernaum as
In the synagogue He taught.
60 His disciples who were listening
  said,
"This is a difficult thought."

61 But Jesus knew their thoughts
  and knew
That His disciples grumbled,
Therefore, He said to all of them,
"Because of this you stumbled?

62 "What if you saw the Son of Man
Rise where He was before,
Would you therefore believe in Him
And serve Him evermore?

63 "It is the Spirit that gives life,
The flesh provides no wealth.
The words I've spoken are of the Spirit,
And they are life itself.

64 "There are some of you who don't
  believe,"
For He knew who they were;
He also knew who would betray Him,
Of this He was quite sure.

65 He said, "I have said unto you,
There's no one can be saved,
Unless it's granted by My Father;
It's not how you've behaved.

66 As a result of what He said
People left Him by the score;
Many followers withdrew from Him
And walked with Him no more.

67 Then Jesus said to the twelve,
"Would you then leave Me too?"
68 Simon Peter said, "Lord, where
  shall we go?
Eternal life's in you.

69 "And we believe and know you are
The Christ of the Living God.
Redemption's found in no one else
And with you we will trod."

70 Jesus answered, said to them,
  "Did I
Not choose the twelve of you?
Yet one of you has a devil who
Determines what he will do."

71 The one of whom he spoke was
  Judas,
Son of Simon of Iscariot,
Although one of the twelve, he would
The Lord's betrayal plot.

Chapter 7

1 Then Jesus walked in Galilee,
Along the peaceful shore
Because the Jews desired His death
And plotted o'er and o'er.

2 The feast of Tabernacles was at hand.
3 His brothers asked, "Would You
Go to Judea so Your disciples
Might see the things You do?

4 "No man does signs in secret if
He would become well known.
If You can do the signs You claim,
The whole world should be shown."

5 His brothers did not believe. He
said,
6 "My time is not at hand;
Your time is always ready, but
You do not understand.

7 "The world cannot hate you, I say;
However, it hates Me,
For I testify that it is evil
And sinful things I see.

8 "You go up to the feast, but at
This time I will not go,
For my time has not fully come
When I must face My foe."

9 And having said these things, He
stayed
Behind in Galilee,
10 But when His brothers had gone up
He went, but secretly.

11 The Jews sought Jesus at the feast,
And said, "Where can He be?"
12 There was grumbling among the
throng as they
Discussed what kind of man is He.

13 Yet no one spoke openly for Him,
For they all feared the Jews.
14 Then Jesus went up to the temple
And there He taught good news.

15 The Jews, who marvelled at His
teachings,
Asked, "How has this man learned?
He has not been taught by our
rabbis,
Yet our respect He's earned."

16 Jesus answered and said unto
them,
"My teaching's not mine alone,
But from the One who sent Me, it
Comes from God's holy throne.

17 "If one would do the will of God
He'll know My teaching's true,
Whether I speak for God or for
Myself in what I do.

18 "He who speaks for Himself then
seeks
For glory of his own,
But he who seeks the One who sent
Him,
No sin in him is known.

19 "Did Moses not give you the Law?
Yet you don't carry it out.
Why do you seek to kill Me and
To bring My death about?"

20 The crowd said, "You must have
a demon;
No one desires to kill You."
21 Said Jesus, "I did one good work
And you marvel at what I do.

22 "Moses gave you circumcision,
In fact from Abraham,
And even on the Sabbath day
You'd circumcise a man.

23 "If a man is circumcised on the
Sabbath
The law will not be broken,
But if I heal on the Sabbath day,
Evil of Me is spoken.

24 "Do not judge by appearances,
But look to God and pray,
Then you can give your judgment
based
On what God has to say."

25 Therefore, some of the people said,
"This man they seek to kill,
26 Yet He is speaking openly
And they are keeping still.

"Do the rulers know this is the Christ?
27 We know where He is from,
But when the Christ appears, no one
Knows from where He will come."

28 Therefore, Jesus cried out in the
    temple,
"You say you know My name
And other things about Me, even
Including from where I came.

"I've not come of Myself, I do
Works I was sent to do.
You know not He who sent Me, but
He who sent Me is true.

29 "I know Him for I am from Him;
And I know that He sent Me.
I wish you would believe My words
And listen to My plea."

30 They therefore sought to seize
    Him, but
On Him none laid a hand,
Because the hour had not yet come
To do what God had planned.

31 Many of the multitude believed
    in Him,
Saying, "When Christ shall come,
What miracles do you expect from
    Him,
That this man has not done?"

32 The Pharisees heard the multitudes
Express these thoughts of Him;
They and the priests sent officers
To bring the Lord to them.

33 Said Jesus, "I'm with you a little
    while
Then go to Him who sent Me.
34 You'll seek Me but won't find Me,
    where
I am you cannot be."

35 The Jews to one another said,
"Where does He intend to go?
There's no place in our nation that
We don't already know.

"Will He then leave our country and
Go out among the Greek?
Will he leave us for them, and in
That place believers seek?

36 "What is this statement that He
    made,
'Soon I'll not be around,
And where I go you cannot come;
Seek Me, I won't be found' "

37 And Jesus stood and cried out when
The feast was nearly o'er,
"If a man comes to Me and drinks
Then he will thirst no more.

38 "He who believes in Me, as
The Scriptures say it's so,
From his innermost part
Shall living waters flow."

39 This he spoke of the Spirit who
Comes to those who believe;
The Spirit was not given yet;
His glory'd not been received.

40 Some of the multitude then said,
"A prophet we now see."
41 Others said, "This is the Christ," or,
"Will Christ come from Galilee?

42 "Has not the Scripture told us that
Christ comes from David's line,
And that His birth in Bethlehem
To us will be a sign?"

43 Because of Him they were
    divided.
The crowd could not agree,
44 Some wanted to arrest Him,
Others, to leave Him free.

45 To the priests and Pharisees went
    the officers;
They returned empty-handed.
The priests said, "Why didn't you
    bring Him in?
This is what we demanded.

46 They said, "We never heard one
    speak
As this man spoke today."
47 The Pharisees therefore answered
    them,
"Have you, too, gone astray?

48 "No rulers and no Pharisees
In Jesus have believed.
49 It is the ignorant of the multitude
That all have been deceived."

50 Nicodemus, being one of them,
The one who came at night,
51 Said, "Our law hears ere
    judging so,
We can decide what's right."

52 They answered and said to him,
    "Are
You also from Galilee?
No prophet ever came from there,
Search Scripture and you'll see."

53 The arguments finally ran their
    course,
The debaters were a sight.
Hungry, tired, and ready for sleep,
They went home for the night.

Chapter 8

1 Jesus went up to the Mount of
    Olives;
2 He came back early the next day;
Into the temple where the people came,
To hear what He had to say.

3 Scribes and Pharisees brought to
    Him a woman,
Caught in adultery,
And having set her in the midst
4 They said, "We ask of Thee,

"This woman is an adulteress,
We know this for a fact;
There is no doubt about it for,
We caught her in the act.

5 "Now in the Law which Moses
    gave
He said stone such a one;
Do you agree with this or not?
Should stoning now be done?"

6 He knew they asked this question so
Accusations could be found,
So He ignored their question; stooped
And wrote upon the ground.

7 But when they kept on asking Him
He said, in a solemn tone,
"Let him among you without sin
Be first to cast a stone."

8 He then stooped down again and
    yet
Wrote once more on the ground,
And when Jesus looked up again
Only the woman was found.

9 The men had heard what Jesus
    said
And quietly slipped away,
Convicted by their conscience
Without a word to say.

10 He rose and straightened up, and
    then
Said, "Woman where are they,
Did none of them move to condemn
    you?"
11 She said, "They went away."

Jesus said to the woman,
"Go, leave your life of sin.
Neither do I condemn you."
Then spoke to them again.

12 "I am the light of the world
And he that follows Me,
Shall not walk in darkness but
Have the light of life in thee."

13 The Pharisees said, "You bear
    witness of
Yourself—it is not true.
You lead the people from the Law
In all you say and do."

14 He said, "Though I bear witness of
Myself, it's true, I know,
Because I know from whence I came
And where I'm going to go.

"But you don't know from whence I
    came,
Will go, or what I've done;
15 You judge according to the flesh;
I judge not anyone.

16 "But even if I do judge, I
Know My judgment is true.
In it, I'm not alone, but with
He who sent Me to you.

17 "In your law it is written:
'The testimony of two men is true.'
18 I bear witness of Myself, and
My Father bears witness of me too."

19 They were all saying to Him, "Your
Father to us please show."
Jesus answered, "If you really
    knew Me,
My Father you would know."

20 Jesus spoke this in the treasury
And some of them believed;
Because His hour was not yet come,
Jesus was not then seized.

21 He said, "Soon I will go away
And you'll seek Me again.
Where I am going you cannot come,
You shall die in your sin."

22 The Jews said, "Will He kill
 Himself?
He goes where we can't go."
23 Again He was saying to them,
"You all are from below.

"I say you all are of this world,
While I come from above.
I am not from this evil world,
I came to show God's love.

24 "I therefore said unto you that
In your sins you will die.
Unless you know that I am He
And My words not a lie."

25 And so they were saying to Him,
"Tell us, just who are you?"
"I'm what I said from the beginning
And all my words are true.

26 "I've many things to say and judge;
He who sent Me is true;
The things I hear from Him, therefore,
Are what I speak and do."

27 That He was speaking of the Father
They did not realize,
Although He had done many signs
Before their very eyes.

28 Said Jesus, "When you lift Me up
You'll then know who I am.
I do naught of Myself, for I'm
The Son of God and man.

"So I do nothing on My own,
I speak as I am taught;
I do these things to please Him, and
His will is always sought.

29 "He is with Me who sent Me;
He's not left Me alone.
I always do what pleases Him,
What comes from His own throne."

30 As Jesus said these words
To all the people there,
Many came to believe
What Jesus had to share.

31 He said to those believing, "If,
You continue in My word,
Truly you're My disciples if
You believe what you have heard.

32 "And you shall know the truth
 and then
The truth shall make you free."
33 They said, "We're the sons of
 Abraham.
Slaves we will never be."

34 He said, "Each who commits a sin
By sin is then enslaved,
And you are not freed from your sin
By how you have behaved.

35 "The slave someday must leave
 the house,
Inside he can't remain.
He has no rights upon the house;
The law makes this quite plain.

"The son, however, can stay home
For he's the father's seed.
36 Therefore, if the Son makes you free
Then you are free indeed.

37 "I know you're seed of Abraham,
And Yet you'd take My life,
Because My word cannot abide
In you, so full of strife.

38 "I speak of that which in
My Father's presence was conferred,
Though you do that which from
Your father's mouth you've heard."

39 They answered, said again, "We are
The sons of Abraham."
Said Jesus, "If he were your father
You'd do the works of him.

40 "But now you seek to kill Me, who
Has told the truth to you;
Truth which I heard from God Himself,
This Abraham did not do.

41 "You carry out deeds of your father."
They said, "Your logic's odd,
We were not born in fornication,
We have one father, God."

42 Said Jesus, "If God were your Father
Me you therefore would love,
Because I have come from God,
Who sent Me from above.

43 "You do not understand, because
My word you cannot hear.
44 You are sons of your father, the
devil,
And his desires you hold dear.

"He was a murderer from the start;
In speech he tells a lie,
For he speaks from his nature, so
Follow him and you will die.

45 "Because I speak to you the truth
You still do not believe;
46 Which of you convicts Me of sin?
Why not My word receive?

47 "Who is of God will hear God's word,
But some of you don't hear;
So therefore you are not of God
To Me it does appear."

48 The Jews said, "You have a
demon, and
A Samaritan must be."
49 "I have no demon," Jesus said,
"And you dishonor Me.

50 "I seek not to glorify Myself,
The judges will come some day.
51 If anyone would keep My words
Death will not come His way."

52 The Jews said, "Yes, you have a
demon;
Abraham and the prophets died;
Yet you say if we keep your words,
Then from death we can hide.

53 "Are you greater than Abraham?
And then the prophets, too?
Who do you fancy yourself to be?
Again we ask of you."

54 He answered, "If I honor Myself,
My honor is nothing at all.
It is my Father who honors me,
The God on whom you call.

55 "But you've not come to know Him, I
Know Him, and this is true;
If I don't know Him, I'd
Be a liar just like you.

56 "Abraham rejoiced to see My day;
He saw it and was glad."
57 They said, "You couldn't have seen
Abraham,
Fifty years you have not had."

58 Said Jesus, "Truly I say to you,
Before Abraham was, I am."
59 Therefore, they picked up stones to
stone Him,
Saying, "Here's a blasphemous man."

But Jesus hid Himself from them,
For His time had not yet come,
So Jesus slipped through the crowd
To complete what He'd begun.

Chapter 9

1 He saw a man, blind from his birth,
As He passed by one morn.
2 His disciples asked, "Did his parents
sin
That blind he should be born?"

3 He answered, "This man's, nor his
parents'
Sins caused him to be blind,
But so God could be manifest
In the works you will find.

4 "I must then work the works of God
As long as it is day;
For night will surely come, when
one's
Work will be laid away.

5 "While in the world, I light the world
So all mankind can see.
And all those who believe My words
A light to them I'll be."

6 Then Jesus spat upon the ground
And from that ground made clay.
He pressed it to the blind man's eyes
And sent the man away.

7 He said, "Go wash in Siloam's pool."
He went and washed as told,
And when he came back he could see;
Could everything behold.

8 The neighbors who knew him as a
  beggar
Asked, "Is not this the one
Who used to sit outside and beg
Under the burning sun?"

9 Some said of him, "Yes, it is he."
Others said, "No, it is not,
Although we all agree that he
Resembles him a lot."

The one who had been blind spoke up,
He said, "I am the one."
10 Therefore, they all asked of the man,
"Just how was this thing done?"

11 "Jesus made clay and did anoint
My eyes and said to me,
'Go to Siloam's pool and wash.'
I did, now I can see."

12 They said to him, "Where is this man,
Where can Jesus be found?"
He said, 'I do not know, for I
Was blind when He was around.'"

13 They took him to the Pharisees
To see what they would say;
14 Now it was on a Sabbath when
Jesus had made the clay.

15 "How is it you received your sight?"
He was asked by the Pharisees.
He said, "He placed clay on my eyes;
I washed, and now I see."

16 Some of the Pharisees then said,
"He breaks the Sabbath day;
Therefore, He cannot be from God.
Look in the Law, we say."

But others there among them said,
"How can a sinful man
Perform such signs as these? We'd have
You tell us, if you can."

17 They asked, "What do you think of
  Him
Since He has made you see?"
The blind man said, "He is a prophet,
At least, it seems to me."

18 The Jews did not believe hit; they
Thought he was never blind.
Therefore, they sought his parents,
The truth they'd try to find.

19 And when they found his parents
  they
Said, "We would ask of thee,
You say this, your son, was born blind;
Tell us, how does he see?"

20 His parents said, "This is our son,
He was born blind, it's true,
21 But how it is that he now sees
We can't explain to you.

"We do not know the place he went,
Or who performed the cure;
Just ask him, for he is of age;
He can tell you, we're sure."

22 They said this for they knew the
  Jews
Had agreed they should cast out
Anyone from the synagogue who
  said,
"Jesus is the Christ, no doubt.

23 "So for this reason," the parents said,
"Ask him, he is of age, this one."
To be cast from the synagogue
Would cause them to be shunned.

24 So for a second time they called him,
The man who had been blind,
They said, "Give God the glory and
You will find peace of mind.

"We know this Man's a sinner; at
Your healing people saw
Him working on the Sabbath day,
Which is against the Law."

25 He answered, "Whether He's a sinner
I really do not know,
But I know whereas I once was blind
I see now where I go."

26 Therefore, they said again to him,
"What did He do to you?
How did He open up your eyes?
This time answer us true."

27 He said, "I told you even now,
And all my words were true.
The story I repeat, would you
Be His disciples, too?"

28 They all turned on him with scorn:
"His disciple you must be.
But we all follow Moses' law
As you can clearly see.

29 "We know that God spoke unto
   Moses,
But as for this strange man,
We do not know where He is from,
Please, tell us if you can."

30 He said, "Here's an amazing thing;
I really am surprised.
You do not know from where He came,
Yet He opened up my eyes.

31 "We know God does not hear sinners,
But ever since time began,
If one would do the will of God
God then would hear that man.

32 "It has been so since creation,
I think that you will find
You never heard of anyone
Who opened eyes of the blind.

33 "If this man weren't from God,
   there would
Be nothing He could do.
If you search in the Scripture, you
Will find that this is true."

34 They answered and said, "You
Were born in sin, no doubt.
And still you try to teach us."
And so they put him out.

35 Jesus heard they'd cast him out,
He looked for him and said,
"Do you believe in the Son of Man?
By Him will you be led?"

36 He answered and said to Jesus,
"My Lord, just who is He?
That I may then believe in Him,
The one who made me see."

37 Said Jesus, "You have seen Him and
He stands before you now.
He is the One who talks to you.
Will you before Me bow?"

38 He said, "Lord, I believe," and he
Then worshipped Him right there.
Although reproved by the Pharisees,
He found great loving care.

39 "For judgment I came," said Jesus,
That all the blind may see.
And those who see will be blind if
They do not believe in Me."

40 Some Pharisees were standing there
And heard Him say these words,
Said, "So, you think that we are blind,
Is that what we have heard?"

41 And Jesus said, "If you were blind
Then you would have no sin,
But you say we see clearly, so
Your sin remains within."

Chapter 10

1 "He who does not enter by
The sheepfold's door I say,
Is a robber and a thief who tries
To climb up some other way.

2 "It's He who enters by the door
Who's shepherd of the sheep;
3 The doorkeeper opens to him.
The sheep he'll safely keep.

"He calls His sheep by name, and they
All recognize His voice;
He leads them out to pastures where
The flock can all rejoice.

4 "When He puts forth His own, before
The flock He will then go,
And they will follow Him, for their
Own shepherd's voice they know.

5 "A stranger they'll not follow; from
A stranger they will flee;
They do not know a stranger's voice,
A stranger's they'll not be."

6 And Jesus used this parable
As to the crowds He spoke;
They didn't understand, for they
Were a hard-hearted folk.

7 Said Jesus, "I say to you of
The sheepfold I'm the door,
8 They were all thieves and robbers,
   they
Who made these claims before.

9 "Yes, I'm the door into the fold,
So you must come through Me,
And if you do you will be mine
For all eternity.

"You shall go in and out,
And dwell in pastures green;
10 The thief comes but to kill and
    steal;
He's of a spirit mean.

"I came that they might have life, and
Have it abundantly;
11 I am the shepherd of the sheep,
For them I die willingly.

12 "He who's a hireling, not a
    shepherd,
Not the owner of the sheep,
He runs away when he sees the wolf,
The flock he will not keep.

"The wolf snatches some of them,
    and all
The rest he scatters wide.
13 The hireling flees because he's hired
And in them has no pride.

14 "I am the good shepherd, as
You all can clearly see;
I know all of My own sheep,
And My own sheep know Me.

15 "Even as I know the Father,
By the Father I am known.
I lay down My life for the sheep,
For them I will atone.

16 "And other sheep I have as well
Which are not of this fold;
I must bring all of them as well
Out of the rain and cold.

"They shall become one flock as soon
As My voice they all hear;
The sheep will have one shepherd, and
To Him they are all dear.

17 "Therefore the Father loves Me; He's
With Me as I'm with men,
Because I will lay down My life
To take it up again.

18 "No man takes it from Me, but I
Lay it down of My own.
I can lay it down and take it up;,
This commandment God made
    known."

19 A division arose among the Jews
Because these things they heard,
20 They said, "He has a demon, why
Do you listen to His word?"

21 Said others, "He is not possessed
As you can plainly see.
A demon cannot cure the blind
Or heal the sick, can he?"

22, 23 Jesus was in the temple area
Walking in Solomon's Colonnade,
Winter in Jerusalem was always when
The Feast of Dedication was made

24 The Jews said, "If you are the Christ,
Don't keep us in suspense;
To desire to remain unknown
To us does not make sense."

25 He said, "I told you who I am,
But My words you don't receive,
Nor the works I did in My Father's
    name
You just would not believe.

26 "But you do not believe in Me
Because you're not My sheep;
27 My sheep know My voice
And all My words they'll keep.

28 "I give eternal life to them
And they shall never die;
No one can snatch them from My hand,
No matter how they try.

29 "My Father's given them to Me,
His only begotten Son.
No one can snatch them from His
    hand.
30 My Father and I are one."

31 The Jews took stones to stone Him,
32 "My good works you did see,"
Said Jesus, "So I ask of you
For which do you stone Me?"

33 "For a good work we stone you not,
But for your blasphemy,
You, being just a man, yet make
Yourself out God to be."

34 "Is it not written in your law?"
Jesus asked, "Have you not read
In Scripture, 'You are gods?' This is
What your own law has said.

35 "If He referred to them as gods
To whom the Word of God came,
And the Scripture cannot be broken,
It always remains the same.

36 "You charge Him Who God sanctified
And sent to earthly sod,
That I blaspheme because I said
I am the Son of God?

37 "Do not believe in Me unless
I do My Father's will.
38 But if I do My Father's work
Believe the works then still.

"These things I do so you'll understand
And make it plain to see,
That I am in the Father, and
The Father dwells in Me."

39 Again they sought to seize Him, so
He thought it would be wise
40 If He went beyond the Jordan to
The place where John baptized.

41 And many came unto the Lord
While He was staying there,
And Jesus taught the multitude
Because for them He cared.

They said, "John has performed no sign
When with us he did share;
It's true what he said about this Man,"
42 And many believed in Him there.

Chapter 11

1 Lazarus lived in Bethany;
Mary and Martha lived there too,
And Lazarus became quite sick
In spite of all they could do.

2 It was Mary who anointed His feet
And wiped them with her hair;
Now that her brother was very sick
She knew that Christ would care.

3 The sisters sent a message, "Lord
He whom you love is sick,"
4 But when He got the message, He
Did not start out very quick.

"This sickness," Jesus said,
"Will glorify the Holy One.
It will not end in death
But honor God's own Son."

5 Now Jesus loved Martha and her
  sister
And He loved Lazarus, too.
6 When He heard Lazarus was sick
He knew what He would do.

He remained two days longer,
7 Then to His disciples said,
"Let us go again to Judea
For Lazarus is sick in bed."

8 The disciples said to Him,
  "Master,
The last time we were there
The Jews all sought to stone You, so
To go, do we really dare?"

9 Said Jesus, "Hasn't the day twelve
  hours
When the sun shines clear and bright?
One does not stumble if he walks then
Because he sees that light.

10 "Only at night there's danger
When a man might stumble and fall.
The reason for that is simple,
Because he has no light at all."

11 Then Jesus also said to them,
"Our friend Lazarus is asleep.
I must go there and awaken him
So his sisters will not weep."

12 They said, "Lord if he is asleep
Then soon he will recover."
13 But Jesus had spoken of his death,
As they would soon discover.

They thought He meant sleep literally,
14 Therefore, He plainly said,
"I did not mean a restful sleep,
For our friend Lazarus is dead.

15 "For your sakes I am glad that
  when
He died we were not there.
So that you will believe in Me,
Let's go to him and share."

16 Said Thomas, who's called Didymus,
To Jesus and his friends nearby,
"Let us also go with Him, that
With Him we may also die."

17 When Jesus arrived in Bethany,
Lazarus had been dead four days.
18 Now Bethany was near Jerusalem,
About two miles away.

19 Many Jews came to the sisters,
To comfort them with a word.
20 Martha went out to meet Jesus
When of His arrival she heard.

But Mary stayed in the house.
21 To Jesus, Martha said,
"Lord if You had been here, I know
My brother would not be dead.

22 "Even now I know what ere you ask
God will bring it about."
23 He said, "Your brother will rise
again
If your faith has no doubt."

24 Said Martha, "I know he'll rise again
On resurrection day."
25 Said Jesus, "I'm the resurrection
And the life, is what I say.

26 Even though one be dead,
A new life he'll receive.
If he believes, he'll never die;
Martha, do you believe?"

27 She said, "Yes Lord, You are the
Christ,
The Son of God. I believe.
And You have come into the world
Sin and sorrow to relieve."

28 Then Martha arose and went her
way
Calling Mary secretly,
"The Teacher has come, He is here,
And He has asked for thee."

29 The Jews soothed Mary in the
house;
30 She quickly rose and left the room.
31 They too went out and followed her;
They thought she was going to the
tomb.

32 When Mary found where Jesus was,
She fell at His feet and said,
"Lord, if You'd have been here, then
My brother would not be dead."

33 When Jesus saw her weeping,
With Jews who wept also,
Jesus was moved in spirit and
Was troubled by their woe.

34 He said, "Where have you laid
him?" They
Said, "Lord, please come and see."
35 Jesus bowed and wept with
them, and said,
"Mary, believe in Me."

36 Some Jews said, "See! How He loved
him."
37 While others who were crying,
Said, "If He opened blind men's eyes
Could He have stopped his dying?"

38 Jesus, therefore, being deeply moved,
Went with them to the tomb;
It was a cave within a hill,
A small and narrow room.

A large stone lay against the cave.
39 Jesus said, "Remove the stone."
And Martha, sister of the deceased,
Said, "Lord, leave it alone.

"He has been dead four days;
The body's begun to decay.
It's better to leave the stone in place;
Outside the cave we'll pray."

40 Said Jesus, "I said if you believed,
God's glory you would see,
So therefore roll the stone away
And leave the rest to Me."

41 And so they moved the stone,
then Jesus
Raised up His eyes and said,
"I thank You that You hear Me even
When I pray for the dead.

42 "I know You always hear Me, but
So the people here can see;
They may observe the things we do
And believe that You sent Me."

43 Then He cried, "Lazarus come
forth."
44 He who had died came out.
He was bound both hand and foot,
With grave cloth wrapped about.

Said Jesus, "Loose him, let him go."
45 And seeing what He'd done,
Many of those among the crowd
Believed He was God's Son.

46 But some went to the Pharisees
And told what they had seen;
47 Therefore, the priests and Pharisees
A council did convene.

They said, "What are we going to do?
For this we do perceive,
48 If we let him go on like this
On Him all will believe."

49 But one of them named Caiaphas,
Who was high priest that year,
Said, "You know nothing at all, but
To me it does appear:

50 "That we must be expedient,
The people we must cherish;
'Tis better one should die for all
Than have a nation perish."

51 He did not say this of himself.
Being the high priest that year,
He prophesied Jesus would die
52 For all people far and near.

53 From that day on they planned
    His death.
54 Jesus walked no more among Jews.
He went away to a city called Ephraim
And there He taught His views.

55 Now the Jews' Passover was at hand
And many to Jerusalem came,
Some got there early to purify
Themselves in God's Holy name.

56 Many were seeking Jesus as
In temple gates they stood;
They said, "Do you think He will come,
Or think He even should?"

57 The Pharisees and priests had
    ordered
If He came to Jerusalem,
They were to report it to the council
So they could seize Him.

Chapter 12

1 Six days before the Passover,
Jesus went to Bethany,
Where Lazarus lived, the one He
    raised
And who death did not see.

2 They made for Him a supper there,
And Martha served each guest,
And Lazarus reclined as well,
Along with all the rest.

3 Mary took a pound of costly ointment
And anointed Jesus' feet.
She wiped them with her hair and
    thus
The whole room smelled so sweet.

4 But Judas Iscariot, one of the twelve,
Was reclining near the door;
5 Said, "Why was this not sold and
    the funds
Then given to the poor?"

6 He had no interest in the poor,
Not even one little bit,
But he controlled the money box
And used to steal from it.

7 Said Jesus, "She anoints Me for
    burial,
So let her alone, I say;
8 The poor will be with you always,
But I'll be gone some day."

9 When the Jews learned He was
    there, they came
Not to hear what He said,
But that they might see Lazarus
Whom He'd raised from the dead.

10 The chief priests all took counsel
    then
To plan what they would do;
They said, "To destroy His teachings,
    we
Had best kill Lazarus, too."

11 Because on account of Lazarus
Many Jews had gone away
And were believing on Jesus Christ;
The number grew each day.

12 The next day, a great mutitude
Had gathered in the street;
When they heard he was near, they all
Went out the Lord to meet.

13 They cut branches from palm trees,
And they began to sing,
"Blessed is He whom God has sent.
Is this not Israel's king?"

14 Jesus found a donkey, on
Which there was put a coat.
Then He climbed upon its back,
Just as the prophets wrote.

15 "Fear not daughter of Zion, see!
When your king will appear
Sitting upon a donkey's colt;
You'll know God's kingdom's near."

16 The disciples didn't understand
    at first;
But when Christ was glorified
They remembered what was
    written and
Things done before He died.

17 The crowd that was with Him when
He called Lazarus from the grave
And raised him from the dead,
All said, "Israel He could save."

18 The crowd went out to meet Him ere
He reached the city wall.
Because He had performed a sign
They said, "He's Lord of all."

19 The Pharisees said to one another,
"We are not doing any good,
The whole world's going after Him,
As we had feared it would."

20 Now there were certain Greeks
    among
The ones who worshipped there
21 They came to Phillip and they said;
"With Jesus we'd like to share."

22 Philip sought out Andrew and
The two to Jesus came.
They said, "Some Greeks would
    meet You, for
They have heard of Your fame."

23 In answer Jesus said to them,
"The time has now appeared
For the Son of Man to be glorified,
The hour that I once feared.

24 "Unless a grain falls in the earth
It's by itself alone,
But if it dies it bears much fruit,
That is how wheat is sown.

25 "He who loves his life loses it
Amidst this worldly strife.
But he who hates his life shall keep it
And have eternal life.

26 "If you serve Me you'll follow, and
Where I am, you're there, too;
I've honor from My Father. Serve
Me and He'll honor you.

27 "My soul has become troubled, and
I don't know what to say,
Shall I ask for deliverance?
No, I was sent this way.

28 "Father, won't You glorify Your
    name?"
A voice like a thunder chain
Said, "I have glorified it before
And I'll glorify it again."

29 The multitude there did hear it,
Said, "It has thundered loud."
Said others, "An angel spoke to Him."
There was division in the crowd.

30 Jesus answered and said to all,
"This voice that you just heard
Was not for Me, but is for you
So you would hear God's word.

31 "Now is the judgment of this
    world;
Its ruler's fall you'll see,
32 If I be lifted up from earth,
I'll draw all men to Me."

33 He said this thing to indicate
The death he was going to die,
And to let His disciples know
The time was drawing nigh.

34 Therefore the multitude replied,
"We have heard in the Law
That the Christ is to remain forever,
To be worshipped in awe.

"You say the Son of Man must rise,
Who is this Son of Man?
Give us a sign so we will know,
Reveal Him if you can."

35 Therefore He said to them, "For a
Little longer you have light.
Walk while the light's among you, don't
Wait for the dark of night.

"The one who walks in darkness will
Quite surely go astray,
He can't see where he goes; therefore,
He cannot find his way.

36 "While you have the Light,
    believe in It
That you'd become God's sons."
These things He spoke unto the crowd,
Then hid when He was done.

37 Though He'd worked many signs,
    yet in
Him they did not believe,
38 That Isaiah's word might be fulfilled,
"Lord, our report is not received."

39 Also Isaiah was inspired to write,
"Although the Lord's arm is revealed,
40 He blinded eyes and hardened
    hearts,
Lest they repent and be healed."

41 These things Isaiah wrote because
He had seen the Lord's glory,
And he wrote down what he had seen;
It wasn't just a story.

42 Many rulers there believed in Him,
But would not dare confess it
Lest they be cast from the synagogue,
By Pharisees unblessed.

43 The Pharisees strove very hard
To be approved of men,
Rather than be approved by God
And have true peace within.

44 Then Jesus raised His voice and
    said,
"If you believe in Me, alone,
You believe the one who sent Me.
This belief leads to God's throne.

45 "And if you have seen Me, you've
    seen
The One by whom I'm sent.
46 I have come as light unto the
    world
That darkness might be rent.

47 "If any hears My sayings and
Then turns and goes his way,
He has One who judges him
On the judgment day.

"I did not come to judge the world,
But that it might be saved.
I know you have rejected Me
By the way you have behaved.

48 "He who does not receive My sayings,
If by him they are rejected,
That one will not be judged by Me
Yet judgment's not neglected.

49 "I have not spoken on My own,
But as the Father commanded.
He sent Me and told Me what to say,
I've done as He demanded.

50 "I know what He has commanded
    and
In the last day you will see,
He has commanded eternal life,
Just as the Father told to Me."

Chapter 13

1 Before the Passover Jesus knew
His hour was at hand,
When He'd depart from this world and
Return to the Father's land.

Having loved His own who were in
    the world,
He loved them to the end;
He would protect and keep them as
A true and loving friend.

2 During supper the devil had
Put into Judas' heart
To betray Jesus, for Judas was
Now ready to do his part.

3 Jesus knowing He came from the
    Father,
And had all things from His hand,
He had come forth from God and
    would
Go back at God's command.

4 Then Jesus rose from supper and
His garments laid aside,
He girded Himself with a towel,
And His disciples eyed.

5 He poured water into a basin
And began to wash their feet,
And wipe them with a towel to cleanse
The dust from off the street.

6 When Jesus came to Simon Peter,
Peter said, "What do You do?
Would You really try to wash my feet
And those of others, too?"

157

⁷ Said Jesus, "What I'm doing now
You do not understand,
But you will later realize
Why this thing I demand."

8 Said Peter, "You'll not wash my feet,
Your servant I would be,"
Said Jesus, "If I don't wash you,
You have no part in Me."

9 Simon Peter to Jesus turned
And this is what he said,
"Then Lord wash not just my feet, but
Also my hands and head."

10 Said Jesus, "He who's bathed is clean
And needs but wash his feet,
And I say most of you are clean,
But one of you does cheat."

11 For He knew who was betraying Him,
And that is why He said,
"Not all of you are clean and by
My Spirit have been led."

12 When He had washed their feet and put
His garments on again,
He said, "I would explain my deed
Before supper we begin.

13 "You call me Lord and Teacher, and
In this thing you are right.
14 If I who am your teacher have
Washed all your feet tonight,

15 "Should you not follow My example,
And do as I have done,
And be a servant to one another,
Minister to everyone?

16 "A servant's not greater than his master,
Neither is the one who's sent.
Greater than the one who sent him, though
For him his life is spent.

17 "If you understand all of these things,
And all these things you do,
Then I will make this promise that
Blessings will come to you.

18 "I do not speak of all of you,
The ones I chose I know,
But that the Scripture may be fulfilled
There's one here who's My foe.

"He says that he is one of us, but
He's not what he claims to be,
Although he eats of My bread He
Lifts his heel against Me.

19 "From now on I am telling you
Of things to come about,
So that when they do occur you will
Believe and never doubt.

20 "Truly, truly I say to you,
When I send you another,
Receive Him and therefore you
Will also receive My Father."

21 When Jesus had said these words He
Was troubled, then testified,
"Truly one of you will betray Me.
It cannot be denied."

22 The disciples looked at one another,
Each of their minds was seeking
To try to tell which one it was
Of whom the Lord was speaking.

23 The disciple whom Jesus loved,
And next to Jesus leaned,
24 Was asked by Simon Peter, saying,
"Tell us of whom He means."

25 The one by Jesus then said, "Lord,
Who is it? Who would dare?"
26 He said, "The one for whom I dip,
The sop I do prepare."

Then Jesus dipped the sop and gave
It to Judas Iscariot.
27 Then Satan entered into Judas.
Jesus said, "Quickly, carry out the plot."

28 When Jesus said these things to Judas,
No one there knew just why,
29 Since Judas had the moneybox
They supposed he went to buy.

Or perhaps He was suggesting that
He give some to the poor.
So, they did not know why he left,
Why Judas went out the door.

30 Once he'd received the morsel, Judas
Went out into the night;
From henceforth he would not walk
With the one who could bring light.

31 When Judas had gone out from
them,
To the others Jesus cried,
"Now glory comes to the Son of Man
And God is glorified.

32 "If God is glorified in Him
He's glorified also;
This will come without delay,
Keep watch so you will know.

33 "Children I'm with you a little while.
You seek Me: I told the Jews,
Where I am going you cannot come
Pay attention to My views.

34 "A new command I give to you
That you love one another;,
35 All men will know you are Mine if
You each show love to your brother."

36 Peter turned and said to Jesus,
"Lord,
Where are you going now?"
Jesus said, "At this time, you can't
come,
But later, I avow."

37 Peter again spoke to the Lord,
"Right now I'd follow You,
For You I would give my life, what
More would you have me do?"

38 Jesus said, "Would you lay down
your life?
For Me are you prepared to die?
Before the cock crows in the morning
Three times Me you'll deny.

Chapter 14

1 "Let not your heart be troubled;
Believe in God, and in Me, too.
2 In My Father's house are many
mansions,
Which I go to prepare for you.

"If this weren't so, I would tell you
3 And if I go to prepare,
Be sure I'll come again, and I
Will come and take you there.

"I want you to be with Me forever,
This is why I say,
4 'You know where I am going, and
You also know the way.' "

5 Thomas spoke and said, "Lord,
where
You go we do not know;
Therefore, how can we know the way
Unless You tell us so."

6 Jesus softly said to Thomas,
"I am the way, you see;
I also am the truth and life;
You come to God through Me.

7 "If you had known Me, Thomas,
You'd know My Father too;
From now on you know Him,
For now I live in you."

8 Said Philip, "Lord, show us the Father
And we'll be satisfied."
9 Said Jesus, "Don't you know Me? I've
Walked daily by your side.

"I've told you if you have seen Me
You've seen the Father, too,
For the Father dwells in Me, this
should
Be apparent unto you.

10 "Don't you believe I'm in the
Father?
In Me, God, you can see.
The things I say and works I do, are
Because He lives in Me.

11 "Believe Me that I'm in the Father
And He in Me does dwell,
Or else believe on account of the
works,
Which do a message tell.

12 "Truly I say to each of you,
Don't doubt, believe in Me.
You'll do the works that I do, and
13 Even greater works you'll see.

"Because I'm going to My Father,
Prayer in My name is done.
I will do this so that the Father will
Be glorified in the Son.

14 "Whatever you ask in My name,
That is what I will do.
15 If you love Me keep My
    commandments
Is what I ask of you.

16 "I will ask My Father, and another
Comforter He will send
Who will be with you forever,
And He will be your Friend.

17 "This friend will be truth's Spirit,
    whom
The world cannot receive
Because it does not know Him, for
In Him they'll not believe.

"Believers all will know Him, though,
For He abides in you,
And He'll be in you always, you
Will know My words are true.

18 "I will not leave you desolate,
19 Soon you'll see Me no more;
I will again come to you but,
Not as I came before.

"Because I live, you shall live and
20 In that day you will know
That I am in the Father and
You are in Me, also.

21 "The one who truly loves Me will
Keep all of My commands,
And he will be loved by the Father,
My love He'll understand."

22 Judas, not Iscariot, said to Him,
"Lord, what has come about
That you'll disclose yourself to us,
Yet leave the world in doubt?"

23 Jesus answered and said unto him,
"He who loves Me keeps My word;
Therefore My Father will love him,
That one He will undergird.

"For we will come unto him,
And there make our abode.
We will ease his burdens,
And also share his load.

24 "He who does not keep all My words
Then Me he does not love;
The words you hear are not Mine,
    but
The Father's from above.

25 "These things I have said to you
    while
Abiding with you still,
26 But the Holy Spirit whom the
    Father sends
Will come and My place fill.

"He will teach all things, then you'll,
Remember what I said,
The days we walked together, and
Along the paths were led.

27 "Peace I now leave with you;
My peace I give today;
Not as the world gives, do I give;
My peace goes not away.

"Let not your heart be troubled,
Nor let it ever fear.
28 You heard Me say I go away,
But that should bring you cheer.

"Yes, I truly will go away,
But come again I will.
I go to be with the Father, because
Greater than I, He is still.

29 "Now I have told you all these things
Before they come about,
So that when they do come to pass,
You'll believe and will not doubt.

30 "I will not speak much more with
    you,
The world's prince does appear,
And he has nothing in Me, but
This prince's time is here.

31 "I'd have the world know I love
    the Father
And do what He demands.
Arise, let's go from here and be
Faithful to His commands."

Chapter 15

1 "My Father is the husbandman,
I am the true vine today,
2 And every branch that bears not fruit
He takes that branch away.

"And every branch that does bear, He
Will carefully look o'er,
And then will He prune that branch
So it will bear much more.

3 "Because of the word I spoke to you
You are already clean,
If you continue to abide in Me
The good fruit will be seen.

4 "A branch must abide in the vine
Or fruit it can't produce.
A branch that's severed from the vine
Is of very little use.

5 "I am the vine, you are branches,
Therefore, abide in Me.
Apart from Me you bear no fruit
For this old world to see.

6 If a man abide not in Me,
As a branch he is cast out.
The branch is withered and
    gathered then,
Cast into the fire without doubt.

7 "If you then abide in Me
And My words abide in you,
Then you can ask whate'er you will
And nothing I won't do.

8 "By this My Father's glorified,
That much fruit you should bear,
And so prove to be My disciples
As with others you shall share.

9 "Just as My Father has loved Me,
Even so have I loved you;
Again I say, continue in Me,
In all you do, be true.

10 "If you keep My commandments, in
My love you will abide,
As I have kept My Father's
    commands
And in His love I hide.

11 "These things I've spoken that
    My joy
May be made full in you,
And that your joy may be full in
The things you say and do.

12 "You know that I have loved you, now
    give you this command
That you love one another. This
    always will demand.

13 "Greater love has not one than
    this
Who gives his life for a friend.
14 If you do what I command you,
    ou're My friends to the end.

15 "No longer do I call you servants,
    for
In your Master's plan you've part,
But I have called you friends for
    you are
So very dear unto My heart.

"All things I have heard from My
    Father
To you I have made known.
16 You did not come and choose Me,
    but
I chose you for My own.

"I appointed you to go bear fruit
And that your fruit remain,
That what you ask My Father, He
Will give you in My name.

17 "Again I give you this
    command,
Love one another true.
18 The world may hate you, but it
    hated
Me before it hated you.

19 "If you were truly of the world,
The world would love its own,
But you are not of this world, so
They won't leave you alone.

20 "I chose you out of all the world
And by the world you're hated.
A servant's not greater than his
    master,
This I have often stated.

"If the world has persecuted Me
They'll do the same to you;
If they keep My Word, then therefore,
They'll also keep yours, too.

21 "All these things they will do to you
If you're true to My name,
For they don't know who sent Me, and
That is their greatest shame.

22 "If I'd not come and spoken to them
Then guilty they'd not be,
But now they've no excuse, for their
Sin everyone can see.

23 "He who hates Me then also hates
The Father just as well.
This is the case because the Father
And I together dwell.

24 "If I had not done among them
Works which none other did,
Then they would not have sin, and so
Their folly would be hid.

"But they have done this to Me and
Have seen My works as well;
They hated both Me and My Father;
This is very sad to tell.

25 "But this had to come to pass
That is written in their laws,
The word which had to be fulfilled:
'They hated Me without cause.'

26 "But when the helper comes from
    the Father,
Which I will send to thee,
The Spirit of Truth and Righteousness
Will witness to you of Me.

27 "He will give power and knowledge,
    then
You will bear witness, too,
Because you were with Me from the
    start
And will do the things I do."

Chapter 16

1 "These things I've spoken to you that
You may be kept from stumbling,
For many things will come to you
Which will be very humbling.

2 "They'll cast you from the synagogue
And some of you they'll kill,
And whoever does the killing
Will think they do God's will.

3 "These things they will do to you, for
The Father they've not known,
And of Me they've no knowledge, they
Think only of their own.

4 "I did not speak these things before
For their hour was not yet here,
But you'll remember when it comes
And these words bring you cheer.

"I did not say this when we met,
When you first followed Me,
Because I was with you then, and
My works you all could see.

5 "But now I'm going to return
Unto the One who sent Me,
6 You do not ask where I am going,
But you're sorrowful, I can see.

7 "But I tell you the truth—it is
Best for you that I go;
It I don't, the Helper will not come
To teach what you should know.

"But if I go I will send Him,
8 He'll come and convict of sin,
And He will teach of
    righteousness
And bring judgment before men.

9 "He will convict men of their sin,
Who don't believe in Me.
That is their key problem,
Which they need to see.

10 "He will convict of righteousness
Then they'll see quite clear
That I've gone to My Father
And no longer am seen here.

11 "He'll convict of judgment, for the
    world's
Prince is judged, I avow;
12 I have more things to say to you,
But you can't bear them now.

13 "But when the Spirit comes to you,
He will speak what He hears said.
He will guide you into all truth,
And tell you what's ahead.

14 "All things the Father has are mine,
He placed them in My care,
15 So the Spirit takes what is mine
And with you He will share.

16 "Soon you will not see Me, then
Soon you will see Me again,
Before I go to My Father,
And you will not see Me then".

17 His disciples said to one another,
"What does the Master mean,
'A little while, you'll not see Me,
And then I will be seen?"

18 So many questions crossed their
    minds,
They all were full of doubt;
"What does He mean by 'a little
    while?'
What does He talk about?"

19 Knowing they wished to question Him
Jesus said, "Why can't you see?
A little while, I won't be seen,
And then again see Me?

20 "Truly I say this unto you,
You'll weep and you will cry,
But all the world will rejoice when
The Son of Man does die.

"Though you be very sorrowful,
It will be turned to joy.
Your joy will succeed your sorrow,
For death I will destroy.

21 "Whenever a woman travails, she
Has sorrow and has pain,
The hour comes for her to deliver,
And her body travails with strain.

"After she gives birth to the child, she
Remembers the pain no more.
A child has been born to her,
And greater joy is in store.

22 "Today I've brought you sorrow, for
I've said I will depart,
But I will come to you again;
You'll have a joyful heart.

"No one can take your joy from you,
23 You'll question not, that day.
Ask the Father in My name,
You'll receive it then, I say.

24 "You have asked nothing in My name,
Just ask, and you'll receive,
So that your joy will be made full
As in Me you believe.

25 "I have spoken in symbolic words,
Someday, I'll make things plain.
26 I do not say I'll ask the Father,
You'll ask Him in My name.

27 "The Father loves you, for you have
Shown love unto Me.
You believe I came from the Father, and
That the Father dwells in Me.

28 "I came forth from the Father, and
Am leaving the world and you.
I am returning to the Father
Once My work here is through."

29 His disciples said, "You now speak
plainly;
We understand Your speech,
30 We realize you know all things;
All is within Your reach.

"We know You've come from God, from
Him
Your commission did receive."
31 Jesus smiled and said to them, "Now,
I know you do believe.

32 "Behold! an hour's coming. In fact,
It is already here,
When you will leave Me all alone
And be scattered far and near.

"Each will go to his own home and
Leave Me to face My foe,
But the Father's always with Me. I'll
Not be alone, I know.

33 "These things I've spoken unto you
So that when darts are hurled,
You will find peace in tribulations;
I've overcome the world.

Chapter 17

1 These things Jesus spoke, then lifted
Up His eyes in prayer;
He said, "Father the hour has come
When glory We shall share.

2 "You've given Me authority
And power over all,
So that I give eternal life.
To all whom You may call.

3 "And this is life eternal, that
The people may know Thee,
The one and only God, and know
To earth You have sent Me.

4 "I've glorified Thee on the earth,
Did what I was sent to do.
5 Now glorify Me with Yourself,
With the glory I've had with You.

6 "I revealed Your name before
The men who now are mine,
And they have kept Thy word;
therefore,
You gave Me what was Thine.

7 "Now they know that all I have
Comes as Your gift to Me.
8 The words you gave Me I told them:
They know I came from Thee.

9 "I only pray on their behalf,
Not on behalf of others;
I ask for those you've given Me,
They're Thine, and we are brothers.

10 "All things of Mine are Thine as well,
And all Your things We share;
I have been glorified in them,
For them I'll always care.

11 "And I am no more in the world,
But here these men remain.
I ask Thee, Holy Father, that
You'll keep them in Your name.

"The ones whom Thou has given Me
That they might be as one,
Just as we are united as
The Father and the Son.

12 "While I was with them I guarded
them,
I kept them in Your name,
Not one of them was lost except
The son of hell and shame.

13 "But now I come unto You, and
These are the things I speak,
That they may have My joy in them
As Your will they do seek.

14 "I've given them Your Word, and so
The whole world hates them all.
Like Me, they are not of the world,
For having heard My call.

15 "Don't take them from the world,
but keep
Them from the evil one.
16 They are no longer of the world,
As I'm not, being Your Son.

17 "And sanctify them in the truth.
Thy word is truth, we know.
18 As You sent Me into the world,
Into the world they go.

19 "For them I consecrate Myself
And my disciples too,
That they may ever dwell in truth
In all the things they do.

20 I do not pray for these alone,
But for all who will believe.
The words which my disciples speak,
Consecration they'll receive

21 "That they may be made one, even
As, Father, You live in Me,
That they all may be one in Us, then
The world will believe and see.

22 "The glory which You have given Me
I now give unto them,
That they be one as we are one,
I will say this again.

23 "Yes, I in them and You in Me
In perfect unity,
That the world may know You love
them,
Just as You love Me.

24, 25, 26 "Father, this is My desire—
that
They whom you've given Me
May be with Me where I am, so
My glory they will see.

"Oh righteous Father, You loved Me
Before the world began;
The world has not known Me, but You
Know Me, the Son of Man.

"They know You sent Me. I have made
My name known unto them,
That the love wherewith You loved
Me, I'll
Make known to them again."

Chapter 18

1 Then Jesus crossed the Kidron Val-
ley,
Once he had prayed this prayer;
He was followed by His disciples
To the garden which was there.

2 Now Judas, who was betraying Him
Knew about this place of prayer,
For Jesus and all His disciples
Often went there to share.

3 Judas with a band of soldiers from
The chief priests and Pharisees,
With torches, lanterns, and weapons
came
At night, Jesus to seize.

4 Jesus, knowing what was coming,
Went forth in manner meek.
He said to Judas and the soldiers,
"Who is it that you seek?"

5 "We seek Jesus, the Nazarene,"
Said the leader of the troop.
"I am He," said Jesus, to the men,
Judas was with this group.

6 When He said, "I am He," they fell
Down on the grass so green.
7 Again He asked, "Whom do you seek?"
They said, "Jesus, the Nazarene."

8 Said Jesus, "I told you I am He,
Take Me, and harm no one,"
9 So prophecy's fulfilled, 'of those
You gave Me, I lost none.' "

10 Simon Peter quickly drew his sword
And struck the high priest's slave,
And he cut off his right ear, for he
Thought he was being brave.

11 Jesus said to Peter, "I would have
You put your sword away.
The cup which the Father has
    given Me
Shall I not drink today?"

12 The Roman soldiers and their
    commander
And the officers of the Jews
Arrested Jesus, bound His hands,
And strong cords they did use.

13 They took Jesus to Annas first;
He was Caiaphas' father-in-law,
Caiaphas was high priest that year.
The Jews held him in awe.

14 Caiaphas was the one who had
    advised
It was best one man should die,
Than have the Romans destroy
    their land
And make the people cry.

15 Simon Peter followed after Jesus,
To see what they would do,
And still another of the disciples
Followed at a distance, too.

The second was known to the high
    priests, so
He entered into the court,
16 But Peter stood outside the door,
Waiting for his report.

The one inside spoke to a servant
Who let Peter go inside.
In these strange surroundings
His fear Peter could not hide.

17 The servant girl to Peter spoke,
And put him on the spot,
She asked, "Are you one of His
    disciples?"
Peter answered, "I am not."

18 Now servants and officers
    standing there
Made a charcoal fire,
As it was cold, Peter joined the crowd;
Warmth was his desire.

19 The high priest questioned Jesus
    about
His disciples and His teaching.
20 Said Jesus, "I've spoken openly,
In the temple did My preaching,

"Or where the Jews together met.
In secret, I've said no word.
21 Therefore, why do you question Me?
Ask them what they have heard."

22 Once Jesus had said this, one of
The officers standing by
Slapped Jesus with his palm, and said
"Is that the way to reply?"

23 Said Jesus, "If I've spoken wrongly
Tell Me what I said.
But if you know I spoke the truth,
Why did you hit My head?"

24 Annas therefore left Him bound and
Sent Him to the high priest,
To find some cause for Jesus' death
Before the Passover feast.

25 Now Peter still sat near the fire,
Which had become quite hot,
When one said, "You are one of them."
Said Peter, "No, I'm not."

26 One of the high priest's
servants came
And gave Peter a fright,
Kin to the one whose ear was cut,
Said, "Weren't you there last night?"

27 Peter therefore denied it again,
Only to hear a sound.
A cock crowed in the distance,
That struck his conscience down.

28 They led Jesus from Caiaphas' court,
To Pilate's judgment seat.
If they went in they'd be defiled
And the Passover could not eat.

29 Pilate therefore went out to them,
Said, "Why bring Him to me?"
30 They said, "If He weren't an evil man
We would not trouble thee."

31 But Pilate said, "Judge Him your-
selves,
Don't bring Him in here to me."
They said, "But sir, you know that we
Can't give the death decree."

32 That Jesus' words might be
fulfilled,
Which He spoke to signify,
What kind of death He was to face,
That He was about to die.

33 Pilate went back inside with
Jesus.
He said, "Some have these views
Against Rome you plan rebellion,
Are You the King of the Jews?"

34 Jesus said,"Do you ask of
yourself?"
"Or do others say it of Me?"
35 Pilate replied, "I'm not a Jew
I hope you can plainly see.

"Your own nation and your chief priests
Delivered You to me.
Now I ask what you've done, for I
Now wish to hear Your plea."

36 "My kingdom's not of this world,
Jesus said,
"Else My followers would appear
To keep Me from being delivered up;
My kingdom's not from here."

37 Said Pilate, "Then You are a
king?"
He answered, "That is right,
For this I was born into the world
To bear witness to truth and light.

"Everyone who is of truth,
That one will hear My voice.
My disciple he will be;
In his spirit will rejoice."

38 And Pilate said, "What is truth?"
Then he sought out the Jews.
He said, "I find no fault in Him
For things which you accuse."

39 But a custom's been established
that
I release someone to you.
Now it's Passover time, and this
Custom I'll carry through.

"Shall I release the King of the Jews?"
40 The mob then loudly demanded,
"Not this man but Barabbas." For
Barabbas was a bandit.

Chapter 19

1 Pilate then had Jesus scourged.
2 Soldiers wove thorns in a crown.
They put the crown upon His head
And at His feet bowed down.

They put a purple robe on Him.
3 And cried, "Hail, King of the Jews."
They also hit Him with their hands;
God's Son they did abuse.

4 Then Pilate came again and said
To those outside the hall,
"I bring Him out that you might know
I find no fault at all."

5 Jesus dressed in a purple robe
With thorns upon His head
Stood there before that angry crowd,
Behold the Man," Pilate said.

6 When the chief priests and the
others saw Him,
They cried out, "Crucify!"
Said Pilate, "Do this deed
yourselves,
No cause He has to die."

7 The Jews answered, "We have a law,
By that law He should die.
He made Himself the Son of God,
That is the reason why."

8 When Pilate heard this statement, he
Became much more afraid;
If he would kill the Son of God
An error would be made.

9 Pilate once more did ask
Jesus from whence He came,
But Jesus gave no answer, would
Not even give His name.

10 Pilate therefore said to Him
"Why do you not speak to me?
I can kill you or release you,
I have this authority."

11 He said, "You've no authority
Over Me, or over men,
Unless it's given from above.
My betrayer has the greater sin."

12 Pilate kept trying to release Him,
But the Jews cried out, "We know
You are no friend of Caesar's if
You would let this man go."

13 When Pilate heard the words
        they said,
He then brought Jesus out;
He sat down on the judgment seat
While crowds stood all about.

14 It was the preparation day
For the Jews' Passover feast.
Said Pilate, "See your King. I think
That He should be released."

15 Therefore the mob cried out to him,
"Take this evil man away;
He should be crucified, and it
Should be done this very day."

Pilate rose and said to all,
"Shall I crucify your king?"
The priests said, "We've no king
        but Caesar;
His favor we would bring."

16 He sent Jesus to be crucified;
For us Christ bore this shame,
17 He bore His cross up the hill,
        Golgotha,
Called by its Hebrew name.

18 On that hill they crucified Him,
It was a gruesome scene.
There was a man on either side
And Jesus hung between.

19 Pilate wrote an inscription there
Which bore the following news:
"This is Jesus Christ, the Nazarene,
Who is King of the Jews."

20 The inscription was written
        three ways—
In Latin, Greek, and Hebrew.
As they were near the city it
Was read by many a Jew.

21 The chief priest said to Pilate, "The
Inscription o'er His head
Should not read, 'King of the Jews,'
        but,
'King of the Jews, He said.' "

22 But Pilate said, "This I have
        written
And I'll not take it down;
It says He was a king, although
He wore no earthly crown."

23 When Jesus had been crucified,
The soldiers made a pile,
Divided Jesus' earthly goods, for
Those who stood guard awhile.

They also took His coat, which had
Been woven from the top.
It was a seamless garment; they
24 Said, "We should rend it not.

"If we should tear it up it would
Be of no use you see.
Let us cast lots for the coat
To see whose it should be."

Thus Scripture was fulfilled,
        "Among them
My garments they divided.
They cast lots for My clothing and
Its owner thus decided."

The soldiers therefore did these things
25 While near the cross was seen
Jesus' mother, Mary, wife of Clopas,
And Mary Magdalene.

26 Looking down, Jesus saw His
	mother and
A disciple whom He loved nearby.
He said, "Look on him as your son,
He'll care for you 'til you die."

27 Then Jesus said to the disciple,
"To you I make this known,
To treat this woman as your mother,
As if she were your own."

From that time that disciple
Cared for Mary in his home.
Though she was the mother of Jesus,
He treated her as his own.

28 Jesus knowing things were
	finished, that
The Scripture be fulfilled,
Said, 'I am very thirsty." So
29 With vinegar a sponge was filled.

They put it on a hyssop branch,
Raised it for Him to drink.
30 Once He received it, Jesus' head
Upon His chest did sink.

Then He said, "It is finished." And
Those standing by could hear it,
He closed His eyes and bowed His
	head,
And He gave up His spirit.

31 As it was the day of preparation
Jews said, "No bodies should be here
When our Sabbath day comes,
And it is very near."

They besought Pilate to command
	his men
That the legs of the crucified be
	broken,
And that the soldiers take the
	bodies away;
This to Pilate was spoken.

32 The soldiers broke the legs of the
	first
Thief crucified that day.
They broke the legs of the other, too
To give death its full sway.

33 But when they came to Jesus, and
Found Him already dead,
They did not break His legs at all
34 But pierced His side instead.

There flowed out blood and water, and
35 The witness would not deceive;
For he is telling you the truth
So you also may believe.

36 For these things came to pass
	that the
Scripture might be fulfilled,
"Not a bone of Him shall be broken
When the Son of Man is killed.

37 "They shall look on Him whom
	they pierced."
Elsewhere these words are read.
All prophecies were thus fulfilled.
He died just as they said.

38 Then Joseph of Arimathea, a secret
Disciple until that day,
Asked Pilate for the body, that
He might take it away.

Pilate gave Joseph permission, who
	then
Took the body from the site,
39 And Nicodemus came with him, who
First came to Christ at night.

Nicodemus brought both myrrh
	and aloes,
A hundred pound in weight.
40 They quickly wrapped the body
	in linen
For it was getting late.

To wrap the body in linen and spices
Was a custom of the Jews,
41 And near the crucifixion spot
A garden was in view.

They took the body to this garden
Where a new tomb had been made.
This tomb, it was nearby,
No one in it had ever laid.

42 Because the preparation day
Was getting very near,
And because the tomb was closeby,
	they
Buried Jesus' body here.

Chapter 20

1 Mary Magdalene came to the tomb,
Right after the Sabbath day,
Although it was still dark, she found
The stone was rolled away.

2 She ran and came to Peter;
She also encountered John.
She said, "They've taken the Lord
away.
We don't know where He's gone."

3 Therefore, Peter went to the tomb,
4 The other disciple ran ahead.
The other disciple got there first,
5 Looked in, but did not see the
dead.

6 Then Simon Peter, who followed him,
Came up and went inside.
7 He also saw the linen wrappings
And the face cloth by their side.

8 The other disciple then entered in,
The one first to the tomb;
He saw the grave cloth there, as well;
He found an empty room.

9 Though they believed all of the
words
Which the Master often said,
Still they did not fully understand
He had risen from the dead.

10 So the disciples went away again,
They went to their own room,
11 But Mary stood there weeping,
then
Stooped and looked into the tomb.

12 She beheld two angels, both
Of them were dressed in white,
Sitting where the body had been
lying
When the tomb was sealed so tight.

13 And they said unto Mary, "Woman,
Why are you weeping so?"
She said, "Because they took my Lord
And where, I do not know."

14 As soon as she had said these words,
Mary turned herself around,
And she saw Jesus, but did not know
Her Lord she now had found.

15 Said Jesus, "Woman, why do you
weep,
Who is it you are seeking?"
Mary thought it was the gardener
To whom she now was speaking.

She said, "What have you done
with Him,
Tell me I humbly pray.
If you tell me where you laid Him,
I'll go take Him away."

16 Then Jesus said to her, "Mary."
She answered, "Rabboni."
Which in Hebrew means My Teacher.
Mary did no longer cry.

17 Said Jesus, "Do not touch Me, for
To My Father I've not ascended;
Go to My brethren, say to them,
That My time here has ended.

"I now ascend to My Father, who
Is now your Father, too;
He is My God, also your God,
He'll tell you what to do."

18 Mary Magdalene came to the
disciples;
She told what Jesus said;
She said, "I've seen the Lord! I know
He's risen from the dead."

19 When therefore it was evening, and
They spoke of the day's news,
They had the doors all tightly shut
For they still feared the Jews.

Jesus came and stood in their midst
And said, "Peace be with you."
20 He showed His hands and side to
prove
Mary's words were true.

When the disciples saw the Lord
They in accord rejoiced.
They lifted up their praise to God;
Their joy they loudly voiced.

21 Jesus therefore said again,
"My peace I bring to you;
The work My Father gave to Me
I send you now to do."

22 Then He breathed on them, said,
"The Holy Spirit you're given.
23 If you forgive sins of anyone
Their sins will be forgiven.

"If you retain the sins of any,
Their sins remain there still,
For sin can only be removed
By doing My Father's will."

24 One of the twelve was not with them
The night that Jesus came.
By the others he was called Didymus,
But Thomas was his name.

25 The other disciples said to him,
"He rose, He did appear.
All of us saw Jesus risen
For He joined us right here."

Thomas said, "Unless I see the nail
    prints
And wounds that He received,
And place my hand on His pierced side
Your words can't be believed."

26 Eight days passed, and the disciples
Met in the room again,
Although the doors were shut and
    locked,
Jesus came and stood within.

He said, "Peace be to all of you."
27 Thomas' doubts I would relieve,
Touch My hands and side, and then
Do not doubt, but believe."

28 Thomas answered, "My Lord and
    My God,
The marks I now do see.
I know you are the risen Lord;
That is enough for me."

29 Jesus said, "Because you have
    seen Me
Have you really now believed?
Blessed are they which have not seen
And yet My words received."

30 Many other signs He did while His
Disciples were around,
But there is not room in this book
To write all of them down.

31 These things I've written down,
    that all
Who hear them may believe
That Jesus is the Son of God
And Him you must receive.

Yes, Jesus is the Messiah and
To earth He really came.
He is the Holy Son of God,
Life's only in His name.

Chapter 21

1 After these things Jesus showed
    Himself
To the disciples by the sea.
He did it in this manner so
They would know it was He.

2 There were Simon Peter and Thomas,
Nathanael from Cana of Galilee,
And two other of His disciples,
Along with the sons of Zebedee.

3 Said Peter, "I am going fishing."
They said, "We'll come with you."
They went out, got into a boat,
And fished the whole night through.

4 Jesus came and stood upon the beach
At the breaking of the day,
They did not know Him for the dark
Had not all passed away.

5 Jesus therefore called to them,
    "You don't
Have any fish, do you?"
When they said, "No," to them, He
    said,
"This is what you should do.

6 "Pull in the net and cast again;
This time throw to the right.
There you will find a school of fish
That you missed last night."

They cast as Jesus told them to,
And though they were strong men
The haul of fish was so great, they
Could hardly pull it in.

7 The disciple whom Jesus loved,
    Said, "It's
The Lord on the beach."
When Peter heard it was the Lord,
For his coat he did reach,

For Peter had been stripped for work,
He put his tunic on.
He left the boat, waded to shore,
In the cool and misty dawn.

8 The other disciples came in the boat,
For they were not far from land,
And dragging along the net of fish,
They were a happy band.

9 And when they had reached land,
they saw
A fire burning near,
And found fish placed upon it. Jesus
10 Said, "Bring your catch right here."

11 Simon Peter drew the net to land,
Full of large fish from the lake.
There were one-hundred fifty-three,
And still the net didn't break.

12 Said Jesus, "Come and eat."
None of
The disciples questioned Him,
Or said, "Who are You?" For they knew
Quite well who was with them.

13 Jesus gave each one some fish,
And also gave them some bread.
14 This was the third time he was
with them
Since He'd risen from the dead.

15 When they had finished
breakfast, He
Said, "Simon son of John,
Do you love Me more than these, or
Is your love for Me gone."

Said Peter, "Lord I love You, I
Am yours—you know I am."
Said Jesus, "Then if you love Me
I'd have you feed My lambs."

16 He said to him a second time,
"I ask you, son of John,
Do you really love Me, and will you
Love Me when I am gone?"

"Yes Lord, You know I love You, and
Your commands I try to keep."
Said Jesus, "If you love Me, then
Simon, tend My sheep."

17 He said to him the third time,
"Simon, do you still love Me?
Can I always count on you, and will
You always faithful be?"

This third time grieved Peter deeply, and
Peter began to weep.
"Lord, You know how I love You."
Said Jesus, "Then feed My sheep.

18 "Truly, truly I say to you,
When you were a younger man
You'd gird your cloak about you, and
Walk according to your plan.

"But when you old and weary grow,
You will stretch out your hands;
Another will gird and carry you
According to their own plans."

19 Now He said this to signify
What kind of death he'd die,
And that this kind of death, His Lord
He would then glorify.

And after He had spoken thus,
He said to Peter, "Follow Me,
Serve God and man as I have served.
My witness you're to be."

20 Then Peter turned himself around;
The beloved one caught his view;
The one who leaned near Jesus' breast
And asked, "Who's betraying you?"

21 Peter therefore seeing the
disciples, said,
"Lord, what is he to do?"
22 Said Jesus, "If he stays 'til I come,
Follow me, what's that to you?"

23 This saying went forth to the
brethren
That this disciple would not die;
Yet Jesus did not say this, and
Neither did He imply.

He only said, "If I want him to remain,
What is that thing to you?"
He meant you are to be faithful,
In spite of what others do.

24 This disciple witnessed all these
things
And wrote them down for you.
As he walked daily with the Lord,
We know his words are true.

25 Many other things Jesus did, but if
They were all written down,
The world could not contain the books
Which would everywhere be found.